WHO and W

GOD IS

THE EVIDENCE & PROOFS

An even more exciting journey of discovery

THIS BOOK CONTAINS ABSOLUTE HISTORIC EVIDENCE THAT PROVE THAT GOD EXISTS AND THAT THE BIBLE IS GOD'S WORD OF TRUTH

"You need not that any man teach you:"

1 John 2:27

ALL YOU NEED TO DO IS TO ASK FOR A LOT OF HELP FROM HIM

By

Brian H. Butler

WHO and WHAT GOD IS

This book consists mostly of prose expressions of the author's view and understanding of the Scriptures. It has many quotations from The King James Version of the Bible which is in the Public Domain, which is generally considered by most scholars to be overall the best translation despite its ancient English, and its many errors of translation which can easily be overcome and resolved by the careful, diligent student.

The publisher of this book may be contacted by email at:

bhb@ernestworkman.com

Perfect bound paperback book ISBN:

978-0-6454042-3-4

eBook ISBN:

978-0-6454042-4-1

Typeset by Brian H. Butler
Formatted by: Angel Key Publications
angelkey.com.au

Published by Ingram Spark
Printed by Lightning Source

DEDICATION

This book is dedicated to the praise of the Almighty God, the Creator and Father of all, with grateful thanks for the inspiration He has provided; To express appreciation for His wonderful works; and to help His human children to establish a closer connection and relationship with Him. Also to bring the knowledge of the correct names of the Father and His Son to the world of Christendom, and to hallow, honour and praise those names.

In our world, it is important for everyone to address human dignitaries by their correct name and title. Human names are very important to people. It is impolite or even rude not to address a person by their correct name and their title if they have one.

How much more important is it to address our Creator and His Son by their correct names?

God the Father chose to inspire the Old Testament in the Bible to be written by His servants in the Hebrew language. In the original Hebrew texts, God's name is expressed in four letters: YHWH, which is the Hebrew verb 'to be' or 'to exist'. The Hebrew word does not include the vowels 'a' or 'e'.

Strong's #3068} hwO;hy] — Yhovah, yeh-ho-vaw'; from 1961; (the) self-Existent or Eternal; Jehovah, (this is incorrect, as explained next) YaHWeH

Probably the most correct word to use for God the Father is 'Yahweh' pronounced 'YahWay'. The word 'Yah' is also used in the Bible to represent 'God'. Notice that the Name of God begins with a 'Y' not a 'J'. There is no

"J" in the Hebrew. Note: No letter 'J' existed in the English alphabet before 1524 A.D.

The world of Christendom calls on the incorrect name of God's Son, everything is done "in His name", but the word they use is not His name. Does this matter? Yes!

Many believe that 'Jesus' is the correct name of God's Son, but that name did not exist before the 17th century. At the time of the Apostles, He would have been called 'iaysooce' or 'iashua' the first two letters pronounced as a 'Y' i.e. 'Yashua'.

The word 'Jesus' appears incorrectly translated 942 times in the New Testament of the King James version of the Bible. That name for the Son of God is not used in this book because it is incorrect. Also, the manner in which it is commonly used by all and sundry is blasphemous. It is a mistranslation of the word 'Yehowshua' which is of Hebrew origin as is explained in Strong's Greek Concordance #2424.

Strong's (2424) ÆIhsou~v, ee-ay-sooce'; of Hebrew origin [Hebrew {3091} (Yehowshuwa`)]. Yah'Shua is the name of our Lord as a man. After His death and resurrection, when He was glorified by the Father, His Son's name became YahwehShua.

In the Old Testament God the Father inspired Moses to write in Exodus about God's Name. While the Children of Israel were still in Egypt as slaves to Pharaoh, God spoke to Moses in the burning bush:

13 And Moses said unto God, Behold, when I come unto the children of Israel, and shall say unto them, The God of your fathers hath sent me unto you; and they shall say to me, What is his name? what shall I say unto them? 14 And God said unto Moses, I Am That I Am: and he said, Thus shalt thou say unto the children of Israel, I Am hath sent me unto you. 15 And God said moreover unto Moses, Thus shalt you say unto the chil-dren of Israel, the Lord God of your fathers, the God of Abraham, the God of Isaac, and the God of Jacob, has sent me unto you: this is my name for ever, and this is my memorial unto all generations. Exodus 3:13-15

In the New Testament, Christ was challenged by the Pharisees, and infuriated them in John 8:58 by saying to them: *58 Jesus said unto them, Verily, verily, I say unto you, Before Abraham was, I am.* The Pharisees knew the Law by heart, and knew that Christ was quoting Exodus 3, and thus claiming to be God.

The word 'Christ', or 'Khristos' in Greek, means the Messiah. Strong's (5547) Cristo>v, khris-tos'; anointed, with oil, consecrated, the Messiah, Christ.

9 After this manner therefore pray: Our Father which art in heaven, Hallowed be thy name. Matthew 6:9

The word 'hallow' is Strong's #37 hag-ee-ad'-zo; to make holy, i.e. (ceremony) purify or consecrate; (mentally) to venerate: to hallow, be holy, sanctify.

The first thing that Christ commanded us to do when we pray is to 'hallow' the name of the Father. So in this book, the name of the Son of God as a man will be expressed as ‘Yah’Shua’ which means God our Saviour; and ‘Christ’, Greek, Khristos, the Messiah.

It is the earnest hope of the author of this book that the information it contains will lead many Christians to a closer walk with God the Father and His Son.

WHO and WHAT GOD IS

THE EVIDENCE & PROOFS

An even more exciting journey of discovery

By

Brian H. Butler

RELIGION	THEOLOGY
GOD GOD'S WORD The Holy Bible	**GOD** GOD'S WORD The Holy Bible
FILTER 1 The Human Mind The carnal mind is enmity against God, for it is not subject to the law of God, neither indeed can be Romans 8:7	THE PURPOSE OF LIFE is to learn about God from the study of His Word & to strive to be like Him. Ask for, and receive it! GOD'S HOLY SPIRIT FLOWS INTO YOUR MIND The 'Light' comes on. New Understanding floods your mind & heart.
FILTER 2 Truth mixed with error Partial truths False Doctrines - Idolatry Human ideas & reasonings	**NO FILTERS** PURE TRUTH DIRECT FROM GOD TO YOU
FILTER 3 Church organisations Priests, Ministers Desire to control followers	
YOU YOUR MIND Your Human Spirit Deceived into believing truth mixed with error Having the understanding darkened being alienated from the life of God through the ignorance that is in them, because of the blindness of their heart Ephesians 4:18	**YOU** YOUR MIND Your Human Spirit Enlightened by the flow of God's Holy Spirit, filled with the truth The eyes of your understanding being enlightened; that you may know what is the hope of His calling, and what the Riches of the Glory of His inheritance in the saints. And what is the exceeding greatness of His Power to us-ward who believe, according to the working of His Mighty Power. Ephesians 1:18-19

Contents

ACKNOWLEDGEMENT

In all my eighty-five years I had often been exhorted to study the Bible, but I had ***never*** been taught ***how*** properly to study.

Dr. Ernest L. Martin, my colleague and mentor, showed me HOW to study. The first essential tool is always to begin by asking for God's help for inspiration and understanding. The wonderful Bible study 'tools' I have learned from Dr. Martin and his tapes, also form the basis of this book.

A personal note from the author:

"I have absolutely no doubt in my mind that in this age, Dr. Martin was a (if not the) most remarkable teacher filled with the Holy Spirit, and that his insights and research were guided directly by God. I have found his work more inspiring than the work of any other man in my now eighty-two years. To be very clear, in no way am I 'following a man', but merely using his tools. I am following Christ's Word, studying the Bible for myself, with God's help".

Dr. Martin hoped that many would 'do him out of a job' by learning with the aid of Christ the Messiah and the Holy Spirit so that we will not even have to learn from him. (Or from me! Ed.) Dr. Martin says we have never really needed him, and that may be true, but I feel that God has used him to help me grow in grace and knowledge by leaps and bounds using the 'tools of the trade' he recommended; compared to sixty years of a lifetime of personal study in my own strength. I truly hope that the same may become true for those who read this book.

PREFACE

How this book came to be written

As a child, my parents used to take me to church. When I was about twelve, I was asked to give the reading which happened to be 1 Corinthians 13, known as the 'Love' chapter. I memorised it, and somehow, its content and the occasion remained with me. Although attending for many years, my whole experience could be summed up by saying, I never really understood anything. The odd parable, or the story of Jonah, but otherwise, nothing.

Once I left home at eighteen when I was called up to do my National Service in the R.A.F., I did not attend any services at all. At twenty-two, I once went to a local church, but was so unimpressed, I never went again. I had always believed in God, and thought of Him as Creator, but I really was not interested at all in any religion. Frankly, even then, I thought, like so many do, that religious activities seemed to be at the root of many of the world's problems and wars.

Then I got the 'flu. Confined to bed, I started to browse some old copies of the Reader's Digest. Some advertisements took my eye. One said in bold lettering, 'Does God Exist? Another offered 'Proof of the Bible'. There was no mention of a 'church', just the offer of some leaflets. I sent off for them.

I was taken by the style of the pamphlets, and that the writer clearly believed that the Bible was actually, really, the Word of God. Something went on in my mind, and I was very keen to learn more.

After a year or so of studying the written material and the Bible, I came to realise that there was an organisation behind it all, a church. I wrote off to them, and to cut a long story short, when I was twenty-five, I was invited to attend.

My first experience in the dingy, dusty hall was not enjoyable at all. The congregation seemed to be a motley group of somewhat miserable people. Anyway, I was not looking for a cosy social club. I was looking for more inspiration to read and study the Bible, and to come to a better understand what this word 'Christian' was all about, so I stuck with it.

Most of the ministers were a sombre lot, and the sermons were long and not very interesting. An exception was a Dr. Ernest L. Martin, who seemed very different from all the others. His approach to the Bible, his historical and chronological knowledge, and the way he told us to read the Scriptures carefully, impressed and inspired me to greater efforts.

At twenty-nine, in 1964, I applied to go to the college which was run by the church, and was accepted for the four year, full time course, to major in Theology and obtain a Bachelor of Arts degree.

During my four years in college, I was privileged to take several courses with Dr. Ernest L. Martin, the Dean of the Faculty. His lectures were always riveting, and the most enjoyable as he made the history, geography, and the chronology of the Bible 'come alive' as I had never experienced in my life before.

After graduation in 1968, I was offered the opportunity to work for the College, and I gladly accepted a position in the data processing department, which was to stand me in good stead as time went on.

I also spent time with Dr. Martin from 1971-1974 after I was appointed a member of the Faculty of Ambassador College, Bricket Wood, U.K.

In 1974, Dr. Martin was the head of the department of Theology at the headquarters of the church in Pasadena, California. His personal studies over several years, independent of the church hierarchy, led him to realise that many of the doctrines taught by the 'church' did not stack up against what the Bible clearly said, and many flatly contradicted the Bible itself.

Dr. Martin attempted on many occasions to bring to the notice of the church doctrinal committee for their consideration, anomalies and deviations from what the Bible plainly showed. His attempts were always met with hostility and rebuttal. As a result of these unresolved differences over most important matters, after forty years of service with the church as a high ranking minister, Dr. Martin saw no other recourse but to resign his position as Head of Theology.

His letter of resignation may be viewed at:

https://hwarmstrong.com/history/history-earnest-martin-resignation.htm

In 1975, my work with that church came to an end. Two years previously, in 1973, I had met and spent time with an American Chiropractor, Dr. John Blossom, who introduced me to a new concept in chiropractic, known as Applied Kinesiology (A.K.) developed in 1964 by Dr. George Goodheart, D.C. I.C.A.K..

For the next twenty-five years I pioneered A.K. in Britain and Europe, ran a clinic of natural health care, and taught thousands the A.K. principles of self-help health care.

In 2000, I retired after those years working in natural health care, helping the sick to work on their health and well-being, I once again turned to the study of Theology. The word Theology comes from two Greek words, Theo meaning God, and Logos meaning Word, hence Theology is the study of God's Word, the Holy Bible.

More recently, in 2013 I began an intense and in-depth study of over two hundred tapes recorded, and articles written by Dr. Martin on the fruits of his many years of intense Biblical research before he died in 2002.

Working with Dr. Martin's material for 40-50 hours a week, using the essential 'keys' to understanding the Bible that he suggested the earnest Bible student employed, I learned more in those three years than I had in over sixty years of my own personal previous study of the Holy Bible in my own strength. Since 2013 I have written well over a thousand pages of notes on Dr. Martin's Biblical doctrinal research. In my opinion this book contains the most important details of the fundamental basis of Christianity.

I became so excited at what I was learning about HOW to study the Bible with God's help, rather than accept what any church or minister told me about it, or trying to study in my own strength. In the years since I wrote 'Why ARE We Here?', 'THE Biggest Lie', Discover More About God, and 'WHO and WHAT IS GOD? In 2020, I embarked on this current volume "WHO & WHAT GOD IS - The Evidence and Proofs" which sets forth the absolute evidence and proof that God exists, and that the Bible is His Word. It also contains the evidence of the deceptions of 'Churchianity', the nonsensical suggestion that 'Everything came from nothing', the 'Theory of Evolution', Human Philosophy, and Science falsely so called.

More importantly, this book that you hold in your hands provides essential 'Keys' on HOW to study, and grow in Grace and Knowledge, and a glimpse of the glorious future we have as Children of God.

INTRODUCTION

The purpose and goals of this book, 'WHO and WHAT GOD IS' is to provide a resource to anyone whose 'eyes and ears' are being opened by our Father, the Almighty God.

God, by means of the flow of His Power, Holy Spirit will inspire their minds to see the clear evidence of deception that 'Yah'Shua', 'Christ' the Messiah warned about in Revelation, the last Book of the Bible He wrote for our instruction.

*And **the** great dragon was cast out, that old serpent, called **the** Devil, and Satan, which deceives **the whole world**: he was cast out into **the** earth, and his angels were cast out with him. Revelation 12:9*

When Christ the Messiah says that Satan has deceived the whole world, He means just that. That includes all organisations of human beings. The Governments, the Philosophers, Scientists, the Religions, are all involved in the greatest deception possible.

There are thousands of separate denominations of what is known as Christianity. Each one claims that their version of the truth, what they believe, teach and practice from their understanding of the Bible, is the correct one. They cannot all be right! There can only be one version of the Truth. The Holy Bible is that Truth.

The original manuscripts, inspired by Yahweh the Father, through His Son Yahweh-Shua were the source of the Bible we have today, and they were perfect in every detail, and were exactly as He intended them to be.

However, **all** human translations contain errors, made either by translators, or by organisations which have altered the Bible to suit their own agendas.

For instance, The King James Version contains the incorrect name 'Jesus' instead of 'Christ the Messiah' nine hundred and forty two times. According to Strong's Concordance, the word #2424 in the original texts, Strong incorrectly adds the word 'Jesus' to the actual words that appear in the texts.

(2424) ÆIhsou~v, — *ee-ay-sooce'*; of Hebrew origin [Hebrew {3091} (Yehowshuwa`)];

Strong's #2424 correctly gives the Aramaic 'iasooce' ('Yaysooce') and the Hebrew origin of the word as Yehowshuwa which came from the Tetragrammaton YHWH or Yahweh which is God's Name in the Old Testament. YHWH is the verb 'to be' or 'to exist'.

There was no letter 'J' in the English language until 1524, so it is clear that 'Jesus' was not the name of our Lord when He was on earth, but it was added by the translators of the King James Version in 1611.

For this reason, the false, incorrect name of 'Jesus' has been crossed out, replaced or deleted in this book.

The earnest student of the Bible need not be concerned too much about the aberrations, as it is perfectly possible, with God's help, to find a way past those errors, and be assured that what they are learning is indeed the Truth.

The King James Version is still probably the most reliable translation, and certainly is the best one for its elegant and poetic expression of texts.

PLEASE READ THIS FIRST

ABOUT EVIDENCE, PROOF, WITNESS, TESTIMONY

The book you are holding in your hand is evidence, proof, and testifies to a number of irrefutable proven facts.

For a book to exist there has to be an idea or concept in someone's mind, an author to write it, a designer to format it, materials like paper ink and glue, a printer and a bookbinder to make it.

The book you are reading is tangible, solid, physical evidence, proof, and testimony of the existence of all these things.

You cannot 'see' the concept, author, designer, printer or the bookbinder who made it, but you know, and know that you know, and have no doubt whatever that they have to exist in order to produce the book you have.

If anyone suggested to you that the book came from nothing and materialised itself, you would doubt their sanity would you not?

Yet, a popular notion among some highly intelligent 'quantum' and other 'scientists' propose that 'everything came from nothing', and nobody questions their sanity. By denying a Creator they make fools of themselves.

We can observe the universe, we experience everything on earth, we know, and know that they exist. Since they exist, there must have been a concept, a designer, and a Creator to make them.

The Bible is full of evidence, proof, witness and testimony that God exists and that the Bible is His Word. So if you study the book God , Yahweh the Father wrote, you will know, and know that you know that God exists and that the Bible is truly His Word.

All the points mentioned in this summary are included with additional information throughout the text pages of the book.

If you intend to consider basing your life on the Bible, it is essential that you start by knowing three things:

1. Know, and KNOW that you KNOW that there is a God.

2. Know and KNOW that you KNOW that the Bible is His Word.

3. Know and KNOW that you KNOW that the three theories which suggest that

i. ‘Everything came from nothing’ and

ii. ‘Everything ‘evolved’ from proteins that formed spontaneously in ‘seas’ that were already there’, and

iii. ‘That inanimate matter sprang into ‘life’ of its own accord;

These are utterly false and without any foundation in fact.

This does not mean that you ‘think’ you know, or ‘believe’ you do, it has to mean that **the absolute conviction that these statements are true for you personally.**

This book claims to offer absolute proofs with rock solid evidence to prove that the first two statements are true beyond all reasonable doubt, and that those unproven propositions in the third have no basis in fact.

For this to work for anyone, they need to be seriously dedicated to applying themselves to reviewing the evidence, and to satisfy themselves that the evidence not only supports these first two propositions, but proves it to themselves beyond any reasonable doubt.

Regrettably, most people think that the Bible was written by men, that it is full of errors, fairy tales and stories of long ago that have no relevance to us today. **As long as a person believes any of those things, and does not really believe that the Holy Bible is God's Word, they will never get any real benefit from reading the Bible.**

To have a solid foundation for a proper relationship with God, a person has to have belief and faith based on actual reliable evidence and solid proofs. The Bible provides that evidence and proof because God caused the Bible to be written through men, and is flawless, accurate and True.

There are two types of belief and faith: One is 'human' belief and faith, and the second type is a God-given Gift of Belief and Faith, they are quite different. In this section, for human belief and faith, a small 'b' and 'f' are employed. To indicate God's Gifts of Belief and Faith, a capital 'B' and 'F' are used.

Human belief and faith cannot bring a person to really know or truly understand Spiritual matters.

God given gifts of 'Belief and Faith' are based on the solid evidence He provides that are required to gain an ever increasing knowledge and experience of Spiritual things. Just hoping for, or praying vaguely for God's gifts is not enough. We need to ask specifically for His Help and Gifts, and then it takes diligent, consistent work to grow and become a mature Christian person.

The solid irrefutable evidence comes in two forms. First, the existence of everything physical in the universe and the 'life essence' that enlivens all things are proof that a Creator exists. Everything had to be 'made', as nothing can come from nothing.

Secondly, we have the evidence in the Holy Bible written by men who were inspired by God, of the many people who were 'eyewitnesses' to the events it contains.

Most people, even the most sincere, that claim to be Christians who base their belief and faith on emotional experiences, or on 'feelings' rather on actual evidence are on very shaky, unreliable ground.

Almost all 'believers' are not aware that 'proofs' are available, they think it just takes 'belief' and 'faith'. This is no truer of spiritual matters than it is of physical matters. We live our lives and act mostly based upon 'evidence' of our own experiences, and on things that others have demonstrated to us are true. When we fail to do this, and act with gullible belief or blind faith we usually pay a penalty of some sort.

To open the door to God's Knowledge, Understanding and Wisdom concerning the real evidence in the Scriptures, it requires each person to ask for the 'keys' of God's gifts of 'Belief and Faith' (Capital letters are used to differentiate 'human belief and faith', and 'Spiritual Belief and Faith'), and for the Spiritual 'gift' of an open mind, and also to have the determination to continue to work at it diligently. Human belief and faith are simply not enough.

Here are two passages in the Bible that help to explain this situation.

[6] For the (carnal, human) mind of the flesh is death, but the mind of the Spirit is life and peace .[7] because the mind of the flesh is hostile toward God; for it is not subject to God's law, neither indeed can it be. [8] Those who are in the flesh can't please God. Romans 8:6-8

[14] Now the natural (carnal, human) man (woman) doesn't (cannot) receive the things of God's Spirit, for they are foolishness to him (her), and he (they) can't know them, because they are Spiritually discerned… 1 Corinthians 2:14

Do the thousands of Christian denominations have the truth?

Thousands of religious organisations claim to base their ideas and teachings on the Bible, but they all differ to one degree or another about what they believe the Bible teaches. Knowing that, it is obvious that they cannot all be correct. All must be in error to one extent or another, and this is true. How can anyone know this or test this?

It is simple, but complicated and time consuming. When considering the beliefs of any group, it would be necessary to check each doctrine or teaching that each group holds to be true against the Scriptures to see if what they say is supported by what it actually says in the Bible. This is not as easy as it might sound, and as a person studies and progresses in their understanding, the several reasons for this will become clear.

Some of the most important sayings of Christ, Yah'Shua the Messiah, are His repeated warnings about **deception**, and being deceived. In this regard, there is an absolute self-evident truth, and that is:

ANYONE WHO IS DECEIVED, DOES NOT KNOW-THEY ARE DECEIVED

If a person did know, they would not be deceived.

How can anyone avoid being deceived? Trust no human, no person, no priest, and no organisation when it comes to 'religion'. Take a grip on your mind, ask God directly for His direct help every step of the way. Do not listen to what anyone may tell you, work it out carefully for yourself by reviewing the evidence, and prove each point for yourself **<u>to your own satisfaction</u>.** This is especially important as you use the vital 'keys' to read and study this book and God's Word. Be assured, the author has done his intentional best to eliminate his own ideas or interpretations, and urges the reader to practice to think very carefully, and to make up their own mind about every issue.

THE EVIDENCE PROVIDES THE PROOFS

1st: How to Know, and Know that you KNOW that there is a God

The Inexplicable 'Energies' and 'Powers' that produce the physical existence of Matter must come from somewhere. Here is a list of some mysterious 'Powers': Love and Ethical thinking; Life-Force; Bio-genesis, the fact that life can only come from life, and the miracle of Biological Design and DNA from which millions of species are formed; The Power of Perpetual Motion that spins the particles within each atom; Gravity, Centrifugal Force, Magnetism, Electricity, the Electromagnetic Spectrum; the 'mystery' of precise design and order in Mathematics; and 'Capillary Attraction' without which no plant could survive and grow.

These are all God's powers, which although scientists can observe, measure, and put them to use in various ways, but nobody can explain exactly what they are, or how they came to be, and there is a very good reason for why they cannot.

That 'Energy' and 'Power' of all these types exist is self-evident, and it makes no rational sense to suggest 'it comes from nothing' or to say "it is just there". There has to be a Source of all these Energies, and we call that Source 'God'. All Energy emanates from God, He is the origin of all Energy and Matter.

It is self-evident that 'matter' exists. The existence of all 'things', solids, liquids, and gases is the observable and experiential evidence of a Creator Force. Nothing in our human experience 'comes from nothing', everything wesee has to be the result of thought, creative planning, design, selection of materials and productive work. The same applies to all matter.

2nd: How to Know and KNOW that you KNOW that the Bible is God's Word

Few, if anyone you have ever met, will have any real idea how the Bible came to be produced. They would have no concept of how it came to be constructed in the form that it is. Most think it is 'just a book'. This is very far from the truth.

Statistically, the laws of probability make it quite impossible for human beings to have been able to have put the Bible together. The 49 (7x7) books in the original Bible were selected from many thousands of original texts written over thousands of years by dozens of different people, yet it is totally accurate and never contradicts itself. How were the original manuscripts (literally hand-written) selected? Here is some solid evidence of their authenticity.

The Bible was assembled and 'Canonised' by Inspiration of God

What does "Canonised' mean? 'Canon' means "a rule or law," or in classical Latin, "a standard of excellence." According to one opinion in a dictionary produced presumably by secular people who were not subject to or bound by religious rule says: “A biblical canon or canon of scripture is a set of texts (scrolls or “books”) which a particular religious community regards as authoritative scripture”. This is not the case with the Holy Bible. It was produced by Divine Authority, and the Direct Action of God through the Prophets and Apostles and protected by them.

The precise choice of books was selected, and their order was ‘canonised’ specifically by The Almighty God as He oversaw the work done by His servants the Prophets and His Apostles. All the people who, under the inspiration and dictation of God wrote the books of the Bible, were aware of the reality of God because of the evidence He had given to them. What they wrote was based on being an eyewitness of circumstances or events. This is true of the New Testament writers who refer to all the evidence included in the Bible, because they were all eyewitnesses of all the things they could testify to and were writing about.

Under the direct inspiration of God, just four people on only two occasions chose each of those books to be included in the Bible. How can we be sure of that? Here is the proof of the procedure.

Originally the Old Testament consisted of 22 books, one for each letter of the Hebrew alphabet. They were selected and ‘Canonised’ by Ezra, the Priest and Prophet of God, in God’s Holy Temple, under God’s direction about 445 years before Christ. Each page was copied by ‘Scribes, then it was given to highly trained priests who were scribes called ‘Sopherim’, or the ‘Counters’.

They examined every letter, word, and each line of each page of the completed copy. If there was any error at all, even just one letter, that page was destroyed under supervision, and the Scribe had to write a new one.

This whole procedure makes an absolute nonsense of statements of critics who question or refute the authenticity of any of the 22 books in the original Old Testament, or the inspiration and accuracy of the 27 books in the New.

They were also meticulously checked by God's servants, the Jewish Authorities under God's Divine direction, so there could be no possible room for error, and kept safely under armed guard, as they are to this day in Israel.

The New Testament books were also assembled and 'Canonised' late in the first century A.D. to a very high standard of excellence by the Apostles James, Peter and John who had been eyewitnesses of all that Christ did. The three apostles were under the direct inspiration of the risen Christ 'YahwehShua' the Messiah who oversaw the selection of the choice of the 27 books of which the New Testament consists. Christ the Messiah ensured that they were all included and 'sealed', no more and no less.

The evidence of fulfilled prophecy proves the Bible is true

No human being can predict accurately any future event. They may make a guess at what will occur and may occasionally be right, but they cannot predict details with any certainty. God says He can and does do that. Here God speaks in the first person:

[22] "Let them (your gods) announce and declare to us what will happen! Declare the former things, what they are, that we may consider them, and know the latter end of them; or show us things to come. [23] Declare the things that are to come hereafter, that we may know that you are gods". Isaiah 41:22, 23

[9] "Remember the former things of old: for I am God, and there is no other. I am God, and there is none like me. [10] I declare the end from the beginning, and from ancient times things that are not yet done. I say: My counsel will stand, and I will do all that I please... [11b] Yes, I have spoken. I will also bring it to pass. I have planned. I will also do it." Isaiah 46:9-10, 11b

The Bible contains literally hundreds of prophecies which include great detail of events hundreds of years before they were fulfilled, and there is absolute evidence that they came to pass. Again, it is impossible for human beings to prophecy accurately anything in advance of it happening. God can and does. This is even more incontrovertible evidence that the Bible is God's Word.

The Spiritual content of the Bible concerning Moral and Ethical issues which would be impossible for carnal human beings to write is further evidence that it is truly the Word of God.

The Bible was not written to be understood by everyone at all times. This will become clear as the reader studies this book. Proper understanding of the

Holy Bible is contingent upon the reader having the Spiritual Gifts to do so.

Even with all this clear evidence available, it is still both possible, and even very likely, that some who read this information will still choose to think that it does not constitute 'proof' and continue to have reservations about the Bible. For anyone who feels this way, further study may not be relevant for them now. God selects those to whom He will reveal His truths at any given time.

3rd: Know that all human 'theories' of 'origins' are illogical and false

Thirdly: Know and KNOW that you KNOW that the three theories which suggest that

1. 'Everything came from nothing' and
2. 'Everything 'evolved' from proteins that formed spontaneously and grew into creatures in 'seas' that were already there', and
3. 'That inanimate matter sprang into 'life' of its own accord; are all utterly false and without any foundation whatsoever in fact

Virtually the entire world's population has accepted one of more of these theories, guesses or modern notions, and almost everyone believes that they are definitely 'fact'. If that is the case with anyone reading this, they may not even wish to look further into them or consider changing their mind about any of it. That is everyone's privilege.

We are here on earth to learn to make wise choices

On the other hand, if someone is sincere about seeking to have God, Yahweh, rule in their lives, they could ask for His help to be able come to 'see' the insanity of these three suppositions. Anyone who has embraced and accepted them, will indeed need a lot of help to 'unlearn' them, and also to resist the pressure of all those around them who will think that they have lost their minds.

It takes work to be a true Christian a follower of the Messiah

Even with the help of the Almighty God it will take a lot of hard work and a considerable amount of thought and research for anyone to be able to be rid of these demonic false ideas.

Once free of them, and enabled to study with an open mind, the glorious and exciting truths of God's Plan for us will flood into their minds.

The freedom of choice is there for each person to weigh up all the evidence for themselves without any interference from anyone with a vested interest.

Hopefully the reading of this first section on 'proofs' and 'evidence' will create an appetite for the reader to desire to learn more.

CHAPTER 1

Who and What God IS
The Evidence and Proofs

GOD'S MANUAL FOR HUMAN LIFE

How can we even begin to learn more about 'Who and What God **IS**'? God actually wrote a 'manual' that tells us all, everything we need to know about everything in this life that we **cannot** find out for ourselves.

The Creator God wrote that all time 'best-seller' called the Bible. More Bibles have been printed than any other book ever published, by far. It is the only Book that explains in detail how the Earth and the Universe was Created by the Creator.

Many say that the Bible is impossible to understand. They say it is full of unbelievable stories, and contains many contradictions. As long as anyone thinks that way they will never even begin to understand it. Interesting, many who express these opinions have never carefully read or studied the Book.

It is crucial that each person satisfies themselves that the Bible is God's Word of Truth. Absolute confidence of this fact is essential before making any attempt to read and understand the Book. To do that, it is important to understand how the Bible came into existence. God the Father, Yahweh, dictated each of the books that the Bible contains, word for word, personally to men. He inspired His servants painstakingly to write these words on the original manuscripts exactly as he wanted them to be written.

Each page was then checked by specialist the professional 'counters' who counted every letter of every page, and if just one letter was missing or incorrect, the page was destroyed. Yahweh wanted His book exactly the way He planned it to be, and the original scrolls are just that.

In a later section, the abundant proofs of the absolute authenticity of the Bible are explained in detail.

Men and women have made hundreds of different translations and they all contain errors, because each one includes human fallible ideas about Yahweh. But that fact does not need overly to concern anyone who really wants to learn the 'truth'. Yahweh can and does make sure that a diligent student will be able learn what He wants them to know at any given time in their lives.

Strange to relate, it is also a fact that the Bible was not written with the intention for it to be read and understood like any other book. The Holy Bible is not just another book, it is the 'Book of Truth' written by the Creator God the Father, Yahweh, which contains the truths we need to know, and are here to learn in order to make a physical and spiritual success of this life. It is the most complex Book in the world, written over centuries by many different people inspired by God, but it all fits together like one huge jigsaw puzzle. But there is no 'picture on the box'.

The study of Yahweh and His Word, and Christianity, those who follow the teachings of Yah'Shua, Christ the Messiah, are not for the religious 'hobbyist' or casual 'believer'. It is a 'Way of Life' that takes conviction, dedication, and a lot of hard work, not to be undertaken lightly, and also the fervent daily application of the practical living principles involved.

So those who truly want to learn about God, Yahweh, have to read and study the Book He wrote, the Manual, very carefully, **and with His help**. Without that 'help', the Bible appears to make no sense to the human mind and is even inexplicable.

So much of the Book appears to be nonsense to the unbelieving reader. It is said that 'seeing is believing' although in Spiritual matters, 'believing IS seeing'. So with God's help and the right attitude we can begin to learn a lot more about Him and how to live from the Holy Bible.

So from the Bible we can learn about 'Who and What God the Father, Yahweh Is'

His Book tells us that God the Father, Yahweh is made of Spirit Matter and Spirit Essence which is invisible and indestructible, as are all His Powers which extend everywhere, and are Omni-present. Yahweh is the Origin of Creation.

The Source of all the Powers of Yahweh are still a mystery to human beings, and always will be. Energy,

Life-Force, Matter, Gravity, Centrifugal Force, Magnetism and Electricity, the Electromagnetic Spectrum including Sound and Light and Radiation, Capillary Attraction, and so on listed in more detail later, are some of the Invisible Omnipotent Spiritual Powers of God's Spirit which is why they will never be completely understood by ordinary carnal fleshly humans beings.

But what we can learn about Yahweh will be only made plain to us if we look in the right place, firstly at our surroundings. Because Yahweh has shown us powerful evidence of His Invisible Power and Design in the tangible forms of all physical matter we can observe in the heavens; and touch, feel, and examine here on earth.

The invisible things of the Invisible God Yahweh are clearly visible to us when we look at and study the creation of the world and the universe. Humans can begin to understand Yahweh by examining the physical things that He has Created and made, and even learn a great deal about His Eternal Powers and Godhead. The tangible evidence of our Creator is everywhere, so if we do not believe, we are without excuse.

All Energy comes from Yahweh. Quantum physics has enabled scientists to formulate many notions of how electromagnetic force operates within the atom, but they still cannot explain its Source. When science is all boiled down, scientists think that all energy we experience on Earth is believed to come from the Sun's energy. Where the Sun's energy originated nobody knows if they deny God the Father.

In a sense, when scientists investigate what 'is', what exists, with more powerful instruments like the electron microscope the Hubble telescope, and now **The James Webb Space Telescope** which is 100 times more powerful than the Hubble, and a million miles from earth in space will change how we see the Universe. They will discover more and more amazing things, whether they appreciate it or not, since everything that 'is' was made by Yahweh, they are actually learning more about Him.

Two absolute laws: "Cause and Effect" and "Biogenesis"

In all our experience of this human life, we know for certain that these two laws are fundamental and true.

There is a Cause for every Effect, and every Effect has to have a Cause.

Logic demands that there cannot be an effect without a cause.

Logic demands that 'life' cannot arise from lifeless inanimate material.

Yet in an attempt to explain the existence of the universe without a Cause, Designer or Creator this earth and all on it, some make three propositions: One, which states that everything came from nothing, and two, that everything developed itself over time, and three that inanimate matter produced 'life' spontaneously.

These three notions can only be entertained if those who propose them suspend or ignore the 'Law of Cause and Effect' and 'Biogenesis'. This is strange, as these two laws are the bedrock of all science.

With their illusions, magicians would have us think that things can 'come from nothing'. In our human experience, nothing comes from nothing. Everything that is made here on earth starts in someone's mind with a mental picture, a thought, or an idea. The idea becomes a concept, a design of 'something'. The materials required to make the 'something' are planned, sourced and assembled. Then the 'something' is then made.

So how could all matter, solids, liquids, gases in the incredibly vast universe, and the millions of living species on our Earth just 'happen' from 'nothing' without there being a Mind that thought of the concept, the ideas, a design and a plan? The very nature of that thinking defies all sane logic.

There had to be a Mind, a Designer, a Plan, and the Powers to execute the Creation of the physical matter and all lifeforms, and to maintain the order and stability of all we know. That 'Mind' we call God the Father, 'Yahweh' is His name.

GOD IS A LIVING SPIRIT BEING

Yahweh is a Spirit made of Spirit Matter, He is All Powerful, with Infinite Powers. All Energy and all Life come from Him. 'Be-ing' is the present continuous of the verb 'to be'. God always 'Was', 'Is', and always 'Will Be'. 'Yahweh'. God is Past, Present, and Future, the simplest English word that expresses this is Eternal.

So the word 'Being', to be' or to 'be existing' continuously, and in the case of Yahweh without beginning or end. As long as they are alive, humans and everything that has 'life', that has 'breath' on Earth are 'be-ings'.

GOD, Yahweh, IS PURE LOVE – Totally Loving concern for Everything He Creates.

Yahweh is Love. Yahweh is entirely Love. Everything He does is motivated by Love, a Loving concern for His entire Creation. Even in everything that is the opposite of Love in this present evil world, the Love of Yahweh is in all. Without evil, we humans could never truly begin to understand Love without His help.

The love of Yahweh is vastly different and not to be compared with Human Love which is only a shadow, a very limited dim reflection of His for all His Creation.

Yahweh is also total Wisdom – Sophia, the female side of Yahweh is His Wisdom. Yahweh is innately 'male' and 'female' so He made His children male and female in His image.

Yahweh's Infinite Powers are the Cause of All Things Here is a list of some of Yahweh's Spiritual Powers:

Love, Mind, Imagination, Moral and Ethical Values, Life-Force, the miracle of human life and each heartbeat and breath we take, the design of all Biological life and the DNA from which millions of species are constructed; The Perpetual Power and the energy contained within each atom; Gravity; Centrifugal Force; Magnetism, Electricity, the Electromagnetic Spectrum of oscillating frequencies, which are an effect expressible as a quantity that repeatedly and regularly fluctuates above and below some mean value. It ranges from very low frequencies (VLF), through those we call 'sound', up to the tiny window of frequencies we call 'light', on up through invisible high frequencies with very short wavelengths like radio waves, ultra-violet, x-rays, gamma rays, nuclear radiation and so on; Also the Mystery of 'Time' itself was Created for Humans, which did not exist prior to 'The Big Bang' according to its proponents;

The 'mystery' of Mathematical Numbers, like Prime numbers, the Fibonacci Sequence, and more recently the discovery of Fractal Mathematics; Capillary Attraction without which no plant could grow, and we could not work properly the way we do with fluids; Photosynthesis which converts light into plant growth energy. True science actually proves that Yahweh's Powers and His Creation exist.

Human beings are able to examine, measure and use Yahweh's Powers in many, but limited ways. What they cannot do if they deny Yahweh, is to know how they came to be, or the true nature of them. This is because they are all Spiritual Powers which cannot be fully understood or fathomed by even the most educated people. That these Powers exist is self-evident and unarguable. Gravity is at work throughout the whole universe, and all His other powers are here for us to observe and work with on earth.

There is no satisfactory physical explanation from science concerning the above Energies, the origin and order of the heavenly bodies, the origin of life, and the Intricate, precision design of everything we examine, the functions of mind, consciousness, human free will and agency, objective moral truth, conscience, or the ability to discern right from wrong.

Human reasoning, scientific or otherwise cannot come up with any sane explanation of the origin of the Cause of all these Effects or these Powers without allowing the existence of a Cause beyond and outside this universe, which we call God whose name is 'Yahweh'.

Yahweh is the Designer and Creator of All Things

On a human level we know that nothing can be created without a design. The same is true of Yahweh. God the Father tells us in His Word that His first creation was His Son, the Word. All His Designs both Spiritual and Physical are capable of producing Infinite Variety of Similar but Different Forms.

God, Yahweh, is the Lawgiver of All Law

All the laws that underpin everything we know flow from the Powers we know are the Laws of Yahweh that are explained in His Word, the Bible.

God, Yahweh, is ALIVE – The Source of all Life - The Life Giver

Yahweh is Alive, He has Innate Life, and has infinite Power to give 'life'. Life can only come from Life. Yahweh is 'Alive' and 'Conscious' and always has been, and always will be. God, Yahweh, gives life, and takes it away. When He takes 'Life' away, it cannot be restored by humans.

Yahweh is the Source of all Life and Consciousness that exists in its myriad forms on Earth. Like all Yahweh's

Powers, the 'Life-Force' is a mystery no human can completely understand. When 'Life' is present in any type of organism, that form is 'alive'. When 'Life-Force' is absent, that organism is 'dead', and cannot be restored to 'Life' except by the 'Life-Giver', Yahweh.

What does Yahweh look like?

Yahweh is Invisible to human beings. However, God's Spirit Matter has form and shape, and occupies space. Yahweh looks like a human being in shape, and has a head, eyes and ears, a body, and arms and legs. His eyes constantly run to and fro over the Earth watching over us. He sits, walks, feels, laughs as we do.

How do we know Yahweh looks like that? The Book Yahweh wrote tells us that He created humans in his own image, in the image of Yahweh created he him; male and female created he them. Therefore human beings look like Yahweh because He formed them so, and they are His children. Each human person embodies male and female elements just like Yahweh does Himself. Since He made humans in His Image, we must look like Him, and He must look like us.

So this is how we can know, and **know** that we know, exactly what Yahweh looks like? The answer is really simple. He looks just like a human being. How can we know that for certain? Here is what Yahweh said when He made Adam and Eve.

[26] And God said, Let us make man in our image, after our likeness: Genesis 1:26

This is not a fairy tale. Yahweh did create Adam, the first man, from the dust of the ground. Sceptics deny that, but Yahweh's Word claims that this account and all within its pages is Truth, and with the clear proofs that Yahweh inspired men to write the Bible we can have confidence in that fact.

The Hebrew words 'image' and 'likeness' in Genesis mean 'image' and 'resemblance'. So Adam and Eve were the 'image of, the likeness of, and resembled God's appearance.

[7] And the LORD God formed man of the dust of the ground, and breathed into his nostrils the breath of life; and man became a living soul. Genesis 2:7

Most people own a scanner these days. Anything you want to copy, you just place face down on the glass and press 'copy'. Out comes a copy, an image so close to the original that it is almost impossible to tell the difference. So when the Scriptures say we are made in the image of Yahweh, it means just that.

Although Yahweh is made of Invisible Spirit Essence, He is not a 'fog', or a shadowy 'wispy' wraith or phantom. Just like a human being, He has a form and a shape, has a head with hair, a body with hands, arms and legs and feet. He talks, walks, sits, eats and drinks.

Yahweh is All in All. Aspects of God's 'Beingness': Yahweh is Immortal; Invisible; 'Alpha' and 'Omega', the 'Beginning' and 'End'; Eternal; Timeless; Omnipotent - All powerful: Omniscient - All seeing: Only Wise, Unsearchable; Kind, Forgiving; Glorious; Holy;

Incorruptible; Light; Immutable – unchangeable; Just; Kind; Merciful; Most High; Past finding out; Perfect; Power; Our Rock.

Where did Yahweh live before the foundation of the World?

Yahweh lives in one place, in His Heaven, closer to the earth than most people think. However God's Holy Spirit Power is Omnipresent and fills everywhere, and everything in the universe is an expression of that Power. God's physical Temple that was built on earth under His direction and to His exact and detailed specification had thrones, furniture, tables and chairs, and was a physical replica of His Spiritual home in Heaven.

24 The God who made the world and all things in it, he, being Lord of heaven and earth, doesn't dwell in temples made with hands. Acts 17:24

Yahweh is Eternal, is not bound by Time, He is an Timeless Invisible 'Spirit', and has 'always' lived in an 'unseen' Spiritual dimension, a 'Heaven' where He has His Throne. We have no way of knowing 'where' that was originally, or indeed if it was a 'where', but there are indications in the Bible as to where He lives in this era Yahweh had a Plan to extend Himself into a Family.

That Plan involved the creation of another Being.

Where does Yahweh live now?

Yahweh is not Omnipresent everywhere as some suggest, He lives in one place in His Palace in Heaven.

However, it is true that His unlimited Powers and His Spirit fill the entire universe and beyond.

Yahweh clearly has the choice to live wherever He chooses in His universe.

[18] To whom then will ye liken God? Or what likeness will you compare unto him? ... [21] Have ye not known? Have you not heard? Has it not been told you from the beginning? Have you not understood from the foundations of the earth? [22] It is he that sits upon the circle of the earth, and the inhabitants thereof are as grasshoppers; that stretches out the heavens as a curtain, and spreads them out as a tent to dwell in: Isaiah 40:18, 21,22.

So where might He have chosen to live now? Surprisingly, it is not far from earth. How close is He to us on the'circle' of the earth? Well, there are several references to God using the world (figuratively) as His Footstool, so His Residence cannot be that far away.

*Thus saith the Lord, The heaven is my throne, and the earth is my **footstool**: where is the house that ye build unto me? and where is the place of my rest? Isaiah 66:1*

Then this verse is quoted in the New Testament for emphasis and which shows that this fact still obtains in our era, YahwehShua Christ the Messiah says in Matthew:

[25] Nor (swear) by the earth; for it is his footstool: neither by Jerusalem; for it is the city of the great King. Matthew 5:25

[49] Heaven is my throne, and earth is my footstool: what house will ye build me? saith the Lord: or what is the place of my rest? Acts 7:49

Yahweh's home is in the heavens, close enough in figurative language to use the earth as His footstool. From His vantage point, He can watch over His children. Where else would a Father choose to live, and why?

[9] For the eyes of the Lord run to and fro throughout the whole earth, to shew himself strong in the behalf of them whose heart is perfect toward him. 2 Chronicles 16:9

Only through Christ the Messiah can we be 'perfect' towards Yahweh the Father, and those who are 'in Him' are perfect as far as the Father is concerned.

[10] For we (human beings) are His (God's) workmanship, created in Christ Yah'Shua the Messiah, unto good works, which God hath before ordained (determined or ordered to happen) that we should walk in them. Ephesians 2:10

The entire universe and the human race are the 'handiwork of God. He made everything.

[27] That they should seek the Lord, if haply they might feel after him, and find him, though he be not far from every one of us: [28] For in him we live, and move, and have our being; as certain also of your own poets have said, For we are also his offspring. Acts 17:27, 28.

So we can find Him close by, as we draw closer to Him He draws closer to us.

In the Book Yahweh wrote, the Bible, He tells us a lot about Himself. There is so much more to learn about Him in the Instruction Book He wrote for His children. It is part of the exciting journey we humans can pursue, by not only reading it, but studying it carefully every day. It is apparent that most people of the Christian faith do not do that, otherwise they would not belong to so many divided groups.

God, Yahweh, is Timeless – but humans are bound tothink in terms of time.

'Before' and 'after' are not words we can really use when talking about Yahweh, and the Word YahwehShua His Son, because they are timeless. Humans are bound into the concept of 'time', but they cannot explain 'time' as it is a Spiritual Power of Yahweh. Yahweh wanted to form a Family of Beings.

God, Yahweh, Created Time for human beings to learn the Purpose of Life

Yahweh created 'Time' for us so that we could learn to exercise our free will over the years of a lifetime to decide whether to love and serve Him, or not to.

The universe, the earth, human beings are all solid evidence that prove the existence of Yahweh

How can we know anything about a Creator God? Simple really. One way is to observe and wonder at the evidence of an incredible mind at work all around us in this world.

The wonderful mystery of our 'life' and the construction and workings of the wonderful bodies we inhabit and how they function, and the 'Life' of the entire fauna, flora. Not to mention the orderly Sun, motions of the Moon, the Planets, Stars and the apparently unlimited vastness of the Universe.

Before the 'Beginning' of all we know

Before the 'beginning' of anything, Yahweh was. Before any 'beginning' we are aware of, and as far as we know, there was only Yahweh.

There is only One Yahweh. Yahweh always was, is and always will be. Yahweh is timeless, and is the 'Beginning' and the 'End' of everything.

'Time'

Yahweh created 'time' for each of His human family to experience the lifelong process of being alive and conscious, and to enable them to learn about 'good' and 'evil'.

Some top brains in the world are wrestling with attempting to understand what exactly 'time' is. They will never work it out, it is one of Yahweh's secrets. Nobody can explain in detail the Nature of any of Yahweh's Powers. That is because they are the Secret Spiritual Powers of Yahweh, and humans will never fathom them no matter how hard they try.

A well-known phrase was composed by William Cowper written in 1773: "God moves in a mysterious way His wonders to perform; He plants His footsteps in the sea, and rides upon the storm".

Human false ideas about the beginning of the universe.

Some theoretical physicists now say that everything came from nothing? Many propose that everything in the Universe came from nothing and it all just formed itself one day with a 'big bang'. But can that truly be the explanation for everything? 'Everything came from nothing' has to be a false idea or belief.

On the other hand, many who subscribe to the 'theory'of evolution give credit for everything to 'Mother Nature'who or whatever that is; or in the case of one brilliant naturalist with a worldwide reputation, who appears to give the credit to each species for being able to develop itself.

These human notions are sacrilege, they steal the credit for Yahweh's Creation and give the credit to a 'Mother' who does not exist, or to a mythical process that 'made everything from nothing'.

Some who support this theory propose that simple 'life' began in the sea. The suggested evolutionary process describes how 'simple proteins' assembled themselves into a form of 'life'.

To start with, there is no such thing as a 'simple protein'. Science tells us that 'simple proteins' are made up simply (?!!) of chains of amino acids held together by peptide bonds and folded or twisted in a specific way. So chains of amino acids joined themselves together? They do not do that in a Petri dish in any lab now.

Are amino acids simple? The term amino acid is short for α-amino [alpha-amino] carboxylic acid. Each molecule contains a central carbon (C) atom, called the α-carbon, to which both an amino and a carboxyl group are attached. The remaining two bonds of the α-carbon atom are generally satisfied by a hydrogen (H) atom and the R group.

How could these very complicated amino-acids then assemble themselves into a form of protein that could navigate around, feed itself, excrete waste products, and reproduce itself? That is a lot to ask of a few chemicals floating around in the sea. They do not do that nowadays in a lab Petri dish either. Need any more be said?

It is even harder to understand how 'primitive' forms of life over millions of years gradually evolved the features they needed to survive without which they would have very quickly become extinct. So why do very intelligent, well educated people 'believe in this proposition?

'Evolution' makes the truth of God's Creation into a lie, and in a sense the whole notion worships the creation and the created instead of the Creator. They exchange the glory and Power of the Incorruptible God who made all things into the physical image of physical humans, birds, four-footed beasts, creeping things and gives them the credit for their own design and development. Where does pragmatic logic come in?

Nothing in our experience on Earth comes from nothing and makes itself. No rational thinking mind would suggest that. It just cannot be so. Magicians would have us think so with ‘rabbits out of hats’ and their illusions, but that is exactly what their ‘magic’ is, illusions, a deceptive appearance or impression that is not real. So if everything could not have come from nothing, then somehow ‘Someone’ made it out of ‘Something’. For ease, that ‘Someone’ we can call ‘God’, and He must have made it all out of ‘Something’. He did. He made it Out of Spirit Matter. Once the notion and existence of a ‘Designer’ is accepted, human beings can appreciate and be in awe of every complex wonder with which we are surrounded on Earth.

‘BEGINNINGS’

Yahweh, God our Father had no beginning, and is timeless, has always been, is, and will always ‘be’ alive.

When one tells a story to a child, it is quite usual to start by saying: “Once upon a time …” In the ‘Instruction Book’ that Yahweh has written for His human children so they could learn about Him, and how to live, He uses a similar phrase which says ‘In the beginning…’

But to help our understanding of Yahweh, it is necessary to go ‘way beyond’ and ‘before’ that ‘beginning’ to when neither ‘time’ and nothing of what we know about existed, and only Yahweh existed. The story we are doing our best to understand began ‘aeons’ or ‘ages’ ‘before’, but none of these words work because there was no ‘time’ before that.

In the Hebrew language, the four letters that represent God’s name YHWH, called the ‘tetragrammaton’, represent the verb ‘to be’. Although there are no vowels in this group of letters, if an 'a' and an 'e' are inserted, 'YaHWeH' is the result.

In this book, after a great deal of prayerful thought, 'Yahweh' pronounced 'YahWay' is the name used for 'God'.

Others use 'Jehovah' but there was no letter 'J' in the English language until 1600 A.D. Incidentally, the name 'Jesus' was not the name of the Messiah for the same reason, it was a made up word from the Hebrew 'YHUShA' for Joshua which was 'iashuah' or 'Yashuah'. Christ is Yah'Shua the Messiah.

This is all simply academic, as everyone knows what the intended meaning is when anyone says God or Christ. The Bible warns us about 'strifes about words', nobody wants strife. The important thing is that we understand what we respectfully mean by any of these words, and that is all that matters.

Yahweh is the Source of all Power and all forms of Life. All humanity knows the 'Law of Biogenesis' that 'Life' can only come from 'Life'. Yet both 'evolution' and the notion that 'everything came from nothing' deny that Law and suggest that 'life' came from inanimate matter and materials. They cannot say how, because it did not, cannot, and never will happen. Some scientists say they are getting close to making bacteria that will reproduce themselves from inanimate matter, but they have not, nor will they achieve their aim.

The absolute law of Biogenesis – 'Life' can only come from 'Life'

Biogenesis is the theory that living things can only come from other living things. It was developed in 1858 by Rudolf Virchow as a counter-hypothesis to 'spontaneous generation'. In 1861, Pasteur conducted experiments in an attempt to support the 'biogenesis theory'.

Biogenesis is NOT a theory. It has never been established that any inanimate substance has become 'alive'.

On one website, an atheist and proponent of evolution says: *"Science is now so close to constructing cells capable of reproduction from a feedstock of simple molecules that we have to acknowledge that it will eventually be done. In principle, such cells are just as alive as we are, because evolution could lead from them to something like us, albeit with a very large number of steps and over a long, long time. None the less, we know that evolution can do this. Evolution goes right the way back to sodium chloride, methane and ammonia. These are our ancestors".*

Although evolution is an unproven 'theory', the article above states categorically that "evolution can do this", that is, produce'life' given enough time. To state that salt and gases were our 'ancestors' would be laughable if it were not sopreposterous. Was all this based on genuine scientific evidence? Clearly not.

The 'Breath of Life'

The 'breath of life' God gave to Adam and to all humans is very special. It has a unique non-physical component that no other form of life is given. The Hebrew word used in this connection is 'neshama', and it means a 'mind' with intellect and the ability to 'choose' how to live.

Animals, fish and birds have a type of 'breath of life' but it does not contain 'neshama'. All creatures act according to activities that are built into their DNA and pre-programmed into their brain that has an 'operating system', a BIOS (Basic Input/Output System) like a computer.

Animals cannot imagine, design or change the way they are programmed to live; they forage, eat, drink, mate, have offspring, fight, migrate, according to instinct. Birds cannot decide to build a different type of nest; whales cannot choose which way to navigate or migrate the oceans, they act on instinct.

When Yahweh made humans in His Image and Likeness He equipped them with qualities of His own type of 'Neshama' Intellect, Design and Creative abilities, but very limited compared to His Mind. With their first breath the 'neshama' in Yahweh imparts a special portion of some of His features to each newborn. For instance, those of 'imagination', 'intellect', 'design' and 'creative' powers, as well as some of His other Powers, like morality, ethics, good and evil and choice. All very limited of course, but we are still like Him as we are made in His Image.

Human beings take pride in their design and creative powers, and usually take the credit for what they produce. They rarely give the credit to God for their abilities, and worse rarely give any credit to Yahweh forall He has Designed and Made. This is sacrilege, the definition of which is 'stealing credit from God'.

The Design of DNA

Consider the creation of the DNA double helix spiral, that amazing 'framework' of all living things. The unimaginable work involved with Creating that 'framework' and in the design of millions of species, all intertwined in the unbelievably complicated, and yet delicate ecological balance that enabled all to reproduce, where all are part of the food chain which ensures all were fed, yet all maintained in a balance without any one species dominating the entire world. It is a fact that the weight of insects is greater than all the people in the world. It is a good job their numbers are under Ecological balance and God's Control.

Just these few details outlined here must have involved an almost infinite complexity of interdependent design. Such is the AWESOME POWER of Yahweh. That is a mind-stopping thought in itself.

God's miracle of design, DNA, is the incredible set of 'keys' that define each form of life.

DNA, or deoxyribonucleic acid, is the hereditary material in humans and almost all other organisms. The three dimensional structure of DNA is the double helix which arises from the chemical and structural features of its two polynucleotide chains.

Astronomers have observed helix-shaped nebula near the centre of the Milky Way that stretches over 80 light years, and looks like the classic image of a DNA molecule. This spiral helix may also be observed in the structure of sea shells of all kinds. Yahweh has a way of doing things according to His Design and pattern,

Nearly every cell in a person's body has the same DNA. They are the same in every cell and retain their distinctiveness throughout a person's life. Human cells contain 23 chromosomes (packets of DNA) from the father and 23 from the mother. Each DNA strand contains a unique sequence or code of genetic information that makes up the individual.

All living things have DNA within their cells. However, DNA does more than specify the structure and function of living things, it also serves as the primary unit of heredity in organisms of all types. In other words, whenever organisms reproduce, a portion of their DNA is passed along to their offspring **'after their kind'**. DNA cannot produce a different 'kind' or species.

Although we cannot 'see' the Invisible God, we can experience Him in everything He has made that we can see and experience if we choose to do so.

Everything that exists, and that includes many things we cannot 'see' but nevertheless are very real, by extension, everything is part of Yahweh, and is maintained and upheld by His Powers.

There are Powers of Yahweh the Creator God which although scientists can observe, measure, and put them to use in various ways, they cannot explain exactly what they are, and there is a very good reason for why they cannot.

GOD, YAHWEH CREATED HIS SON, THE WORD from His Own Spirit Matter

In a 'timeless beginning', God became the 'Father' when He created His Son, the Word, from God's own Spirit Matter. There is only One Yahweh, and He created His Son from His Own Spirit Essence and thus the Godhead became a family of two, God the Father and His Son who was the Word, which together were and are One God.

[1] In the beginning was the Word, and the Word was with God, and the Word was God. [2] The same was in the beginning with God. [3] All things were made through him. Without him, nothing was made that has been made. John 1:1-3

The Word, His Son YahwehShua, who God appointed heir of all things, by whom also he made the worlds. Everything was Created by the Word,

[16] For by him all things were created in the heavens and on the earth, visible things and invisible things, whether thrones or **dominions** *or principalities or powers. All things have been created through him and for him. Colossians 1:16*

[1] God (the Father), who at sundry times and in divers (different) manners spoke in time past unto the fathers by

the prophet has in these last days [2] spoken unto us by his Son, whom he has appointed heir of all things, by whom also he made the worlds; [3] who being the brightness of his glory, and the express image of his person, and ***upholding all things by the word of his power****, when he had by himself purged our sins, sat down on the right hand of the Majesty on high: Hebrews 1:1-3*

[6] You are Yahweh, even you are Lord alone. You have made heaven, the heaven of heavens, with all their army (host), the earth and all things that are on it, the seas and all that is in them, and you preserve them all. Nehemiah 9:6

Preserve, Strong's 2421 chayah, khaw-yaw'; a primitive root to live, literally or figuratively; causatively, to revive: vigourously keep alive, certainly, give (promise) life, nourish up, preserve (alive), quicken, recover, repair, restore (to life), revive, save alive, and be whole.

This makes clear that Yahweh not only created all things, but now He through His Son very actively, vigorously and continuously sustains and maintains everything by the use of His Powers.

THE PLANNING PHASE OF YAHWEH AND HIS SON

There is no record of 'when' our timeless God created His Plan. With Yahweh there is no time, but for humans to think of things happening without including the element of 'time' is difficult. So we can imagine that His Plan was devised over 'timeless aeons' and further planned and defined together with his Created Son, the Word. They planned the entire formation and the development of the Plan of God.

The incredible complexity of God's plan

These 'aeons' of developing God's Plan included the design of the Periodic Table of elements from which all physical things would be built.

DNA, Deoxyribonucleic acid is a molecule composed of two chains that coil around each other to form a double helix carrying genetic instructions for the development, functioning, growth and reproduction of all known organisms and many viruses. All the myriad variety of all the Earthly animal fauna, flora and human beings in all their complexity. The crowning part of the Plan was how human beings would eventually become a part of the Creation of the Greater Family of the Children of God.

'Then' Yahweh and the Word, His Son YahwehShua, began an indeterminate 'period' of planning during 'eonian times' however long that was. But as humans, we can only imagine anything in the context of what we know as 'time', yet 'before' God created 'time', God the Father and the Word who are One, explored the concepts and design of everything spiritual and physical that we are aware of now ***before*** any of what we know was Created and came into existence in those two forms of 'Life'.

It was the 'time' when God the Father, Yahweh, was working with His Created Son and instructing the Word in the matters concerning the 'how's' of all the detailed plans that were to be involved with the Creation of all things by the Word.

The plans included first the Creation of all spiritual beings, and after that, all the physical matter of the entire universe.

Everything on Earth, in the heavens, and the universe, spiritual and physical were planned in every detail before they were Created.

This included the creation of the millions of invisible spirit beings. Then the entire physical universe with all the galaxies, stars and planets, the Earth and our Solar System. Our earth with all the millions of species of flora, the plants, the trees; the fauna, animals, fish and birds, a million types of insects, and a trillion types of bacteria.

The pinnacle of all was the Creation of God-man, 'hu-man' beings which they planned and were designed ultimately to become God and part of The Godhead.

It is illogical, even insane to suggest this complexitycould 'design' or 'evolve' itself

Everything that is made by human beings begins its life as a mental thought, then a picture is built up in the mind of the person. As this picture develops, the design is perfected. Then the materials and methods involved in the physical production of the design are carefully planned. Then the object is then put together and made.

Nothing we know of in our human world ever came to be without a 'designer' and a 'manufacturer'.

Yet many in the 'scientific' world argue endlessly, and many teach, that there was no 'Designer' of our fabulous Universe, our incredible Solar system, our Earthly home, or our human minds; no 'Manufacturer', 'it all just happened over billions of years all by itself'.

If anyone were to suggest that the watch on your wrist, that chair you sit in, or that motor car, or that jet plane 'just happened', or 'came from nothing', everyone would think they were crazy, mad, or insane. People around hearing that statement would probably send for the men in white coats to take them away.

What a tragedy it is that so many 'educated' people gullibly accept the theory of evolution, or state that 'everything came from nothing', and thereby commit 'sacrilege', which is defined as 'stealing from God'.

'After' Yahweh and the Word 'completed' their Planning and Design, Yahweh the Father appointed the Word to be His Chief Executive Officer, and to be the actual Creator of all things, and ultimately the Heir (with us) of all things.

Nothing was created from nothing, everything was Created from Yahweh's Spirit Matter Power. The Word would use all God's Secret, Invisible Powers to Create all things. Powers like His unlimited Mind, Infinite Intellect, Spirit Power, 'Gravity', the 'Electromagnetic Spectrum' and the many more listed in the pages of this book.

The incredible Sacrifice of God the Father and The Word His Son made for us.

Here is a staggering, mind-blowing thought. During this planning 'time', another almost incomprehensible part of God's Plan, that is virtually unknown by anyone in the world of 'Churchianity', was discussed in Heaven by Yahweh and His Son before the Creation of all things.

The Plan included the incredible fact that God's Son the Word, at a specific 'time' in history, would relinquish His awesome position of Power in the Godhead, be formed into a man by his Father Yahweh, a man who would be willing to die for the whole human race. The pain involved for the Father and the Son are beyond any human comprehension, and we KNOW that God feels sadness and pain.

The enormity and extent of this sacrifice is not something that many have ever understood, but now some who are reading this may begin to have more appreciation for what was planned and later done for humanity by our God and His Son the Word.

Just these few details outlined here must have involved an almost infinite complexity of interdependent design. That is another mind-stopping thought in itself.

The next chapter explains that God the Father appointed the Word, His Son, to create all things.

CHAPTER 2

THEN GOD THE WORD BEGAN TO CREATE ALL THINGS

[1] In the beginning was the Word, and the Word was with God, and the Word was God. [2] The same was in the beginning with God. [3] All things were made through him. Without him, nothing was made that has been made. John 1:1-3

God the Father, Yahweh, had appointed the Word to be His Chief Executive Officer, CEO, to create and sustain everything.

[15] He (the Word) is the image of the invisible God, the firstborn of all creation. [16] For by him all things were created in the heavens and on the earth, visible things and invisible things, whether thrones or dominions or principalities or powers. All things have been created through him and for him. [17] He is before all things, and in him all things are held together. Colossians 1:15-17

We repeat here for emphasis the first verse in the book of Hebrews where it shows that the Father causes the Son to uphold all things with His Power. [1] God (Yahweh the Father), who at sundry times and in divers (different) manners spoke in time past unto the fathers by the prophets, [2] Has in these last days spoken unto us by his Son (the Word), whom he has appointed heir of allthings, by whom also he made the worlds; [3] Who being the brightness of his glory, and the express image of his person, and upholding all things by the word of his power, when he had by himself purged our sins, sat down on the right hand of the Majesty on high: Hebrews 1:1-3

It is by reason of 'Faith', which is a Spiritual gift from Yahweh that is given to those He chooses, that anyone can begin to understand that the world and all the stars and planets were constructed and framed in their specific positions in the universe by the Word of God, and that things which are 'seen' were made of invisible material, 'Spirit Matter', which cannot be seen.

[3] By faith, we understand that the universe has been framed by the word of God, so that what is seen has not been made out of things which are visible. Hebrews 11:3

Notice, the Word created all that is visible to us, but also He created all those spirit principalities and powers that are invisible to us.

[16] God and His Son created the heavens, the Universe: For by him were all things created, that are in heaven, and that are in Earth, visible and invisible, whether they be thrones, or dominions, or principalities, or powers: all things were created by him, and for him, and they are all similar and different. Colossians 1:16

The Three 'Heavens' of the Bible

The Word Created the heavens and the Earth. There are three 'heavens' mentioned in the Bible.

The first 'heaven', is the sky where the birds and planes fly in the atmosphere surrounding the Earth; then there is the second 'heavens' where countless galaxies are spread across the universe which is constantly expanding. These are the physical 'heavens'.

There is nothing in His Word to tell us where God lived before He Created His Son, and appointed Him Creator and Heir of All Things, but since He is Spirit, His dwelling place is in the 'third heaven' the Spiritual Realm that is invisible to human beings, which has been shown to be closer than many think.

First, the Word, YahwehShua created different types of invisible Spirit Beings and the 'Sons of God'

Before the Word created the physical heavens and the Earth, God the Father, Yahweh, gave of His Spirit Matter and Essence to His Son to create millions of powerful Spirit beings who had the power to choose to be faithful and supportive to God or not. He Created angels, archangels, cherubs, and the 'Sons of God' who were very powerful high ranking beings that were to have a part in ruling the physical creation.

God also created 'Lucifer' and many other types of Spirit Beings with free will

God the Word, YahwehShua, created many powerful Spirit beings of different ranks and powers with free will. Lucifer whose name meant 'shining star of the dawn' was created with choice. Lucifer allowed himself to become power mad, and to think that he could take over from

God. So Lucifer made himself into Satan the Adversary. God did not create Satan 'evil'.

[12] How are thou fallen from heaven, O Lucifer, son of the morning! how are you cut down to the ground, which did weaken the nations! [13] For you have said in your heart, I will ascend into heaven, I will exalt my throne above the stars of God: I will sit also upon the mount of the congregation, in the sides of the north: Isaiah 14:12-13

Part of the Plan of God was for the Word to create Lucifer who had the option to become the Adversary and lead the millions of spirit beings who use their power of choice to choose to be at war with God which many did.

Why did Yahweh do that? It is a part of our Father's Wisdom concerning His Plan. Yahweh is Love, Satan and his cohorts are the opposite of love. Without light we cannot understand darkness. Without silence, we cannot appreciate sound. So without knowing 'evil', we would never be able fully to comprehend 'good'. This reveals the purpose of human life, we are here living this life in a constant state of having moment by moment to use our free will to make and exercise the choice either to love and obey God or not. God, Yahweh, wants us to choose 'Life' and love Him.

Yahweh formed the light, and created darkness: He makes alive and kills. He made peace and good, and the opposite. This truth may present difficulties for many 'religious' type people who do not allow God's

Word, the Holy Bible to lead their minds into a true understanding of God.

God, Yahweh, is in complete control of all things, the 'good' and the 'evil'

God created good and evil, and it is very important to keep in mind that God the Father is in complete charge and is firmly in control of the entire creation, the 'good' the 'bad' and the 'ugly'.

This knowledge helps to explain the answer to the question so many have in their minds. "How can a God of Love allow all the horrendous evil that exists in this world?"

The experience of the horrors of this present evil world is a vital part of Yahweh's Plan to show human beings the awful result of breaking His Laws of Love. Choice, the continuous exercise of free will, is an essential part of the experience of the life of both Spirit Beings and human life which will ultimately lead each individual or person to come to appreciate the Love of God and the vast extent of His Plan for all His Creation.

Throughout history, invisible Satan and his unseen spiritual cohorts have always been, and still are, working at every level of government of the Earth. Satan has managed to convince many in the whole world that he does not exist. How clever is that? He, the defected Sons of God, and all his demons are still hard at work to influence and lead people astray, and to encourage them to break the Laws of Love. They subtly cause almost all on Earth to ignore God in their lives, and to follow their own lusts. Human beings have to learn the lesson that to break the Laws of Love inevitably causes terrible suffering.

Yahweh uses 'evil' to bring about the ultimate 'good' of His loving purposes. Yahweh does not 'sin' in His use of evil. He can use His laws in whatever manner He chooses to achieve His ultimate aims. Yahweh has the Authority to use evil for good, but this option is not open to human beings.

We cannot easily fathom this with our human minds without God's help. However, we have to trust our loving Father God, Yahweh, that if there had been a 'better' way to achieve His purpose, He would have done it differently.

Yahweh knew from before the 'beginning' that to create a Family would involve enormous suffering. Human beings are made in His image, and He built in us the same desire He has, to make a family.

To have a family, people are willing to go ahead and to endure the pain of childbirth. Despite the fact that parents know full well that bringing up children will inevitably involve a lot of emotional and even physical pain as they grown up, pain both for themselves and their children that still does not deter them from that wonderful purpose. God, Yahweh, is the same way.

The Word used God's Creative Powers to form all things physical

Yahweh gave the Word, His Son a 'portion' of His Spirit Matter and His Unseen Powers of Light, Gravity, Centrifugal Force, Magnetism, Electricity, Radiation, the Elements, Capillary Attraction and so on, all His Secret types of Energy to His Son from which to Create all things.

At the Father's direction, the Word then created Space, the physical heavens, galaxies without number, the Earth and its Solar system by using Yahweh's Invisible Secret Powers of Creation.

[5] Thus says God Yahweh, he who created the heavens and stretched them out, he who spread out the earth and that which comes out of it, he who gives breath to its people and spirit to those who walk in it... Isaiah 42:5 (WEB)

[12] I have made the earth, and created man upon it: I, even my hands, have stretched out the heavens, and all their host have I commanded. Isaiah 45:12

The Creation of the Physical Universe

One cannot even begin to imagine the complexity of creating all the designs involved in Yahweh's Plan. The extent of the expanding universe is beyond our comprehension, yet Yahweh has a name for every heavenly body, and calls them all by name.

[1] Praise Yah... [4] He counts the number of the stars. He calls them all by their names. [5] Great is our Lord, and mighty in power. His understanding is infinite. Psalm 147:1,4-5

Ancient writings penned millennia ago say Yahweh stretches (expands) out the north over the empty place, and hangs the Earth upon nothing. In the same texts a word speaking of the heavens being 'formed' actually means a twisting motion. Galaxies are now seen to be spirals.

[8] He alone stretches out the heavens, and treads on the waves of the sea. [9] He makes the Bear, Orion, and the Pleiades, and the rooms (areas) of the south. Job 9:8-9

[7] He stretches out ***the*** north over empty space, and ***hangs the earth*** on nothing. Job 26:7

In another attempt to explain 'Energy', in 1998 some scientists discovered that the universe is not only expanding, but that its expansion is accelerating. The leading theory to explain the accelerating expansion is the existence of a hypothetical repulsive force called 'dark energy'. They say 'dark energy' may possibly be composed of some so far undiscovered subatomic particles that accounts for 85% of the matter in the universe, and about a quarter of its total energy density. One day we shall know.

Although modern physics now proposes that the Universe is expanding, this is apparently contradicted by the notion that 'gravity' actually pulls everything together, and would slow expansion down. So some suggest that 'dark energy' is actually a kind of "antigravity" that pushes the universe apart more strongly than gravity pulls it together.

Now 'black holes' have been 'discovered' where gravity is so strong that nothing can escape out of them.

'Worm holes' are another conjecture, and are thought to exist due to a twisting action of some kind.

There is apparently no end to human attempts to explain the inexplicable. Yahweh's Secret Spiritual Powers are all beyond our limited human understanding even with his help.

How is it that the Earth stays in its orbit where it is with such precision? Should we really put this down to the random effect of 'Gravity' on the forming of our Planet since the 'Big Bang'? Or just admit that something as precise as this needed to be Designed and continually Maintained?

Humans continue to wrestle with some of the mysteries they have uncovered in the search for ever more knowledge. Of black holes, dark energy, the red shift, the rate of expansion of the Universe. So many 'theories', ideas, guesses that are not fact, and so little appreciation of the awesome Powers of the Creator.

The Cosmos – the universe, a system with design and order

Yahweh declares, proclaims, and reveals clearly for all His children to see, that the evidence and proof of His existence is the entire universe. When we look up into the heavens, Yahweh is 'talking' to every one of us, every day and every night, in every language, all over the world, revealing the knowledge about our Creator and His Wonderful Works.

[1] The heavens declare the glory of God. The expanse of the universe shows his handiwork. [2] Day after day they pour out speech, and night after night they display knowledge. [3] There is no speech nor language, where

their voice is not heard. [4] Their voice has gone out through all the earth, their words to the end of the world. Psalm 19:1-4

We had a new view of the skies thanks to the repairs done to the Hubble telescope. Now, in 2022, the new James Webb telescope will reveal even more astounding colour pictures of thousands of galaxies never before seen in human history.

All this had to be created, it could not have 'just happened'. Every day the 'heavens' talk to us, and every night there is teaching in them for us. The word 'heard' is not in the Hebrew, but was added by the KJV translators, because we cannot 'hear' what they are 'saying', yet what they reveal is known to those of every tongue and language in the entire world.

Look up, and wonder at the glory of what we can see, and praise and thank Yahweh every day and night for everything we can observe of what He has made.

These are the generations or history of the heavens and of the earth when they were created, in the day that the Lord God made the earth and the heavens. Genesis 2:4

In the original descriptive Hebrew language of the manuscripts it becomes apparent that the origin of the universe was a progression. First everything was 'planned, then 'designed', then 'made', then 'created', and then 'formed'. Everything was gathered together and 'made', then 'created' in its original form, then 'formed' much like a potter makes a pot.

There are various theories and estimates as to when the universe began, and how long it took, but all these ideas are just that, theories. Recent discoveries put old ideas into a different perspective.

Only a generation ago, the scientific belief of the time stated categorically that there was only one Galaxy, the one in which we live. It was called the Milky Way. Some say it gets its name from a Greek myth about the goddess Hera who sprayed milk across the sky. Also like many words we use today, the English name of our galaxy is derived from its Latin name: Via Lactea. Translated, that means "the road of milk."

When we gaze up at the night sky with the naked eye, on a clear night the band of light across it does look 'milky' because so many of the stars in it are so small they appear to us as a milky fog. The Romans actually got the name from the Greeks, who called our galaxy "galaxias kyklos" or "milky circle". It is said to have a radius of 52,850 light years, and contain 250 billion stars or 150 billion give or take a billion or so. Bigger telescopes, especially the James Webb Telescope, which is now outside our atmosphere, a million miles from earth in space, and thereby provides a much clearer view of the universe, which has caused scientists to have continually to revise their understanding of the Cosmos. It is now thought that there are as many Galaxies as there are stars in the Milky Way. Yahweh's cosmos got larger? Yes, it was expanding, and also humans just made better telescopes.

In 2022 'scientists' have announced that they now have to revise their notions of the Universe starting with a very violent bang, and that the heavenly bodies and planets being formed by crashing into each other. They have now decided all the solid bodies in the universe 'came together gently', slowly being attracted to others, and quietly joining themselves together. Our world was formed this way, they say. The 'science' of yesterday made nonsense again? A light year is about 9.5 trillion kilometres or 5.9 trillion miles. It is the distance that light travels in vacuum in one Julian year (365.25 days). A 'Light year' is nothing but the distance (it is said that it is not a measure of time {?}) that the light travels in one year. The closest two main twin stars to the Earth are Alpha Centauri A and Alpha Centauri B, and are an average of 4.3 light-years from Earth.

So when theoretical Astro-physicists talk about the universe being about 13.7 billion years old, and say that light reaching us from the earliest known galaxies has been travelling, for more than 13 billion years, are they contradicting the definition of a Light year which is the 'distance', with the 'time' it took for light to travel?

Are we at all sure that all that information they publicise is actually factual, or are scientists going to find out over time how wrong they may have been in their calculations? This has certainly been true of the journey of so many scientific 'discoveries' over the last couple of centuries.

Then the Word created everything inanimate, all matter like the 'Periodic Table' of over a hundred different elements, the gases, liquids and solids like air, water and rock, all were created by the Word, and everything is continually maintained and empowered by God's Invisible Powers.

Then He made everything that is 'animate' that lives that has inherent 'Life' which is one of the Spiritual Powers and Gifts of Yahweh. Only Yahweh has 'Life' in Himself, and only He can make anything alive.

Scientists know the existence of these many powers of Gravity, Centrifugal Force, the Electromagnetic Spectrum, Magnetism, Radiation, etc., but they call them 'The Laws of Physics'. This is pure 'sacrilege', which means they are literally stealing the credit for the Design and the Act of Creation from God who used these Powers to create all we know.

[29] The secret things belong to Yahweh our God; but the things that are revealed belong to us and to our children forever, that we may do all the words of this law. Deuteronomy 29:29 WEB

These secret powers belong to God. They are in existence forever and are used continually to uphold and sustain the Universe. And he has given His children a glimpse of them, and the use of them, but complete understanding of them is impossible for the carnal mind, because they are Spiritual Powers.

Our Solar System is different and very special

Scientists are often heard to 'surmise', which means 'to suppose' that something is true without having evidence to confirm it'. They suggest that because the number of

Galaxies and stars is so 'astronomical' (pun intended) it is virtually a 'mathematical certainty' that there are, and indeed 'must be' other places in the Universe where 'Life' like ours exists. It is clear that this is pure conjecture. We have no inspired evidence to prove that.

Of all the Astro-physicists interviewed in a special programme about 'SETI', the 'Search for Extra-Terrestrial Intelligence', not one of those scientists even mentioned or referred to a 'Greater Power' or God. Without exception, they were all of the so far unsupported opinion that we are not 'alone' in the Universe. Some voiced the notion that inside all human beings there is a desire for that 'feeling' to be true, and that there is 'someone' out there. NASA even includes records of sounds and music in their space probes. This 'feeling' of 'alone-ness' is partly what gave rise to the billions spent on 'SETI', the Search for Extra-Terrestrial Intelligence.

The fact is, it is almost certainly true that at some level most people feel 'alone'; and that 'feeling' is part of the make-up of the mind and spirit of human beings, and that it was put there by Yahweh. Why? Because Yahweh wants us to search for Him, and to seek Him. This is because at some level the 'god-part' of us wants to unite with our Creator. What a pity it is that all those involved with SETI are looking in the wrong direction.

God *Is* the Extra-Terrestrial Intelligence our inner 'soul' is seeking, and He has been right here, close to the Earth all the time.

The Design of our Solar System and the Earth

The Sun is 864,400 miles (1,391,000 kilometres) across, and about one hundred times the diameter of Earth. It is so large that about 1,300,000 planet Earths could fit inside it.

There are eight planets in the Solar System, which are in increasing distance from the Sun: Mercury, Venus, Earth, Mars, Jupiter, Saturn, Uranus, and Neptune.

The Sun's heat and radiation are immense. Earth is about 94.5 million miles (152 million km), from the Sun. If there were not protective layers between the Sun and the Earth, everything would burn up. Sunlight takes about eight minutes to arrive at the Earth and provides the energy and warmth needed for life to exist. The Earth's orbit around the Sun is oval or elliptical. Because the Earth is tilted slightly, the amount of sunlight reaching the Earth varies and gives us the seasons, Spring, Summer, Autumn, and Winter, all greatly affected by the Moon that God so carefully placed for us.

'Perpetual Motion' of particles in atoms is absolute proof God, Yahweh, exists

All scientists, and most people know, that there is no such thing on earth as a machine that can run with 'perpetual motion'. Without the addition of energy in some form being supplied, all machines will run down and stop. This is a scientific fact and easily observable.

However, we live in a world of the unseen 'perpetual motion' of particles in atoms that do not 'run down' or 'slow down' because their momentum is sustained and upheld by Yahweh's constant stable Powers. This movement is what produces the 'illusion' of matter being solid. If this was not true and constant, matter as we know it would cease to exist. Everything material would collapse, and there would be no 'solids, liquids or gases'.

With the discovery and construction of these more powerful microscopes, it is only relatively recently that scientists have been able to observe the atoms and particles in ever greater detail and discover more types of them.

Within every atom of every element so far defined by the 'Periodic Table (and they keep finding more elements!), particles of many sorts, electrons, neutrons, positrons, quarks (and they keep finding more particles!), all rotate about a nucleus at a remarkable and constant perpetual speed that does not 'run down'.

An atom is 99.9999999% empty space, and it is the nature and number of these particles and their activity that enables us to observe physical matter to appear to be stable solids, or liquids or gases.

People who do not believe in the Prime Cause, Yahweh, or 'scientists' who do not respect their own fundamental 'Law of Cause and Effect', have no explanation for where this constant supply of energy comes from, or how it sustains this movement.

Scientific observers state that all particles that make up matter are constantly in motion because they have 'kinetic' energy. But here we enter the world of circular reasoning:

"Particles move because they have kinetic energy. But why do they have kinetic energy? Because they move".

Nobody can explain where the 'kinetic energy' comes from but it is evidently there. All who reject that God is that Source of that force and all Power, can have no other explanation as to how atoms contain so much perpetual energy.

The Energy of and within Matter

Einstein's 'Theory of Relativity' can only be really understood by one who has studied advanced mathematics, but even then they must remember that it is just a 'theory'. Theories are simply 'guesses', which at best are assumptions, conjectures, hypotheses, and suppositions. Many take Einstein's ideas as a basis from which to form more 'theories', although others question as to whether or not it is true.

But we can learn something about the Awesome Power of God from Einstein's work. Even if it is not entirely accurate, the truthful core of his notions can give astonishing insights into the awesome Power of our Creator.

How much energy did it take to create the Universe?

Einstein's Theory (guess) of Relativity is expressed as $e=mc^2$ where E is energy, M is mass, and C^2 is the speed of light squared.

Simply stated, this theory (which actually has great truth in it) suggests that it takes an almost unbelievably vast amount of energy to make a very small amount of matter. The energy inside the atom is huge, as witnessed when the power of an atomic or Hydrogen bomb is released from just a few grams or ounces of a uranium isotope.

From our knowing this, when Yahweh through the Word created all the Matter there is, we could deduce that it must have taken more Energy to do so than it is possible for humans to count or express in any terms. Yahweh is the source of all that energy. When all this fantastic amount of energy was released at the time of Creation, perhaps there was a 'Big Bang', but who knows? There was nobody to hear it! Humans have never really understood where the energy that sustains the rotation of particles 'inside' each atom comes from. They cannot because it is one of God's secret things. The electromagnetic spectrum may be observed in action in many ways, but it is still a mystery.

Only a few decades ago previous scientific thought suggested that there were three basic subatomic particles: Electrons, protons, and neutrons. With the advent of the electron microscope and other amazing devices like the new huge particle accelerators, more particles were 'discovered'. Scientists now grapple with many 'new' particles they have now 'discovered'. Which particles, of course, have been there all the time. The more 'scientists' probe into the minutiae of matter, the more they discover about God's incredible Mind, but they will never be able to understand it completely.

Nuclear Energy and Weapons

Einstein developed the basic law of relativity which states that it takes a very large amount of energy to make a very small amount of matter.

Scientists turned his theory around to state that *'a very small amount of material contains an enormous amount of energy'.*

Armed with this new information, it was not long before they were able to manufacture and explode an atomic bomb. Einstein was a pacifist, and was horrified that his discovery had resulted in such a misuse of power, and he spent the rest of his life preaching pacifism.

The two bombs that were dropped on Hiroshima and Nagasaki in 1945 exploded with the power of 12-15,000 tons of TNT high explosive. The more than 9,000-pound bomb contained only 0.6 of a gram of uranium-235, a tiny amount of matter that contained an enormous amount of energy. The second bomb weighed 10,000 pound and had the power of 22,000 tons of TNT but it only contained 0.8 of a gram of uranium-235.

Atomic bombs are now stockpiled by a number of nations around the world. These bombs have the potential to release power the equivalent of millions of tons of TNT. If only a few were detonated, it would mean the end of all life on earth.

In the 20th Century more lives were lost and more people maimed than in the previous 19 Centuries of wars. A staggering thought. We are not learning from experience. On the contrary, the evil side of human nature is running rampant with wars, and feeds on incessant 'news', fake and otherwise, fuelled by the Media, the Internet and 'Social Media'. Everything is 'Millennial'. Now is seems the whole world is being run by the 'Me' generation of under thirties who hold positions they are neither experienced in, nor mature enough to manage with balance and wisdom.

In the Bible in Matthew 24:22 Christ, (khris-tos'; from (5548) (cri>w); anointed, with oil, consecrated, i.e. the Messiah.) said in 30 A.D. that if the events at the time of the 'end of the age' were not 'shortened' or prevented from reaching their conclusion, "no flesh would be saved alive". This only became possible in the 1960's when the more powerful H-bombs were developed and manufactured.

It is estimated that around 15,000 such bombs exist, and that if only a very few of them were detonated it would indeed erase all life from the earth. And the U.S. and Russian governments are currently in 2022 apparently planning to make more. A sobering thought.

Since those detonations, there have been a number of 'accidents' with nuclear power plants, including Chernobyl and Fukushima with devastating results on the local areas. But also with terrible unseen and largely unacknowledged effects on the atmosphere of the whole planet. It is incredible that humans cannot appreciate that the dangers of using nuclear energy are affecting their lives much more than they think. Now Russia has bombed the largest nuclear power station in the

Ukraine, potentially endangering all of Europe if not the whole world.

People who do not honour Yahweh and His Powers are quite unable fully to understand this energy in matter because it is one of the Spiritual Powers of God which cannot be discerned by the human mind.

[14] *But the natural (carnal) man receives not (cannot fathom) the things of the Spirit of God: for they are foolishness unto him: neither can he know them, because they are spiritually discerned. 1 Corinthians 2:14*

With all the ingenuity of brilliant minds, no human being can understand fully all about this life of ours, unless they have the Spirit of God, and even then we are limited in the scope of our comprehension of the Mind of Yahweh.

Mathematics is a Spiritual Power of God

What is called 'mathematics' is actually another of the Mystery Powers of God. The 'laws of maths' are really another branch of the Laws of God. God used His Laws of Mathematics to create the universe and all things in it. The incredible patterns that exist in numbers formed by those laws are not just 'there', they were designed to be there. We can use them, we can even think we understand them, but how they are the way they are is another mystery.

There are a lot of very clever mathematicians in our era. They are performing wonderful feats of calculations using complex formulae they have discovered how to do amazing things like plotting the trajectory of satellites and space modules even to the Moon and back and beyond. But do they give credit for Mathematics to its Creator? Rarely if ever.

But how is it that there exists such a fact as ‘Prime Numbers’? The first five prime numbers are: 2, 3, 5, 7 and 11, there are many more. A prime number is a whole number that has only two factors 1 and itself. Put another way, a prime number can be divided evenly only by 1 and by itself. Prime numbers also must be greater than1(one). Nobody knows how, they just know they exist, and because Mathematics is Spiritual they never will fathom it completely.

Why is there what is called the ‘Fibonacci’ sequence, such that each number is the sum of the two preceding ones, starting from 0 and 1? The first few are 0, 1, 1, 2, 3, 5, 8, 13, 21, 34, 55. They continue ad infinitum. Mathematicians can work out the sequence of these numbers, but they cannot explain how they came to be for the same reason as they cannot explain the ‘how’ of Prime Numbers.

‘New’ Geometry reveals ‘fractal’, another aspect of God’s Spiritual Powers

Geometry is another branch of mathematics which until recently was entirely based on books written by the Greek Euclid in 300B.C. Geometry is a branch of mathematics concerned with whole shapes of one, two and three dimensions, like lines, triangles and cubes; and the size, relative position of figures, and the properties of space.

In the last century many explored a new concept of shapes and dimensions concerning the possibility that the three dimensional world we think we live in may have a 4th or 5th or more. Also that the number expressing the dimension of shapes could be a fraction rather than a whole number. Fundamental suppositions of the centuries old accepted 'rules' of geometry were being challenged.

After some years of research by many Geometers, in 1975, the word 'Fractal' (The word 'fractal' means 'self-similar but different') was coined by a Frenchman, Benoît Mandelbrot, perhaps not so much discovered, but finally put into words. He explained 'Fractals' as being geometric shapes that when divided into parts, each part would be a similar, but smaller replica of the whole shape.

The new word 'fractal' was coined to embrace a new concept of shapes, before that equations were solved one at a time, and that shapes might be defined by repeating a fractional equation in a feedback loop. The concept behind it opened up a completely new field of Geometry.

A 'fractal' is a structural object which is irregular on all scales of length, and therefore appears to be 'broken up' in a radical way. Each of these different types of 'fractal' object display self-similar structure over an extended, but finite, scale range. All identified because of similarity, but different in the detail of the structure.

Observations of apparently chaotic shapes and patterns in nature and even in our business world led to further research. The shape of coastlines, trees, surfaces of broken rocks, frequency of earthquakes, floods, even market prices over long periods, all seemed to occur with a 'regular irregularity'. Was there a principle of Yahweh's Order within the apparent chaos observed that could be discovered? Indeed there is.

It is now clear that everything in the physical realm is structured along the lines of fractal geometry. Mathematicians had discovered another of Yahweh's Invisible Laws.

Fractals are common in the natural world and are found nearly everywhere. An example is broccoli. Every branch of broccoli looks just like its parent stalk, similar but slightly different. The surface of the lining of your lungs has a fractal pattern in their surface area that allows for more oxygen to be absorbed. Such complex real-world processes can now be expressed in equations through fractal geometry.

Most people learned at school that no two identical snowflakes have ever been observed among countless numbers examined. They are all similar but different. DNA is another example of a 'pattern' that is always similar, yet can contain an infinite number of irregularities. Put simply there are no two humans, cows, frogs, or any other creature that are the same in every respect.

When Yahweh Creates, He reveals a part of His Nature that is 'Fractal', in that there are no two things exactly the same in Creation but are 'similar'. How wonderful is that?

For thousands of years, mathematicians with all their brain power have only been able to make one calculation at a time. With the recent development of computing power, humans can now make billions of calculations a second.

The Mind of God who designed and 'Is' the Laws of Mathematics has always had the Power to make an infinite number of calculations simultaneously for Eternity. What awesome Power.

God's Creation is 'Fractal', all 'similar' but 'infinitely' different

Approximate fractals are found everywhere in God's Creation. The development of ever more powerful microscopes has led us to greater understanding of the awesome nature of the design of His universe and all it contains. Yahweh does not 'mass-produce' every type of thing to be all exactly the same. This is phenomenal 'new' information which should lead human beings to a greater appreciation of the Wonder and Power of our Creator. All snowflakes have a distinctive but slightly different shape. Molecules of water that form each tiny ice crystal naturally arrange themselves into a hexagonal (six-sided) structure. The result will be a snowflake with six sides or six arms but incredibly, they are all similar but different, and so are 'fractal'.

With this concept of 'fractal' in mind, it is completely mind-boggling to appreciate that of all the countless trillions of sand particles there are, no two are exactly the same.

This applies also to trees. Each part of a tree has similarity to the whole. Each branch, each twig is a smaller 'fractal' of the whole tree. Yahweh has created an ever growing number of trees, and there are not two the same.

Due to advances in technology, we have moved on from regarding fingerprints as all similar but not the same, to being able to 'read' the human DNA genome, which although all have similarities, no two humans have exactly the same structure. For that matter, no two of any of the hundreds of millions of different species are the same. No two animals, no two birds, no two fish, no two animals in the ten million species of coral, indeed no two of any species of any type have exactly the same DNA structure. What words are we to use to express our appreciation of the awesome, amazing, incredible Mind of God and His Powers of Creation?

So how can we absolutely KNOW that there is an invisible God?

Yahweh is Spirit, and yes, God and his Son the Word are indeed Invisible. So how can we know that 'They' exist? The fact that we ourselves exist, and everything we know about that exists, is all concrete evidence that there is a Creator who made us. For every effect there has to be a cause, God is that cause. Here repeated, is part of the explanation He gives to us in His Word:

[20] *"For the invisible things of Him (Yahweh) from the creation of the (physical) world (and the entire universe) are clearly seen, (Yahweh) being understood (is evidenced or known) by the (physical) things that are*

made, (and in a sense make visible) even His (Invisible) eternal power and Godhead;" Romans 1:20

So Yahweh through Paul clearly states that the visible physical world **is the evidence** that an Invisible God exists. How else can anyone account for 'what is'. Puny human minds have recently come up with two basic ideas. One is that 'everything came from nothing'. Everything just happened, no design, no maker, just one day there it all was. Another suggests that everything evolved of its own accord from materials in the seas.

To a logical Spirit filled mind, when either or both of these theories, guesses or notions are examined thoughtfully, they just do not stand up to scrutiny. Neither can 'stand up in court', simply because neither is true. The problem is that most people are not sufficiently interested to look into these notions objectively for themselves, they simply accept them and get on with life. One day they may live to regret that approach. Again...

26 "To whom then will you liken me? Who is my equal?" says the Holy One. Lift up your eyes on high, and behold who has created these things, that brings out their host by number: he calls them all by names by the greatness of his might, for that he is strong in power; not one fails. Isaiah 40:26

Humans cannot even begin to imagine the Mind Power of a Being that can not only create all the billions of celestial bodies, but the Creator has a name by which He calls each one. What a breathtaking thought! With all our powers of thought, that task would be out of the question even if we could see them all which we certainly cannot. God also knows each of the seven billion human beings by name, the number of hairs on their heads, and everything about them, what they do, and what they think about.

Has the rapid development of computers led to a greater appreciation of Yahweh's Mind, and the mind of His children?

It does not seem so. Sadly most humans take the credit for their own 'brilliance'. Since the rapid development of computers from bytes, to kilobytes, to megabytes, to gigabytes, to terabytes and beyond, we now see that humans are able to work with vast amounts of information with their tiny brains that have Godlike characteristics of design and development. Our brain, just three pounds of fat and water, operates on about 25 watts of electricity that it makes itself from glucose fuel extracted from what we eat. A 'power station' activating our brain that can perform incredible wonders of Intellect from the moment of being given the first breath. Did that brain 'evolve' from primordial slime, or did it 'just come from nothing'? The very idea is ludicrous, and demeans those who are of that opinion.

No, as this book will explain later in greater detail, that brain is descended from the first perfectly structured man Adam who Yahweh made from red earth, passed on to us by the astounding 'magic' of DNA, who He enlivened with the 'breath of life', when He also gave him the gift of 'neshama' which is one of the unique qualities of God that bestows the ability to use 'intellect' and 'mind' on to His children.

In the 'beginning', God, Yahweh, created the beautiful heavens and the earth

The Earth was Created beautiful, perfect as are all God's Creations.

[11] He has made every thing beautiful in his time: also he hath set the world in their heart, so that no man can find out the work that God makes from the beginning to the end. Ecclesiastes 3:11

In the Bible, God speaks in the First Person to Job:

[4] "Where were you when I laid the foundations of the earth? Declare, if you have understanding. [5] Who determined its measures, if you know? Or who stretched the line on it? [6] What were its foundations fastened on? Or who laid its cornerstone, 7 when the morning stars (3556 kowkab, spirit princes) sang together, and all the Sons of God shouted for joy?" Job 38:4-7

Strong's {3556} bk;wOK — kowkab, ko-kawb'; a star (as round or as shining); figuratively, a prince(s):

When Yahweh created the earth, He knew that many spirit beings were witnessing the event, and saw how they reacted at the sight, and He recorded it in His Word.

The powerful 'Sons of God' were among the millions of spirit beings that the Word created before the creation of physical matter, and they sang and shouted for joy at the beautiful sight when the earth was formed.

The astronauts were very much moved, even awestruck by the beauty of the earth viewed from outer space. We know that everything God does is perfect and beautiful, but sadly not everything stays that way due to the sin of humans.

Human beings have an inbuilt limit as to just how much they are able to understand God and His works.

Our Earth was Created with the environment needed for habitation

The earth was created beautiful, and the following verse in Isaiah states that the earth was not created 'tohuw' which means an empty waste.

[18] For thus says the Lord that created the heavens; God himself that formed (yatsar) the earth and made it; he has established it, he created it not in vain (tohuw), he formed it to be inhabited (yashab): I am the Lord; and there is none else. Isaiah 45:18

The earth was formed by God to be inhabited, but the Bible does not say what it was inhabited by initially immediately after it was formed.

The next chapter offers a possible explanation concerning the time when the millions of fossils that have been discovered all over the earth were living creatures. The fossil evidence testifies beyond all doubt to the existence at some time, of our planet being covered with 'flora' and populated by 'fauna' of very different kinds from that which exist today.

CHAPTER 3

THE DINOSAUR AGE EXPLAINED?

THE CREATION OF THE EARTH – BEAUTIFUL – THEN DISASTER

Then apparently at some time after it was first created, nobody can be sure how long after, the beautiful earth suffered sudden destruction because the second verse in the Bible says:

[2] The earth was formless and empty (Hebrew tohu and bohu). Darkness was on the surface of the deep, and God's Spirit was hovering over the surface of the waters. Genesis 1:2

Those words 'formless and empty' in the original Hebrew were 'tohu' and 'bohu' which means chaotic and a desolate ruin in darkness covered in water.

Strong's Concordance is used to provide the meaning of each of the Hebrew words in these passages.

[18] For thus saith the Lord (YahwehShua) that created the heavens; God himself that formed (yatsar) the earth and made it; he hath established it, he created it not in vain (tohuw), he formed it to be inhabited (yashab): I am the Lord; and there is none else. Isaiah 45:18

So the earth was created beautiful, and also to be inhabited.

When Yahweh made the earth He lovingly formed it like a human potter might make a beautiful object out of clay.

The Bible **NEVER** contradicts itself. God does not lie, and cannot lie. Christ quoted words the Psalmist wrote hundreds of years previously.

[34] Christ, Yah'Shua the Messiah, answered them, "Isn't it written in your law, 'I said, you are gods? (Psalm 82:6)' 35 If he called them gods, to whom the word of God (Yahweh) came and the Scripture can't be broken, John 10:34-35

What did Christ the Messiah mean by that statement? The 'canonised' Scriptures cannot be 'broken' or shown in any way to be incorrect, they are truth, God the Father, Yahweh, has ensured that. In Christ's prayer to His Father just before His crucifixion, He emphasised that fact.

[16] They are not of the world even as I am not of the world. [18] Sanctify them in your truth. Your word is truth. (quoted from Psalm 119:142) [18] As you sent me into the world, even so I have sent them into the world. John 17:16-18

Yahweh's Creation of the world was beautiful, not an indistinguishable ruin. Since it was beautifinitially when it was Created, something drastic must have happened to ruin it. It is not a matter of the translation of the tense of the verb. If something was beautiful and became ugly, something must have caused the change.

Absolute scientific Law: There is a cause for every effect.

Was there a Prehistoric period of life on the world?

The irrefutable evidence says yes!

The following story is built upon some indications in the Bible, and on the evidence of the Fossil record that is incontrovertible, but the narrative that follows is an idea, a thought, a conjecture, and is not intended to be taken as a proclamation of 'truth' but merely to offer an explanation of the 'Dinosaur' period which is a proven reality.

How old is the earth?

Theories about the age of the Earth are very conflicting. Some claim that the Earth is only 6000 years old, others say it is 58–100 million years old based on fossil evidence. Others say the universe is 4.3 billion years old based on various dubious dating methods. Who is right? Or are any of these theories correct?

One problem is that methods of dating archaeological and palaeontological artefacts often provide results that appear to contradict each other. 'Scientific' estimates of the age of the universe, our galaxy, the earth and of fossils differ wildly from millions, or hundreds of millions, to many billions. Can we actually know, and know that we know what happened when over past aeons? And does it really matter if we can or cannot do so? In the opinion of this author, we cannot know absolutely or definitively, and it really does not matter for the purpose of this story.

There is probably good reason why the 'Prehistoric' or "dinosaur" era is not explained in Yahweh's Word. The whole Bible is the story about human beings, God's Children, the first of which was Adam. So therefore there could not have been any human creatures that existed before the six days of Creation recorded in Genesis and the forming of Adam about 6000 years ago.

What is important is that we give credit for the existence of absolutely everything to Yahweh, the Creator God. It is of crucial importance that God's children take advantage of the Manual Yahweh wrote through his servants the Prophets and Apostles that tells us about Him, about His Plan, and **everything** we need to know about living this life that we **cannot** learn by any other means.

One thing is certain, the Creation exists – in it we live and move

Yahweh is Timeless. He has always existed, He exists now, and will always exist.

Yahweh **IS**, and it is interesting that the English word 'exists' which means being (alive or be in existence) has **IS** in the middle of the word – ex**is**ts.

In a beginning, whenever that was, it was certainly a very long time ago indeed as we humans count the 'Gift' of time, God the Father, Yahweh, Created His Son, theWord, out of His Own Spirit Matter Essence. The Father and the Son were and are One God.

Then God the Father, Yahweh, through His Son the Word, the 'CEO' of all things, created the heavenly host of spirit beings, the Seraphim, Cherubim, the 'Sons of God', archangels, angels, all created with free choice, or at least He created them with the power of 'choice' whether to love and respect Yahweh, or to rebel against Him.

These 'Sons of God' and other angelic beings were present later at the time of the subsequent creation of the physical heavens and the Earth, they sang and shouted with joy at the incredible spectacle. Who were these 'Sons of God'? What were their activities in the past? And what are they doing now? This is covered in detail later.

Who and what were these 'Sons of God'.

Were they spirit 'beings'?

What was their part in Yahweh's Plan? Some of these created spirit beings, were those who remained faithful to God who look after His and our best interests. Also those who became rebellious and are now adversaries against God. Both currently have ruling positions on Earth in our era.

[12] For our wrestling (literally our fight) is not against flesh and blood, but against the principalities, against the powers, against the world's (spiritual) rulers of the darkness of this age (both then when Yahweh through Paul wrote, and now in our era), and against the spiritual forces of wickedness in the heavenly places. Ephesians 6:12

These invisible rebellious spirits still have great power, and exercise influence over many world leaders. Yahweh appoints humans in positions of

power, but Satan uses his spirit forces for his own ends, and the result is chaos in the world.

Was there a prehistoric period before YahwehShua Created Adam?

Was the creation we know about in Genesis 1:1 when Yahweh created the heavens, our Solar system, and the Earth which was so beautiful that all the angels and the Sons of God sang and shouted for joy, made for a specific purpose that existed for a period, but suddenly came to an abrupt destructive end?

Was there another previous 'beginning' or an initial 'first phase' of Yahweh's Creation on this Earth before He created Adam and Eve that He has not given us much information about in His Word?

Because the very next verse states that the earth was or had become a ruin, a devastated chaotic planet in darkness under water, with Yahweh's spirit moving unhappily over the waters. What could have happened to turn such a beautiful creation into a wreck?

The 'Dinosaur' Era

Millions of fossils have been discovered all over the world, they are concrete evidence that a completely different world did exist at some time. The evidence of the fossil record is undeniable. The remains of completely different types of plants and animals attest to the fact that they lived on earth at some time, and were suddenly destroyed.

If that period was a 'trial' creation or a previous plan, did Yahweh and His Son initially appoint some of His then faithful angelic host to be in charge of that very different world in the same way He has done in our world today?

First, in **a** beginning the Earth was definitely **formed to be inhabited, but the Bible does not *say why, when or by what and whom?*** At the outset, again it must be made clear that this section on 'prehistory' is offered and proposed as a conjecture, speculation, or a hypothesis based on very careful analysis and profound respect for the Scriptures. God our Father, Yahweh, has not seen fit to provide many details of this period of history in His Word, but the evidence of millions of fossils all over the world does.

Science 'explains' the fossil record – but not really

A 'scientist' writes:

"Fossils, the preserved remains of animal and plant life, are mostly found embedded in sedimentary rocks. Of the sedimentary rocks, most fossils occur in shale, limestone and sandstone. So most fossils are found in sedimentary rocks, where gentler pressure and lower temperature, over time, allows preservation of past life-forms. Fossils become a part of sedimentary rocks when sediments such as mud, sand, shells and pebbles cover plant and animal organisms and preserve their characteristics through time. Mud forms when larger rocks erode into tiny, usually microscopic, particles. These particles settle in the calm waters of lakes, swamps and the ocean, covering creatures that live

there. Mud and clay combine with minerals and other particles over time to harden into shale. The hard parts of the creatures covered with mud undergo preservation as fossils when consolidated with other materials inside the shale. Shale splits easily into layers to reveal any fossils inside. Fossils inside shale often include brachiopods, fossilized plants, algae, crustaceans and arthropods trapped in the hardened mud. The very small mud and clay particles allow small details of organisms to be preserved, like the rare fossils of soft-bodied organisms found in the Burgess Shale".

Note: The fossils described above could not all have been deposited over ages of time, they would simply have rotted away. To be preserved, extreme pressure, and not a little heat, over a short period of time would have been necessary. Other creatures were trapped in the ice that suddenly formed due to the Sun being obscured, and remained frozen from that time until the recent Climate Change began to melt areas that have been frozen for many millennia.

Prehistory was the period of time when plants similar, but very different from those we know now, like ferns, mosses and lichens, but also many different types of creatures existed. We know that once upon a time, whenever that was, Mammoths, Sabre Toothed Tigers, and Apes of various types lived on earth which have been misidentified as being our human ancestors. The fossils prove that many different types of Dinosaurs also inhabited the Earth.

It is said that Sabre Tooth Tigers along with Woolly Mammoths, American lions and other giant animals used to live in the American grasslands during the Pleistocene Epoch (23 million to 10,000 years ago). Again we state, that these stated dates are highly questionable due to the inaccuracies of the various dating methods. This group of animals are known as the “Megafauna”.

In the Tundra permafrost, a historically permanently frozen layer of ground (now melting), a Mammoth in remarkably good condition was found frozen and embedded in ice with grasses still in its mouth. For this to have happened, there had to have been an instant fall of temperature to well below freezing. What could cause that? If there was a cataclysmic event in our Solar System which caused the light of the Sun to be completely obscured, the Earth would be suddenly be engulfed in darkness, and everything would immediately freeze. Verse 2 of Genesis 1 says darkness covered the earth.

When did this happen?

As suggested at the outset, frankly there are only guesses and theories to go on, but it certainly was a very long time ago, and it is not important for us to know exactly ‘when’ in relation to this story.

The word ‘prehistoric’ is the story of events long before written human history began. The word history from Greek ‘historia’ meaning inquiry, is now written knowledge, and ‘history’ actually means ‘his-story’, the story of humankind. The human era began at a later time, in another 'beginning' which we know as the six day time period explained in Genesis when God reformed the Earth in six days, and created a different perfect environment upon which Adam the first human, and His Children could live, experience life and time, ultimately to become part of His Family.

The word Human is made up of two words – 'Hu' ancient word meaning God, and Man. Human, hu-man beings are literally God-man (and Wo-Man) beings, because we are Yahweh's children and are destined to become part of the God Family.

Many Bible scholars tend to analyse and dissect the Scriptures in great detail, but rarely in the overall context of, or with regard to Yahweh's plan for His children. Nor do they appear to be really seeking to grow in the knowledge of the truth.

16 "as also in all of his letters, speaking in them of these things. In those, there are some things that are hard to understand, which the ignorant and unsettled twist, as they also do to the other Scriptures, to their own destruction". 2 Peter 3:16

An example of this is their scholarly analysis of the 'gap theory', where there is much disagreement as to whether there is a time 'gap' between Genesis 1:1 and Genesis 1:2. As far as this author is concerned, the question of whether the Hebrew word should be translated 'is', 'was', or 'became' is irrelevant. Such 'debating' is a fruit of the flesh and actually a sin against the Law of Love.

The clear indisputable fact is that in Genesis 1:1 Yahweh says that the Earth was created perfect and beautiful, and that in Genesis 1:2 the Earth was a chaotic ruin in darkness under water. Something must have happened to cause that change!

The reader may want to check out (or frankly not take the time) what those many 'scholars' for and against the 'gap' theory suggest. The 'gap' theory, said to be first proposed in the 1800's, is said to relate to the time that appears to have elapsed between Genesis 1:1 and 1:2. It is mostly just an argument about words. They give no real explanation for the change.

Prophetic events have three fulfilments: past, present, future

In consideration of prophecies in the Bible, it is always important to appreciate that there are usually at least three fulfilments of any prophecy, past, present and future.

A look at Jeremiah 4. Could the 'past' original occurrence of this prophecy in Jeremiah 4 possibly be referring to the cosmic destruction that led to the beautiful world of Genesis 1:1 becoming the ruin of Genesis 1:2? Was the 'past' in this fulfilment of a 'previous' fulfilment before Jeremiah's time when God through him was also predicting another during his time, and thirdly a time to come as our earth comes close to the collapse of the ecosystem, and the possible future events of all-out war in this era?

Is this passage in Jeremiah figuratively referring to this previous prehistoric time? There are certainly some indications that it could be.

[23] *I beheld the earth, and, lo, it was* **without form, and void** *(tohu and bohu); and* **the heavens,** *and they* **had no light.**[24] *I beheld the mountains, and, lo, they trembled, and all the hills moved lightly.*[25] *I beheld, and, lo,* **there was no man,** *and all the birds of the heavens were fled.*[26] *I beheld, and, lo, the fruitful place was a wilderness, and all the cities (Strong's: 'places') thereof were broken down at the presence of the Lord, and by his fierce anger.*[27] *For thus hath the Lord said, The* ***whole land shall be desolate; yet will I not make a full end.*** [28] ***For this shall the earth mourn, and the heavens above be black;*** *because I have spoken it, I have purposed it, and will not repent, neither will I turn back from it. Jeremiah 4:23-28*

We absolutely know that the world was not Created 'tohu' and 'bohu', chaotic and ruined, but became that way. Was it as a result of Yahweh punishing the rebellion of whoever the powerful spirit was that He had put in charge of the prehistoric era? The rebellion of this powerful spirit against Yahweh was long before He Created Adam and Eve. His rebellion seems to have resulted in the mass destruction of a planet, possibly the disturbance of other planets, the formation of the asteroid belt, and the peppering of the earth and the moon with debris.

[7] *Then the earth shook and trembled. The foundations also of the mountains quaked and were shaken, because he (the powerful spirit being that God, Yahweh, had put*

in charge) was angry. 8 Smoke went out of his nostrils (figuratively). Consuming fire came out of his mouth (figuratively). Coals were kindled by it. [9] He bowed the heavens also, and came down. Thick darkness was under his feet. [10] He rode on a cherub, and flew. Yes, he soared on the wings of the wind. [11] He made darkness (the opposite of Yahweh who is Light) his hiding place, his pavilion around him, darkness of waters, thick clouds of the skies. [12] At the brightness before him his thick clouds passed, hailstones and coals of fire. [13] Yahweh (in response) also thundered in the sky. The Most High uttered his voice: hailstones and coals of fire. [14] He sent out his arrows, and scattered them. He routed them with great lightning bolts. [15] Then the channels of waters appeared. The foundations of the world were laid bare at your **rebuke,** *Yahweh, at the blast of the breath of your nostrils. Psalm 18:7-15*

Rebuke of whom? A rebellious spirit being? Did Yahweh's wrathful Power cause destruction, and a catastrophe in our Solar System,

How old is the Earth?

Rocks brought back from the Moon, (if indeed this is true) have been dated at a maximum of 4.51 billion years old. 'Martian' meteorites that are said to have landed upon Earth have also been dated to around 4.5 billion years old by 'lead dating', but is this a 'truth' or another theoryor guess? Again, for the purpose of this story the period of time is not relevant or important.

It is variously said that "the Jurassic period spanned 56 million years from the end of the Triassic Period 201.3 million years ago to the beginning of the Cretaceous Period 145 million years ago". And "Dinosaurs went extinct about 65 million years ago (at the end of the Cretaceous Period), after living on Earth for about 165 million years". And "Tyrannosaurus, Velociraptor, Apatosaurus, Stegosaurus, or Triceratops, were still alive. These, and all other non-avian dinosaurs became extinct at least 65 million years ago at the end of the Cretaceous Period". Opinions differ.

Some palaeontologists claim that the first human ancestors appeared between five million and seven million years ago, *probably* when some apelike creatures in Africa began to walk habitually on two legs. They were making crude stone tools by flaking rocks 2.5 million years ago. Then some of them spread from Africa into Asia and Europe after two million years ago. These ape-like animal creatures are found in the fossil record, **but they were definitely not human**, because this assumption conflicts with Yahweh's True Biblical record of the creation so very much later of the first human being, Adam.

It is suggested that the Stone Age is also divided into three different periods. Palaeolithic or Old Stone Age: from the first production of stone artefacts, about 2.5 million years ago, to the end of the last Ice Age, about 9,600 BCE. This is the longest Stone Age period. Palaeontologists suggest that the Stone Age is the first of the three-age system of archaeology, which divides 'human technological' prehistory into three periods: the Stone Age, Bronze Age, and Iron Age. The Stone Age lasted roughly 3.4 million years, from 30,000,000 BCE to about 3,000,000 BCE, and ended with the advent of metalworking.

So many confusing and seemingly contradictory statements are made by 'expert' scientists that do not appear to be very 'scientific' at all. Questions regarding 'time' are covered next.

The Prehistoric fossil record reveals a very different world

Whenever there appears to be an apparent contradiction in the Bible, this should always bring us to an immediate halt, as it signals the need to dig deeper to find the real meaning that is not immediately obvious, because there are no contradictions in Yahweh's Word.

One of the best ways to dig is to consult the Scriptures in the original language in which they were written, and to employ the powerful study tools suggested by Dr. Ernest L. Martin, which include using the interrogative pronouns, *who what where when and how* to arrive at the meaning God intended us to have of any passage.

Yahweh wrote the original Scriptures through men in the Hebrew language which is much more descriptive, lyrical, figurative and expressive of the Writer's in-depth emotions in an imaginative and beautiful way than is possible in the English language.

So from perfection and beauty – to a chaotic ruin

One wonders how sad Yahweh was when He beheld the destruction of this beautiful, perfect earth that He had lovingly created? So beautiful that the angels and the Sons of God sang with joy.

Genesis 1:2 describes such a completely different scenario and condition which is not at all beautiful. The Earth was not created that way. Something had to happen to make it void, empty and ruined, and covered with water.

For every effect there has to be a cause.

Arguments about whether the Hebrew 'was' meant 'became' or arguments about the 'gap' are pointless scholarly gobbledegook. Clearly the situation in verse 2, 'was' has to mean 'became' as a result of some terrible catastrophe in view of other scriptures saying that the world was Created perfect and beautiful. Strong's Hebrew definitions again help build a picture.

Genesis 1:2 And the earth was became ***'without form',*** *8414* **tohuw**, *to'-hoo; meaning to lie waste; a desolation of surface, desert; figuratively a worthless thing, in vain, confusion, empty place, without form, nothing, a thing of nought, vain, vanity, waste, wilderness; and* ***'void'.***

922 **bohuw,** *bo'-hoo; from an unused root (meaning to be empty); a vacuity, i.e. (superficially) an indistinguishable ruin, emptiness, void; and* ***'darkness',*** *2822* ***choshek,*** *kho-shek'; from 2821; the dark; hence (literally) darkness; figuratively, misery, destruction,* *death, ignorance, sorrow, wickedness, darkness, obscurity. (This was not just darkness, a lack of light, it also implies misery, sorrow, sadness at the state and degree of destruction), was upon the face of* ***the deep.***

8415 ***thowm****, teh-home'; or µhoT]* ***thom****, teh-home'; an* ***abyss*** *(as a surging mass of water), especially the deep, the main sea or the subterranean water supply, deep place, depth.*

And the ***'Spirit'*** *7307* **ruwach**, *roo'-akh; wind; by resemblance breath, a sensible or even violent exhalation; figuratively, life, anger, by resemblance spirit, of a rational being including its expression and functions, air, anger, blast, breath, courage, mind, spiritual, tempest of* ***'God'*** *430 '****elohiym,*** *el-o-heem'; gods in the ordinary sense; but specifically used here of the supreme God (Yahweh); and sometimes as a superlative to Sons of God and angels;* ***'moved'*** *7363* ***rachaph,*** *raw-khaf';* ***to brood****, by implication to be relaxed, flutter, move, shake upon the face of the waters.*

God's Spirit, 'ruwach', was moving or fluttering over the 'darkness' of this empty place, an indistinguishable ruin, figuratively in misery, sadness and sorrow at the sight of the waters, and 'brooding' about the ruinous devastation of His previously beautiful creation.

The Hebrew word rachaph includes the sense of the English word 'Brooding' which can involve many sad feelings within that one word. To 'brood' is to think deeply about something that makes one unhappy, angry, or worried, to agonize over, languish over, feel despondent about, grieve over, eat one's heart out over. Especially when this destruction had perhaps been caused by the rebellious wickedness of a powerful spirit being to whom He had entrusted the task of looking after it. Is this a case of anthropomorphising Yahweh? No.

Yahweh shows in His Word that He has feelings, and when He made us in His image He installed a measure of those feelings in us. To meditate and think about God our Father who gives us every heartbeat, every breath and all the blessings we enjoy, having to bear all those sad feelings, and more when observing the dreadful ruined state of His beautiful Creation, is enough to bring tears to one's eyes

This 'story' happened untold millions of years ago, and may help to explain the events that may have occurred long before the next 'beginning'.

The next stage of Yahweh's plan to extend His Family, was when in a wonderful 'new beginning' God cleaned up, and in six days reformed the Earth much as we know it today.

The next chapter tells how Yahweh made it to be a perfect home and eco system for His children, repopulated it with completely new fauna and flora, and created Adam and Eve, the first of His 'hu-man' children formed in His Image and Likeness.

CHAPTER 4

A NEW BEGINNING AND A REFORMED WORLD

Then God reformed the Earth to make it habitable for His Children.

We are told plainly the Lord created the heavens and the Earth; Yahweh himself formed the Earth and made it and established it. We are clearly told that He formed it to be ***inhabited***, according to His Plan.

[18] For Yahweh who created the heavens, the God who formed the earth and made it, who established it and didn't create it a waste who formed it to be inhabited says: "I am Yahweh. There is no other (God). Isaiah 45:18 WEB

We really do not know when the Earth was first formed. There are estimates, but can anyone really know? Certainly it was clearly a very long time ago as we measure time.

The Word of God, the Bible which is Truth, provides us with the true record of the generations of the heavens and of the earth when they were created, in the day, or at the time that the Lord God made the Earth and the heavens.

[4] This is the history of the generations of the heavens and of the earth when they were created, in the day

that Yahweh God made the earth and the heavens. Genesis 2:4 WEB

In its new 'beginning' after the destruction of the 'Dinosaur Era', the Earth is described as being almost without form, covered in water and darkness probably because of the dust and debris surrounding it. There is still a lot of 'debris' in space, asteroids, meteorites and 'dust' in the atmosphere, but not enough to be of concern. Yahweh began His work of reforming it.

Yahweh began to reform and mould the Earth's land so that the seas were contained by its shores, and still are, that is an amazing phenomena. Salt water is undrinkable, and would drive anyone who drank enough to go mad and die. The waters of the sea evaporate, form clouds, and the snow, rain and dew provide pure distilled water for Yahweh's children to drink.

God populated it with all the fauna and flora, and everything that would be needed to provide a perfect home for human beings was completed in six days. It is unwise to dismiss or reject this statement. God does not lie, a day is a day in this instance, and this is clearly true.

Carefully examine the 'days' of creation, and it immediately becomes apparent that those 'days' could not be thousands or millions of years as some sceptics suggest. All the different plants and creatures on the Earth are part of an intricately balanced ecological system. If the different species of plants, insects and animals of that system came into being separately over aeons of time, pollination could not have occurred and the balance of all life on Earth as we know it could not have come into existence.

God the Word reformed the Earth to be inhabited in six days

The inspired record tells how the Spirit of God the Word 'moved' upon the face of the waters. The Hebrew word here for 'moved' included the sense of brooding of moving in a caring relaxed way to clean up and clear the atmosphere that surrounds our Planet. The air was cleared and was adjusted to contain the perfect balance of Nitrogen, Oxygen, Carbon Dioxide and trace element gases for all air breathing life, and the trees and plants on Earth. So the first thing God did in the reformation of Earth was to Create Light.

Day One – God created light. He is Light

[5] *This **is** the message which we have heard from him and announce to you, that **God is light,** and in him **is** no darkness at all. 1 John 1:5*

The very first thing Yahweh did through the Word was to create 'light' and banish the darkness by clearing the atmosphere of debris. By creating 'light', which is part of the Electromagnetic Spectrum on the Earth, Yahweh was putting His Power and Presence here.

The 'Light' enables our eyes which Yahweh designed for us to be able to see and appreciate all the incredible design and beauty of everything He made in glorious colours. Sight is truly a miraculous gift to His children.

Also the invisible infra-red frequencies of Light provide the warmth and the heat that are essential to life on this planet, and small doses of the ultra-violet rays are necessary for the production of Vitamin D.

The Sun and the Moon 'creates' our day and night and seasons as the Earth rotates.

[19] He appointed the moon for seasons. The sun knows when to set. [20] You make darkness, and it is night, in which all the animals of the forest prowl. Psalm 104:19-20

So what is light? Is it a wave, a particle, photons, and things not yet discovered? Or is light all of those and more? Does light only travel in straight lines, or can it bend with the influence of other Powers of Yahweh? Some suggest that it does.

Light is a tiny window, the visible part of the entire electromagnetic spectrum (EMS) which is largely an invisible Energy. The EMS exists from below the lowest invisible ifrequencies of infrared heat, to radio waves, and up to the higher frequencies of TV and communications, the shorter wavelengths of ultraviolet light, and above that of dangerous x-rays and lethal gamma rays.

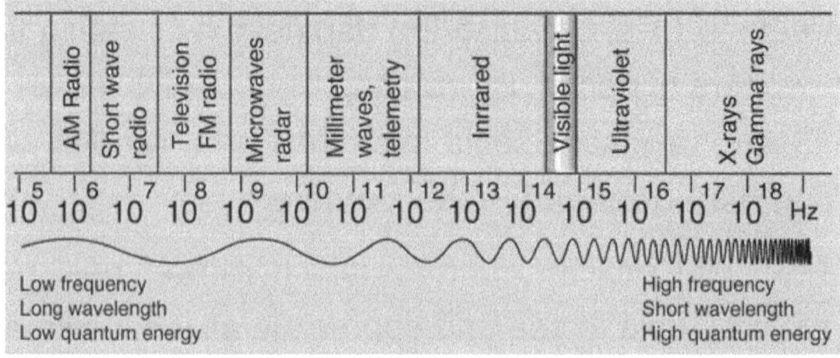

Without the light and heat of the Sun, life on Earth would be impossible. But part of the light of the Sun that it gives out consists of invisible frequencies that are lethal to Life, so life on earth has to be shielded from them.

The Earth's magnetosphere, its magnetic field and other layers, protect us here on Earth from the effects of the plasma, the deadly ionised gas of the Sun's 'flares', and blocks it safely from reaching the surface of our planet. The sun gives off a great number of bands of radiation that would destroy life on Earth were it not for the ozone and other layers. How amazing are Yahweh's Works.

The notion put forth by many modern 'scientific' communities that humans could establish a home on other planets in our Solar system that have environments totally hostile to life is completely ludicrous. There is a lot of talk nowadays about 'terraforming' or making an 'Earthly home' on Mars and transporting millions there from Earth. This is a nonsensical idea for several reasons. Since the radiation levels on Mars, which is not protected like the Earth is, would 'fry' humans in an instant even if they were protected to some degree by their space suits, but few would live the period of the journey. We have everything we need to enjoy a wonderful life here on Earth and keep it thriving, but clearly, we are failing miserably to do this even though we have, or did have perfect conditions. From the results of the way we have misused the fauna, flora, and mineral wealth, it appears now that we have damaged our environment beyond repair. Not content with that, we plan how we can get to another planet and no doubt, if we succeed, will proceed to spoil that place too.

Day Two – God the Word divided the waters, made the 'firmament' land and sky

The word 'firmament' means expanse of the land including the arch of the sky. Yahweh divided the waters that are above the land in the sky, and the waters on the Earth, and the waters that are under the land. A picturesque description of the reality we know.

Yahweh called the dry land earth, and the gathering together of the waters He called Seas. The seas are another miracle. They are contained by the sandy shores of the Earth.

Sand was not broken down rock over billions of years as the God rejecting evolutionists and scientists claim.

[21] *Hear this now, foolish people without understanding, who have eyes, and don't see, who have ears, and don't hear:* [22] *Don't you fear me?' says Yahweh 'Won't you tremble at my presence, who have placed the sand for the bound of the sea, by a perpetual decree, that it can't pass it? Though its waves toss themselves, yet they can't prevail. Though they roar, they still can't pass over it.'* [23] *But this people has a revolting and a rebellious heart. They have revolted and gone. Jeremiah 5:21-23*

Sand was made that way and placed in position on the shores by Yahweh. Amazing too is how the particles of all the sand are much the same size. Each grain was created 'fractal', all similar but different. The wonders of God's creation are endless.

Yahweh also created the Moon to be exactly the right size and placed it at precisely the right distance from the Earth so that its gravitational pull would cause the oceans to be tidal. Twice each day, by Yahweh's Powers, the entire seas of our Planet move back and forth which is essential for the health of the life of the sea and everything in it. How incredible is that?

The seas are a solution of just the right amount of salt which is a purifier. The seas contain abundant life in many forms and the salt, and the motion of the seas keeps the seas 'alive' and prevents the waters becoming putrid. Anyone who has taken home some sea water with little crabs and tiny fish in it knows the disappointment of how quickly the life dies, and the water begins to stink. The way Yahweh created movement of the seas ensures that all life in it will survive. Tragically human activities are now progressively 'killing' the seas with pollution, plastic debris, fishing methods and discarded or lost equipment.

[3] yes, the fishes of the sea also shall be taken away. Hosea 4:3

Professional fishermen are finding it increasingly difficult to make a living due to the ever decreasing catches.

The seas also provide the miracle of fresh water as vapour rises from the sea and creates clouds which release purified distilled water in little droplets of rain. Rain becomes streams and rivers that beautify all the country through which they run, and then flow into the sea.

This we all know, but mostly take it for granted, however this process is a miracle that enables 'life' on our Earthly home. Apart from some bacteria, none of the flora and fauna on Earth can live without that pure water.

Pure water also enables cleanliness and hygiene. Many people around the world collect rain and store it in tanks. Why is that not common practice, and built into all new homes? Where millions in many countries have abundant water clean enough to drink, they waste trillions of gallons every day by flushing it down toilets. Some countries have learned that it is perfectly possible to make odourless dry toilets which breakdown human waste into a usable product. Why not every place on earth?

Where greedy humans have made huge dams, they stop the natural flow of pure water, and thereby steal it from those who would benefit from it downstream. This causes another serious problem. Dams stop the natural rise and flow of water during the seasons causing rivers and streams to stagnate. Pure water has to flow or it 'dies'. It grows green algae which take all the oxygen out of the water and the fish and all life in it dies. This is happening wherever man-made dams exist.

Tragically where water is scarce on Earth there is a lack of cleanliness and hygiene, so diseases flourish. If humans really cared for one another this need not to be the case at all. Proper creative water management could solve that.

Day Three - God created the grass, herbs and trees

The records tells how Yahweh had designed, formed and prepared all the varieties of flora, the plants and the trees before they were ever put into the ground by Him. The Bible record says

[4] This is the history of the generations of the heavens and of the earth when they were created, in the day that Yahweh God made the earth and the heavens. [5] No plant of the field was yet in the earth, and no herb of the field had yet sprung up; for Yahweh God had not caused it to rain on the earth. There was not a man to till the ground, [6] but a mist went up from the earth, and watered the whole surface of the ground. Genesis 2:4-6 WEB

All this work was prepared by Yahweh before He created Adam.

Seeds discovered stored in the pyramids for thousands of years still contained that miracle of 'life'. When discovered and were sown, they sprouted and produced healthy plants. The miracle of 'life' encapsulated in seed should cause us to thank and praise Yahweh.

To confound those who deny Creation, seeds often have two or three protective coatings, and for this to have occurred spontaneously by itself is clearly impossible. Also that trees yield fruit and nuts whose seed is inside it, another incredible design feature without which they would not survive.

All the plants and trees were to reproduce themselves 'after their kind'. We know the utter reliability that all seeds will reproduce the plants they came from. Animals also reproduce after their 'kind', birds make birds, fish make fish, dogs make dogs, elephants make elephants, monkeys make monkeys, and humans make humans. Each can produce a number of varieties within species, but they are still birds, fish, dogs, elephants, monkeys and humans.

There is no record whatsoever of one species morphing into another. This is another unsubstantiated fabrication of proponents of the evolutionary theory. The supposed spontaneous development of the number of differences in the DNA needed would make this impossible.

Even Darwin himself was plagued with serious doubts until his death because he could not reconcile the problem of the design he observed in all things as opposed to his idea that they all occurred spontaneously of their own accord. His 'theory' remains a 'theory' a guess, and unproven idea, yet it is believed to be fact by billions of intelligent but unthinking people. When the subject comes up almost everyone seems to have an almost religious fervour, an intense and passionate feeling about evolution.

Yahweh had substantially now created the fauna and flora, but the next day brought the wonderful mechanism by which everything lives and grows.

Day Four – God created 'lights', day, night, seasons, days, months, years

So Yahweh organised the Earth to be at a certain angle of tilt and to rotate so that the Sun and the Moon would produce Time, days, months, years and seasons. God said in His own language:

14 God said, "Let there be lights in the expanse of the sky to divide the day from the night; and let them be for signs to mark seasons, days, and years; 15 and let them be for lights in the expanse of the sky to give light on the earth;" and it was so. 16 God made the two great lights: the greater light to rule the day, and the lesser light to rule the night. He also made the stars. 17 God set them in the expanse of the sky to give light to the earth, 18 and to rule over the day and over the night, and to divide the light from the darkness. God saw that it was good. Genesis 1:14-18

In our era the destructive actions of Yahweh rejecting human beings has interfered with the weather patterns and the seasons so that they are often more extreme. Droughts, floods, storms and cyclones now affect the growing cycles.

23 "But this people has a revolting and a rebellious heart. They have revolted and gone. 24 They don't say in their heart, 'Let's now fear Yahweh our God, who gives rain, both the former and the latter, in its season, who preserves to us the appointed weeks of the harvest. 25 "Your iniquities have turned away these things, and your sins have withheld good from you. Jeremiah 5:23-25 WEB

Day Five – God made all creatures that have life

God said and is recorded by Moses in Genesis 1

20 God said, "Let the waters abound with living creatures, and let birds fly above the earth in the open expanse of the sky." 21 God created the large sea

creatures and every living creature that moves, with
which the waters swarmed, after their kind, and every
winged bird after its kind. God saw that it was good. [22]
God blessed them, saying, "Be fruitful, and multiply, and
fill the waters in the seas, and let birds multiply on the
earth." [23] *There was evening and there was morning,*
a fifth day. [24] *God said, "Let the earth produce living*
creatures after their kind, livestock, creeping things, and
animals of the earth after their kind;" and it was so. [25]
God made the animals of the earth after their kind, and
the livestock after their kind, and everything that creeps
on the ground after its kind. God saw that it was good.
Genesis 1:20-25

The plants made in day three could not have survived without the insects and birds being involved in their pollination, in day five.

Everything was to produce offspring after their 'kind' or 'genus'. A genus can include more than one species. When biologists talk about a genus, they mean one or more species of animals or plants that are closely related to each other. No genus or species can change into another. And so it is to this day.

And the evening and the morning were the fifth day.

Day Six – Then the Word created the human man and later the woman

And God said, [26] *"Let us make man in our image, after our likeness": Genesis 1:26*

The phrase 'let us' implies that there was communication and discussion between the Father,

Yahweh, and His Son the Word when the time came to begin to make their first human child.

The word in Hebrew translated 'make' is 'asah', literally to do or make, in the broadest sense to accomplish, to bring forth.

The next part of the record says God 'created *man in His own image. In the image of God created He him, male and female created He them. Genesis 1:27*

This word 'created' in Hebrew is 'bara' to create, select or feed.

And then further detail adds that God *"formed man of the dust of the ground and breathed into him the breath of life".* The simple phrase in English *"breathed into him the breath of life"* does not contain the exciting and amazing information and incredible nature and functions of the 'breath of life' that is covered later in this book.

The Hebrew word for formed is *yatsar*, to press, to squeeze into shape); to mould into a form; especially as a potter; figuratively, to fashion, frame, make. And the word *ground* in Hebrew is *adamah* meaning red soil, or clay, country, earth, ground, husband (-man) husbandry, land, hence the name Adam.

God then formed Adam perfectly in every detail of his structure, his bones, his muscles, his sinews, and all his organs including the lungs to process air, extract oxygen and exhale carbon dioxide, the heart, liver, the spleen, the kidneys, the intestines, and so on. All absolutely miraculous in the intricate operation of their functions.

His brain empowered with the *'neshama'* mind with a God-type of Intellect so he would be conscious, and be able to think, plan, create, and can experience moral and ethical concepts which are Godly powers. Consider the amazingly complex digestive system, and even the discrete design of the waste disposal system. Now, in our era, we understand quite a lot more about how the human body works, and we should wonder at its amazing complexity. This gives us another opportunity to express daily appreciation and thanks to Yahweh.

God formed man of the dust of the ground, and breathed into his nostrils the breath of life; and man became a living soul or being. As already stated, human beings are made in God's image, in His form and shape. The word Hu-man is derived from an ancient word root where 'Hu' means God. So Humans are 'God-men' and women. In what sense are we 'God'? We are made in God's, Yahweh's image, and we have the potential to join Him in His God Family one day.

At the end of five days of reformation, God says 'behold it was good'. However, after the sixth day, God proclaims everything He has made is 'very good'. Having made his first children, He is even more satisfied with His Work.

Virtually everyone has seen the series of pictures depicting the gradual development of hairy apes on all fours to a man standing upright with very little hair on his body. These images are indelibly imprinted in our minds, but they are a tragic travesty, a perversion of the truth invented by God-rejecting people. The 'missing link' is still missing. They misrepresent what really happened in a false, absurd, and distorted way. In truth these pictures are a horrific parody, a caricature with striking characteristics that ridicules and makes a mockery of God's Creation of the first human beings.

Those pictures deny the magnificent Creation by God of Adam, the first human being. Yahweh created Adam, the first man who was perfect in every detail. The account tells of that creation in poetic language that is literal and figurative at the same time.

[7] God created Adam from the 'dust of the ground'. It also says that God formed man of the dust of the ground, and breathed into his nostrils the breath of life; and man became a living soul or being. Genesis 2:7

These words in bold are different words with deep meaning in the original Hebrew language.

Human beings, Yahweh's children, are made in His Image

God created Adam and all human beings in His Image and in His Likeness, so we look like Him, and He looks like us. The word Hu-man is formed from an ancient root where Hu means god, so we humans are actually god-man (and women of course) because we were formed by God to become God's children so in English we carry His name.

The Father YHWH, Yahweh through the Word, the 'Potter', the future Christ the Messiah formed Adam the first man out of dust, the most sterile part of the ground. The word formed in Hebrew is Yatsar.

Formed Strong's 3335 yatsar, yaw-tsar'; probably identical with 3334 (through the squeezing into shape); to mould into a form; especially as a potter; figuratively, to determine (i.e. form a resolution): earthen, fashion, form, frame, make, potter, purpose.

In forming Adam, the Word followed the intricate design of their first human child that He and Yahweh the Father had planned aeons before. The more we examine the anatomy and physiology of the human body, the more we should wonder at the intricacies of its design and functions.

God, Yahweh and His Son gave Adam and all his descendants the wonderful five senses of sight, hearing, touch, smell, and taste. Together they give human beings the ability to experience the richness of life's experiences.

God's Gift of the Miraculous Power of Sound.

We take for granted all the sounds we can hear with our ears. The incredible variety of sounds we hear are so much a part of our human experience that most us hardly ever stop to think how it comes about. Yes, we know about the structure of the ear, the tympanic membrane that vibrates and sends signals to a part of the brain that can decipher them. Signals from the right ear travel to the auditory cortex located in the temporal lobe on the left side of the brain.

Signals from the left ear travel to the right auditory cortex. The auditory cortices sort, process, interpret and file information about the sound.

How do your favourite sounds get from your ears to your brain?

Sound waves from the natural world, an instrument or a sound system, travel through the air, and are 'captured' by the outer ear. In the middle ear, the sound waves cause the eardrum and tiny bones attached to the drum to vibrate. The middle ear passes these vibrations to the inner ear. The inner ear includes the snail-shaped cochlea. Inside the fluid-filled cochlea are 20,000–30,000 tiny hair cells. These hair cells are of different sizes that react to different tones and pitches. The inner ear translates vibrations into electrical signals that are carried into the brain by nerve cells called neurons via the cochlear nerve system. The signals travel along the cochlear nerve system to the brain's cerebral cortex. Like a supercomputer, this part of the brain. Other areas of the brain add their power to analyze different elements within the music, such as rhythm, pitch, and dynamics.

The Brain: Once the nerves deliver musical signals inside the skull, the brain goes to work. Researchers now realize music is not just processed in one part of the brain. Performing and listening to music gives many parts of your brain a workout.

Rhythm: The 'belt' and 'parabelt' are located on the right side of the brain. They are mainly responsible for figuring out a song's rhythm. When creating rhythm by tapping toes or beating a drum, the motor cortex and cerebellum get involved.

Pitch and Tone: The recognition and understanding of pitch and tone are mainly handled by the auditory cortex. This part of the brain also does a lot of the work to analyse a song's melody and harmony. Some research shows that the cerebellum and prefrontal cortex contribute, too.

Anticipation: Research shows our brains create expectations when listening to a song. For example, it would figure out if a beat is steady or the melody makes sense. But we especially like it when songs surprise us with exquisite harmonies. This analysis takes place in the brain's prefrontal cortex.

Memory: People have an amazing ability to remember music. Chances are you can recognize your favorite song after hearing just a fragment. These memories are stored in the hippocampus.

Performance: Musical acts like reading music, playing an instrument, and dancing fires up the cerebellum, motor cortex, sensory cortex, and visual cortex.

Emotion: Music has the power to trigger a wide range of feelings in listeners that enrich our lives.

Pause and wonder at the Creativity of our Loving Father and His Son.

The Intricate design of our wonderful bodies.

The closer the different design of each of the myriad different types of cells are examined, the bony structure, the muscles ligaments and tendons; the blood, the heart and blood vessels; the lymphatic system; the organs; and especially the brain; the perfection and the intricacies of these systems are beyond our comprehension. We can only stand back in wonder and offer praise and worship to the Creator.

The Created Adam was the most perfect specimen of a human being in every detail, but lifeless until God breathed into him the breath of life. Pause for thought. Compare the modern 'scientific' thought that "everything came from nothing".

The 'Breath of Life' and its components

So God the Word then breathed into Adam's nostrils 'the breath of life'; and Yahweh has subsequently 'breathed' the 'breath of life' into every human child that has ever been born and drew its first breath. This simple statement in English has unimagined meanings in the original manuscript which are explained next.

The original narrative was written in the Hebrew language which has a number of subtle, lyrical, poetical and descriptive features that do not exist in the English language. So a look at the original Hebrew words in the Old Testament brings out meanings that are completely lost when those Hebrew words are translated into English. Strong's Concordance of Hebrew words, each numbered for easy reference, is a useful work to enable us to gain greater understanding of what God wants us to understand from His Word.

God breathes 'Life' into all who have breath, but 'neshama' Intellect and other 'God Mind' abilities are bestowed only to humans.

God using His Power, ruwach, of His Holy Spirit breathed (5301 naphach) into Adam's nostrils the breath (5397 neshama) of life (2416 chay) and he became a living soul (5315 nephesh).

God breathed these seven components of the 'Breath of Life' into Adam

1. 'breathed' naphach is to puff, inflate, blow hard, air, oxygen, breath.

2. 'breath' neshamah is 'life' consciousness, making alive, 'chay' living, the essence of 'life' as opposed to 'death'.

3. 'breath' neshamah is an electrical stimulus to enliven the brain to control the whole body, and think sub-consciously.

4. 'breath' neshamah is divine inspiration of the 'spirit in man' that links us to God via the 'Silver Cord'. Ecclesiastes 12:6-7

.5. 'breath' neshamah is the thinking 'mind' which permeates and activates every cell of the body, and can cloud intellect with emotion rather than logic.

6. 'breath' neshamah is 'Mind', 'Intellect', the God-like faculty of imagining, reasoning, our power of choice and decision making, understanding objectively, planning, designing, ability to create, especially with regard to abstract matters, as in ethical and moral capacity; and

sensitivity to whom and what we are, awareness of our potential, which enables us to grow mentally and spiritually, develop abilities and talents, and can 'change' attitudes of the emotional mind.

7. 'breath' neshamah is also the spiritual conduit of the Holy Spirit from God the Father to us. John 20:22.

Human beings are not animals, and why they cannot be.

God also breathes the 'breath of life', 'naphach', into all animals that have breath, air, oxygen, and they have an animal spirit 'ruwach' of God's Power, but they do not have 'neshamah' which only God and humans have. The animal spirit 'ruwach' is the 'operating system' that runs the animal brain, and enables it to have the instinct of self-preservation, to forage and find food, mate, take care of young, fight, and it also supplies all the other instincts special to each genus like nest building and migration patterns.

[38] But God gives it a body as it has pleased him, and to every seed his own body. [39] All flesh is not the same flesh: but there is one kind of flesh of men, another flesh of beasts, another of fishes, and another of birds. 1 Corinthians 15:38-39

Each species of animal has its own type of flesh and its own different specific type of spirit 'ruwach'. All have a body and brain and something that gives each species its characteristics and within each species, individual characteristics.

To say that some animals are 'domesticated' is sacrilege, stealing the credit from Yahweh. Human beings did not 'domesticate' animals, Yahweh designed them to be the way they are for His human children so we are able to have a safe and beneficial relation-ship with them. Cows, sheep, goats, dogs, horses, and some other animals have a very specific type of 'ruach' that enables them to relate to human beings in a different manner from 'wild' animals. 'Wild' animals can be trained to a degree, but their 'ruach' remains 'wild' and therefore possibly dangerous.

In another later account more information tells us that male and female created He them. God has male and female characteristics, and humans are created in God's image, therefore humans male and female embody both, and it also reveals what God looks like.

How are human beings exercising 'dominion' over God's Creation?

[26] God said: And let them have dominion over the fish of the sea, and over the fowl of the air, and over the cattle, and over all the earth, and over every creeping thing that creeps upon the earth. Genesis 1:26

To have dominion over anything means being in charge of something or to rule it. Hundreds of English words contain the three letters 'dom'. Many are to do with defining a type of or area of 'realm' or 'reign', such as domain, domestic, domicile, kingdom.

As with every other gift, human beings have a choice in regard to how they exercise that dominion. Yahweh wants his children to exercise loving, caring dominion over His Creation and ‘dress it and keep it’. That phrase means to look after it carefully and well.

We were given dominion over the Earth to preserve the habitat of living creatures, not destroy it; to till the soil and build its ‘heart’, not pollute it with chemicals, herbicides, pesticides, poisons; to treat all animals with kindness and respect, not treat them harshly, be cruel and or terrify them when driving them with helicopters and quad bikes, house them in ‘prisons’ under awful conditions, feed them hormones, and other foodstuffs that are not suitable for them to eat; to treat the oceans with respect and enjoy the fishes of the sea, not dredge the sea of all its living creatures and throw much of it back dead, not pollute it with untreated sewage, nor dump millions of tons of plastic in the oceans which endangers all marine life. What on God’s Earth do we think we are doing? Clearly Yahweh’s selfish children do not care about exercising loving dominion.

God the Father, Yahweh, has given Christ the Messiah dominion over the entire works of His hands, has put ‘all things under his feet’, or within His domain, and He is heir of all things. So how does Christ exercise that dominion? Does He control everything under His dominion? No, He does not. Yahweh and Christ want every human being, willingly to put themselves under their rule. Yahweh does not make or force us to comply.

The 'Mind' of Christ the Messiah is our example of Godly 'dominion'.

The mind of Christ is summed up by: 'He who would be greatest of all, should be the servant of all'. Dominion is not about dominance, or rule by any type of pressure or force. It is based on the Law of Love. The ideal is for us to be in 'service' to everyone with Love, Respect, Consideration, Kindness, and Humility'. This is the Mind of Christ.

Everyone thinks about their own things, and that is good and right. However, everyone needs also to think, to consider and be aware of the needs and things of others while taking proper care of ourselves. Our daily focus and responsibility is to emulate the Love of God and Christ to the maximum of our ability.

Most of humanity has lost sight of, and respect for the God of Creation. They worship false gods in their places of worship. The perverted thinking of ministers of Churchianity teach falsehoods and lies, and misrepresent the God they claim to serve.

30 "An astonishing and horrible thing has happened in the land. 31 The prophets prophesy falsely, and the priests rule by their own authority; and my people love to have it so. What will you do in the end of it? Jeremiah 5:30-31 WEB

The end result is that when everything goes wrong as a result of aberrant human behaviour, people tend to blame Yahweh.

It seems that most human beings have no shame when it comes to the way they abuse and mistreat this wonderful home called Earth. This is mainly because so few believe in, or have any respect for the God of Creation who plainly is no longer in the hearts and minds of so many.

Yahweh is not far away, although we cannot see Him He is 'out there' and near to us. So close, He figuratively uses the earth as His footstool. Christ said so.

[34] but I tell you, don't swear at all: neither by heaven, for it is the throne of God; [35] nor by the earth, for it is the footstool of his feet; Matthew 5:34-35

The solid evidence and the proof of His Reality is all around us here on Earth. Yahweh's invisible 'cloud' Heaven surrounds the physical Earth which is suspended within that 'cloud'. Yahweh's Life Power lives in us and we literally live in Him. "In Him, within His Power, we live and move and have our being for we are His offspring", His children.

Yahweh's Life Power gives us every breath we breathe by activating the muscles of the diaphragm which draws air containing oxygen into our lungs. The miracle of Yahweh's Life Force Power energises the particles within each oxygen atom and causes them to rotate around the nucleus. The oxygen is separated from all the other gases in air by the fractal design of the lungs, and it enters and vitalises the haemoglobin molecules in the blood. As the 'spent' blood returns to the lungs, which then miraculously separate the carbon dioxide, and it is exhaled into theair that plants use to make the fuel to grow and thrive. Incredible but true, how wonderful is our Creator.

MASKS ARE A HEALTH HAZARD – Doctors know that.

While wearing a mask, the gases we breathe out including Carbon Dioxide CO2, water vapour laden with the toxic waste products of metabolism, are restricted from leaving the body. As a result, these actually poisonous gases are partly reabsorbed back into the lungs. This may impair the immune system, and make the person more prone to infections.

All the references on the Internet to masks in connection with the so-called Covid pandemic refute any suggestion that masks impair the immune system, but this is considered to be false propaganda by other scientists and doctors. Anyone who has spent hours in a crowded room with the doors and windows closed knows how drowsy they become because of the increase level of CO2 in the air.

Our 'Life' is in the blood

Our blood is composed of complex red (44%) and white cells and platelets (1%), plasma (55%). Haemoglobin is the protein molecule in red blood cells that carries oxygen from the lungs to the body's tissues and returns the carbon dioxide from the tissues back to the lungs.

The 'haeme' molecule contains one iron atom, the bind point for oxygen. Iron is vital for the production of blood. One oxygen molecule (O^2, or two oxygen atoms) binds to each iron atom via a covalent bond. Thus, each haemoglobin molecule is capable of carrying up to 4 oxygen molecules.

God's Life Power causes the muscles of the heart to contract and relax as it pumps the oxygenated blood around the body. Every heartbeat is a gift from Yahweh. All the blood is contained in blood vessels, and is not in the other tissues of the body.

From the main arteries of the heart, the blood vessels divide up into smaller arteries, and then into tiny capillaries. Capillaries are so small that blood cells containing the life giving oxygen can only move through them one at a time.

The portion of blood plasma that escapes from the capillaries is called interstitial or extracellular fluid, and it contains oxygen, glucose, amino acids, and other nutrients needed by tissue cells. The lymphatic system removes this fluid and these materials from tissues, returning them via the lymphatic vessels to the bloodstream.

The lymph is a non-cellular fluid that bathes all the tissues of the body with oxygen and nutrients where the large blood cells cannot go. This is how oxygen and nutrients get into every cell of the body and are used to generate the energy of life. As the oxygen 'burns' in the cells it produces carbon dioxide. The lymph picks up the carbon dioxide from the cells and it is reabsorbed from the lymph back into the capillaries. The carbon dioxide laden blood is transferred into the lung tissues, extracted, and breathed out. More of God's incredible design work.There are twice as many lymphatic vessels in the lymphatic network as there are blood vessels, and twice as much lymph as blood in the body. About eight pints of blood and sixteen pints of lymph depending on the size of the person. The blood is pumped around the body by the heart, but the lymph is circulated throughout the body by the movement of the muscles which surround the lymph vessels. This is why exercise is so very important for health.

The lymph also collects all the waste products from cell metabolism and transfers them to the main lymph drains in the neck. The waste is transferred into the blood circulation system to be excreted by the kidneys. How marvellous are the works of Yahweh our Father! Human be-ings are god-men and women in a continuous state 'being-ness' or existing 'Life' with all these incredible bodily functions operating moment by moment until death.

How many people on this Earth ponder, wonder, or think about the miracle of 'life' they have? Are they consciously aware that every heartbeat is a continuous gift and an Act of Yahweh? That every breath they take is also a continuous gift and an Act of Yahweh? And does this cause them to acknowledge, thank and praise Yahweh.

Day Seven – God finished the heavens and the earth and rested

[1] Thus the heavens and the earth were finished, and all the vast array of them. [2] And on the seventh day God ended His work which He had made; and He rested on the seventh day from all His work which he had made.
[3] And God blessed the seventh day, and sanctified the Sabbath, or set it apart, because that in it He had rested from all his work which God created and made. Genesis 2:1-3

In the olden times people were very physical in outlook (and most still are), and Yahweh gave them a set of laws which regulated their conduct. These laws had to be kept by His people on pain of death if they did not. The Sabbath days kept them in mind of Yahweh, and they needed the physical rest. The laws of what they could do and should not do on the Sabbath and indeed all the days of the week were very detailed and very restrictive.

After Christ (Yah'Shua') came to Earth, He kept all those laws perfectly, paid the penalty for human sin, was resurrected and restored to His position with Yahweh the Father in heaven, who then sent Yahweh's Holy Spirit, the Comforter, to dwell in the minds of those who are the 'called'.

The 'called' are not required now to keep those old physical laws, including the physical Sabbath, but to strive to keep the far more difficult Laws of the Spirit which include love, joy, peace, kindness, forgiveness, longsuffering, and all the fruits of the Spirit. Those who have God's Holy Spirit have entered into a different type of 'rest', a spiritual 'rest' which continues every day of the week.

God planted a garden in Eden for Adam when he was made.

[8] And the Lord God planted a garden for Adam eastward in Eden in the area of the Euphrates river; and there he put the man whom he had formed. And a river went out of Eden to water the garden. Genesis 2:8

In order to grow, plants and trees have to have water, but how do they draw water out of the Earth? It is by God's miracle Power of 'Capillary Attraction'.

CAPILLARY ATTRACTION – A POWER OF YAHWEH THAT DEFIES GRAVITY

Capillary attraction is yet another miraculous law of Yahweh's Power. What is capillary attraction? Capillary action is the ability of a liquid to flow sideways in narrow spaces and upwards in opposition to the external force of gravity.

When it rains (another miracle), water soaks into the ground. But in addition to just retaining water, capillarity in soil also enables the horizontal and upward movement of water within the soil particles, as opposed to the downward movement caused by gravity. The smaller the soil porous texture, the higher the capillary rise in the water level.

Why is this such an important phenomenon? Because if this flow of liquids did not happen in this way, nothing would grow. Plants would not 'suck up' moisture from the soil against the force of gravity.

Transpiration is the process where plants and trees absorb water upwards against gravity by capillary attraction through the minute tubules in their roots and as water evaporates through the many pores on the leaf surface it makes room for more water to travel upwards. The rate of transpiration is directly related to the surface area of the leaves.

Through Capillary Attraction, trees draw water up through their roots and then up the tiny capillary layer all around the tree just under the bark of the trunk. A mature oak will transpire up to 50 gallons of water per day weighing around 500 pounds, which flow upwards to 80 feet or more up in the air against gravity. As the liquid vaporises and transpires through its leaves, more water is drawn up the trunk. Some huge trees transpire a great deal more. Amazing.

Those who deny the Designer can observe the way that Capillary Attraction works. Perhaps they may talk about surface tension and the meniscus effect, and so on, but how this Spiritual Power happens against gravity is a miracle that scientists cannot really explain at all. Yet another miraculous secret Power of God.

The miracle of Photosynthesis – power and energy from light, air and water

As plants and trees draw water up to their green leaves by Yahweh's Power of Capillary Attraction, another miracle of His Power called Photosynthesis occurs. This is the process by which the energy of sunlight on the chlorophyll in the leaves of green plants synthesizes nutrients from Carbon Dioxide and water, an amazing process invented by God our Father, Yahweh, Creator, the Master Chemist. Interestingly, the chlorophyll molecule has a structure very similar to the life giving blood molecule in animals.

During Photosynthesis, in green plants the light energy is captured from the Sun, and Carbon Dioxide from the air, and these are used to convert water and dissolved minerals into Oxygen, Glucose and energy-rich organic compounds. This process also produces free oxygen released from the water.

The Photosynthesis chemical equation is expressed:

6O2 6CO2 + 6H2O + light energy = C6H1206 + 6O2 that is, six Carbon Dioxide molecules + six water molecules + energy from light produces six molecules of Glucose and six molecules of Oxygen.

In this way, green plants use up Carbon Dioxide from the air, and use it as a fuel, but also produce Oxygen. This is important because all living things need oxygen to survive. In the food chain, all plants make oxygen and sugar for creatures that breathe oxygen and live by eating plants, then carnivores eat animals that eat the plants.

Because Photosynthesis produces Oxygen as a by-product it is part of the way that the balance and proportions of these two gases in the atmosphere is maintained.

The destruction of rain forests and other trees reduces the amount of Carbon Dioxide taken out of the air, and the increase in the number of cattle bred in those areas produce more methane. The profligate use of fossil fuels by thousands of planes, millions of trains, billions of cars, lorries, tractors, and munitions for wars over the last hundred years has led to the steady increase in the proportion of 'greenhouse-effect' gases like Carbon Dioxide that heat up the atmosphere.

For instance, in a journey from London to Los Angeles, a jetliner may use 300,000 pounds of fuel which burns its own weight in Oxygen and fixates some 727 kg. Oxygen for every ton of CO2 produced.

This universal use of fossil fuels that warm the atmosphere has led to the current 'Climate Change' which threatens the collapse of the entire eco system of the earth within a few years.

Adam the gardener

And the Lord God, took the man, and put him into the Garden of Eden that He had planted for him to dress it and to keep it.

9 And out of the ground in the garden the Lord God made every tree to grow that is pleasant to the sight, and good for food; the tree of life also in the midst of the garden, and the tree of knowledge of good and evil. Genesis 2:9

Then God the Word gave Adam strict instructions concerning the trees in the garden. God's first generous statement was to tell Adam that he could freely eat of any and all the trees in the garden, except one. But of the tree of the knowledge of good and evil, God the Word told Adam, you shall not eat of it: for in the day that you eat of it you shall surely die. Adam must have understood that clearly. This instruction about the forbidden tree was given to Adam before Eve was formed.

God the Word had another interesting job for Adam to do. He brought all the animals and birds to Adam for him to name them.

[19] And out of the ground the Lord God (had) formed every beast of the field, and every fowl of the air; and brought them unto Adam to see what he would call them: and whatever Adam called every living creature that became its name. Genesis 2:19

So Adam gave names to all cattle, and to the birds of the air, and to every beast of the field; but for Adam among all the animals there was not found a helper that was suitable for him.

God Creates Eve

Then God the Father said to the Word: "It is not good that the man should be alone; I will make a suitable companion for him".

Then God the Word told Adam that it was not good for him to be alone, and that He would prepare a companion to be with him in his work.

[21] The Lord God caused a deep sleep to fall upon Adam, while he slept He took a part of Adam out of his

body, and then closed up the flesh. From that part of Adam's body; God made a woman, and brought her unto the man. Genesis 2:21-22

Instead of enjoying and appreciating the story of Adam and Eve and learning from it, many people scoff at the account the Creation of Adam and Eve, even to the point of making the ludicrous suggestion either that everything came from 'nothing' or 'made itself'. Those who reject God. He calls fools.

*[1] The **fool** hath said in his heart: There is no God. They are corrupt, they have done abominable works, there is none that doeth good. Psalm 14:1*

And the 'rib', or with whatever portion the Word had taken from Adam's body (the Bible does not say) He made a woman, and brought her to the man. And Adam said, 'This is now bone of my bones, and flesh of my flesh: she shall be called Woman, because she was taken out of Man. And they were both naked, the man and his wife, and they were not at all ashamed'. And why would they be?

At that time, God the Word explained to them the institution of marriage.

[24] for this reason a man will leave his father and his mother, and shall cleave (have intercourse) unto his wife: and they shall be one flesh. Genesis 2:24

No doubt the Word also explained to them all about the gift of sexual intimacy in marriage. He gave detailed instruction to the couple, how they would come together, become 'one flesh' and have children. Yahweh who is male and female is also One. And since God the father produced a Son, they are still One. So when a man and a woman become 'one', they are figuratively 'one' in the same way that God is One. In human terms, we produce children during the loving God-given sex act which should be deeply revered, honoured, and respected. Sadly sex is far too often dragged into degradation by God rejecting people.

Marriage is certainly one of the most wonderful gifts that God has given to men and women. Historically many married people enjoyed a lifetime of mutual love, togetherness, respect and support. Sadly that is becoming rare in the 'developed' countries. Tragically, Satan has been hard at work in our modern era to destroy that wonderful institution. More marriages are breaking down and couples are separating and getting divorced than ever before.

Even more tragically, the whole idea of marriage is losing popularity as more men and women 'get together' in a loose arrangement with virtually no commitment to one another. They live separate lives together, with separate bank accounts. It appears that no longer does a man consider it his privilege and duty to be the provider in the home.

In 1858 Emmeline Pankhurst started the women's rights movement to get the vote for women. In the '70's people used to talk of the 'Battle of the Sexes'. As time has gone on, because women have continued to be disrespected, been held back in business, and generally treated as second class citizens or worse, women have felt the need to continue the fight for 'equality'.

The whole idea that a man and a woman should be 'equal' is not reasonable. They certainly should be treated with respect in every aspect of life. But men and women are very different in so many ways. Men are generally bigger and stronger that women, and women have talents of motherhood that men do not possess. Men and women can no more be 'equal' than an apple is equal to an orange. 'Equality' is a myth, everyone is 'fractically' different.

Yahweh wants all His children to love and respect each other. Satan wants to foment and stir up universal strife and discord. There should be no 'battle' between anyone, especially not between men and women. Yahweh does not want strife or disrespect between any, but in lowliness of mind, in humility He wants everyone to hold others in high esteem, and as being better than themselves.

Courtship used to follow a pattern. Two people attracted to each other spent time together. Then a period of 'courting' where sex before marriage was considered immoral and unacceptable. Then a couple would get 'engaged', save up for accommodation and plan their life together. When financially secure and able to maintain a home, only then would they consider starting a family.

The modern approach is different: Meet, have sex, get pregnant, have one or more babies, then perhaps think about getting married, or even then realise they do not even like each other. God's precious gift has been ungratefully consigned to the bin. A travesty or what?

Now 'same sex' marriages are approved by some governments. In the past when Godless people experimented with sexual practices that are against natural law, they suffered extreme consequences. The modern situation of LBGTQI+ confuses the whole identity and functions of males and females. People may think they are free to behave as they wish with impunity, without any penalty, but time will tell. One wonders how much sadness these immoral behaviours and all human rebellion causes our Father?

God the Word gives Adam instructions about his responsibilities

[9] And out of the ground the Lord God made to grow every tree that is pleasant to the sight, and good for food; the tree of life also in the midst of the garden, and the tree of knowledge of good and evil. Genesis 2:9

When the first man Adam was formed by God the Word, his work on Earth and that of all his descendants that would follow was clearly defined. Then God gave His first commandments to Adam, spelling them out carefully. He was to take good care of the garden, to dress it and keep it well.

The Word gave Adam a job to do, to take good care of the garden, and by extension the whole Earth, make it even more beautiful, and keep it in good condition. This is extended to all humans in the whole world who should have, and should now be, 'dressing and keeping' the whole world in good condition.

Rebellious, selfish, greedy humans are now currently systematically destroying the fauna, flora, the climate and weather of our earthly home, and even disturbing the fabric of the Earth's skin with 'fracking' and other ill-advised and destructive mining practices.

[26] For wicked men are found among my people. They watch, as fowlers lie in wait. They set a trap. They catch men. [27] As a cage is full of birds, so are their houses full of deceit. Therefore they have become great, and grow rich. [28] They have grown fat. They shine; yes, they excel in deeds of wickedness. They don't plead the cause, the cause of the fatherless, that they may prosper; and they don't defend the rights of the needy. [29] "Shouldn't I punish for these things?" says Yahweh. "Shouldn't my soul be avenged on such a nation as this? Jeremiah 5:26-29

Greed and the lust for power drives Godless human behaviour at the expense of caring for planet earth.

THE BIGGEST LIE – you shall not die

Satan in the form of the serpent was in the garden. Then in accordance with God's Plan for His children to come to know clearly the difference between 'good' and 'evil', the snake speaks to Eve.

Eve was walking alone in the garden and met Satan. Satan then told Eve the first and biggest lie.

[4] If you eat of the fruit of the tree of the knowledge of good and evil, You will not die for God knows that in the

day ye eat that fruit, then your eyes shall be opened, and ye shall be as gods, knowing good and evil". The serpent said to the woman, "You won't really die, [5] for God knows that in the day you eat it, your eyes will be opened, and you will be like God, knowing good and evil. [6] When the woman saw that the tree was good for food, and that it was a delight to the eyes, and that the tree was to be desired to make one wise, she took some of its fruit, and ate. *Genesis 3:4-6*

The serpent was selling deceptive knowledge and false 'wisdom' by offering Eve the opportunity to be like God immediately, she was duped, fooled into obeying the Serpent. She had lost sight of the fact that being like God would be her ultimate destiny according to God's Plan.

[6] And when the woman saw that the tree was good for food, and that it was pleasant to the eyes, and a tree to be desired to make one wise, she took of the fruit and ate it, and gave also unto her husband with her; and ate some as well. Genesis 3:6

The lure of 'wisdom' was the bait, and Eve took it. There is a certain false 'wisdom' that Satan is able to make appear all he does attractive to people. It always looks good, is appealing, offers 'new' information, but within all Satan's offerings there is a 'hook' and motive to work against God, Yahweh, and His purpose that has dreadful results in the long term.

Adam knew full well that God the Word had commanded him not to eat from that tree, but he failed to obey God or exercise leadership, and gave in to the wishes and persuasion of his wife.

[7] *And the eyes of them both were opened, and they knew that they were naked; and they sewed fig leaves together, and made themselves aprons. Genesis 3:7 Satan had begun his work of 'polluting' the purity of sex in their minds.*

Later, God went looking for them in the garden but Adam and Eve were hiding because they knew they were naked and had disobeyed God and were afraid. God found them, to Eve He said, [16] *I will greatly multiply thy sorrow and your conception; in sorrow thou shall bring forth children; and your desire shall be to your husband, and he shall rule over you. Genesis 3:16*

And to Adam He said, [17] *Because you have listened to the voice of your wife, and have eaten of the tree of which I commanded you, saying, You shalt not eat of it: cursed is the ground for your sake; in sorrow shalt thou eat of it all the days of thy life; 18Thorns also and thistles shall it produce; and you shalt eat the herbs of the field; 19 In the sweat of your face shall you eat bread, until you return unto the ground; for out of it you were taken: for dust you are, and unto dust you shall return. Genesis 3:17-19*

And Adam called his wife's name Eve; because she was the mother of all living. Unto Adam also and to his wife did the Lord God make coats of skins, and clothed them. It is interesting that the true Bible record mentions that God made them clothing from the skins of animals.

So Adam and Eve learned the difference between Good and Evil.

God the Father said to God the Word: *See, the man is become as one of us, to know good and evil: and now, in case he takes also of the tree of life, and eats from it, and gains eternal life for ever. We will expel him from the garden. Genesis, 3:22-23*

Actually as a result of their eating of the fruit, Satan's 'wisdom' and his 'knowledge of good and evil' would actually lead to total confusion. People to this day do not understand clearly the difference between 'good' and 'evil' because they do not study God's Word and learn His definitions of what they are. Their wilful human nature which is enmity to God ensures that most of the time, people follow their own desires regardless of right and wrong. The result is the current state of the world, total chaos. As a result of their rebellion the Lord God banished him from the Garden of Eden, to till the ground from whence he was taken.

[22] Yahweh God said, "Behold, the man has become like one of us, knowing good and evil. Now, lest he reach out his hand, and also take of the tree of life, and eat, and live forever—" [23] Therefore Yahweh God sent him out from the garden of Eden, to till the ground from which he was taken. [24] So he drove out the man; and he placed cherubim at the east of the garden of Eden, and a flaming sword which turned every way, to guard the way to the tree of life. Genesis 3:22-24

The Truth about Life and Death: When God says you die, you are dead

Satan's 'biggest lie' "You will not die" has most of two billion people in Christianity, and the rest of the world in other religions on Earth fooled. They share a belief that when you die you are not dead, but go straight to 'heaven' or 'hell', or continue to 'live', are 'reborn', 'reincarnated' or exist in some other form.

The idea that we go to heaven when we die, or the concept of an ever burning hell (Dante's inferno written in the 14th century A.D. about hell and purgatory) have no basis in the scriptures whatsoever. Hell is a notion that was thought up by religions to control people by holding them in perpetual fear if they did not meet the requirements of the church's teachings.

What then is the mechanism of life and death? God formed man of the dust of the ground, and breathed into his nostrils the breath of life and his human spirit; and man became a living soul.

Dust + Breath + Human Spirit = Living Soul Living Soul – (minus) Breath - Human Spirit = Death

When the breath leaves the body the person is unconscious, unaware, and has ceased to exist as an entity. It is not living a 'floaty' existence in another dimension. When a man dies:

4 His breath goes forth, he returns to his earth; in that very day his thoughts perish. Psalm 146:4

A dead person has no thoughts because their brain is dead.

[5] For the living know that they will die, but the dead don't know anything, neither do they have any more a reward; for their memory is forgotten. [6] Also their love, their hatred, and their envy has perished long ago; neither do they any longer have any part forever in anything that is done under the sun. Ecclesiastes 9:5-6

[10] Whatsoever your hand finds to do, do it with your might; for there is no work, nor device, nor knowledge, nor wisdom, in the grave, where you are going. Ecclesiastes 9:10

All humans have a human spirit

Humans have a hu-man, a god-man 'spirit' breathed into them with 'the breath of Life' at birth. This human spirit was designed so that God's children would be able to relate to and communicate with Yahweh via His Holy Spirit. When a human being dies,

[7] and the dust returns to the earth as it was and the spirit returns to God who gave it. Ecclesiastes 12:7

[4] His spirit departs, and he returns to the earth. In that very day, his thoughts perish. Psalm 146:4

God stores this human spirit with all its experience of that person until the time comes for that person to be resurrected to human life.

Human beings also have a built in carnal or fleshly human nature which is biased against Yahweh, and indeed at some level is at war with the God of Love. Of course all humans are capable of human love and affection, of kindness, and to a limited degree of exhibiting many of God's qualities, but also can succumb to their lower nature.

But the human spirit is also susceptible to suggestion and influences from Satan and his billions of spirit cohorts. We have only to look at the horrendous, horrible activities of so many human beings on this Earth at this time to know that is true. Satanic inhumane activities are pandemic. Wars, criminal activities, rape, sexual degradation of all forms, torture, all the worst aspects of human inhumanity to humans exist on a vast scale. If we are honest with ourselves our rational human mind can certainly see clearly the universal presence of evil at work all over the world if it is willing to admit it.

These horrors lead everyone at one time or another to the inevitable question: "If there is a God of Love, why does He allow all this cruelty?" We are here on Earth to learn a lesson. That lesson is that when humans break God's Spiritual Laws of Love, pain of all kinds and suffering are inevitable. Once all humans have learned this lesson, and decide to follow God's Way, evil will be destroyed forever. God certainly does not want us to suffer forever. All humans will eventually love and appreciate God for eternity. That time will come.

What happens to the human spirit when we die?

When we die, the dust returns to the earth from which it came: and the spirit returns to God who gave it. The spirit of man has no life and has no consciousness without the body. The analogy of a DVD may help some understand this concept. The personality and the events of a person's life are recorded on the 'DVD' (the human spirit), but cannot be played back or viewed without a TV (the body).

When people die they do not go to heaven, or exist in any other 'state', nor 'be' anywhere else, as the spirit has no consciousness at all. In fact no human being has ever ascended into heaven as the Word of God emphasises more than once.

[13] No one has ascended into heaven but he who descended out of heaven, the Son of Man, who is in heaven. John 3:13.

God stores the human spirit of every human being until it is time for them to be resurrected. When the person is resurrected, God creates a new body for the person out of His Spirit Matter, and re-creates the person by reuniting the new body with their spirit, which contains all the information of their previous existence. How wonderful is that?

What about the resurrection Yahweh promises to all?

If it was true that people 'go to heaven' when they die, what is the purpose of the promised resurrection? That does not make any sense at all.

As Christ died on the Tree, He gave up the 'ghost', that is He died, and His human spirit which had all His human experiences recorded on it returned to God the Father. He was stone dead, Then He was wrapped up and placed in a grave where He remained for three days and three nights. He did not go anywhere.

After His three days in the grave He was resurrected to human life and Yahweh the Father placed His human spirit and the Holy Spirit in Him. Christ then spent time with some people, and was seen by at least five hundred as proof of His resurrection but He did not allow them to touch Him until He ascended to the Father.

As He ascended to the Father in heaven, His physical body 'died'. and He was clothed once more with His Immortality. In the sacrificial system that involved animals and birds, it was the spilling of their blood that symbolised forgiveness for the person.

The now Immortal living YahwehShua then returned to Earth but in physical human form. He then showed himself to His disciples who finally recognised Him. Christ's resurrection was not 'done in a corner', it shook the whole world, and later thousands saw Him alive. The entire event is an irrefutable historical fact. The evidence that the world's calendar was changed attests to that.

There is so much historical supporting evidence, testimony and proofs to everything about the work life, death and resurrection of Christ that there is no excuse for anyone not to be convicted by it.

The 'Fall of Adam' was part of God's Plan

However it was Yahweh's planned intention that Adam and Eve, His very first children, should eat of that tree so that they would have Satan's version of the knowledge of good and evil. Having this knowledge was, and is, an essential part of Yahweh's plans for all His children. With that knowledge of evil and good, all human beings would be able to learn from their human experience that Satan's ways are the ways of death; and that Yahweh's Laws are the only true way to life and happiness.

Everyone on Earth would do well to recognise that God is indeed close to us, watching over each and every one of His embryonic family, and that Yahweh is not at all far away as some suggest. Our very existence is actually in God within the area of His 'Heaven' that surrounds the earth.

In a sense, the whole human race is in Yahweh's 'womb', the Earthly home within His Invisible Heaven that we have been born into. Eight billion people are not really even remotely aware that they are alive and exist consciously as a gift from Yahweh, or that we are God's Offspring, or that a Father/child relationship exists between Yahweh and all humanity. How does God our Father feel about it do you think?

However, Yahweh has allowed all but a few humans to be blinded to Him by Satan and their own minds, so that God does not hold them fully accountable for their ignorance or arrogant defiance.

[3] Even if our Good News (of the Gospel) is veiled (obscured), it is veiled in those who are dying, 4 in whom the god of this world has blinded the minds of the unbelieving, that the light of the Good News of the glory of Christ (Yah'Shua), who is the image of God, should not dawn on them. 2 Corinthians 4:3-4

[15] for this people's heart has grown callous, their ears are dull of hearing, and they have closed their eyes; or

else perhaps they might perceive with their eyes, hear with their ears, understand with their heart, and would turn again, and I would heal them.' Matthew 13:15

Christ (Yah'Shua) the Messiah quoted this from the words He, the Word, inspired Isaiah to write in chapter 6:9-10

According to Yahweh's Plan, this is not the time for most people to be given the gift of 'seeing' the true nature of the relationship that humans can have with the Creator God. Most humans in their puffed up vanity do not appreciate that they are indeed 'tiny', and so very miniscule compared with the Great God their Father.

[11] God has made everything intricately beautiful and He has put the eternity (complexity) of the world in the heart and mind in such a way, so that no human can fathom the work that God created in every detail no matter how hard he (or she) tries. Ecclesiastes 3:11

Yahweh keeps secret His Spiritual knowledge, and He exposes as nonsense the words of those who reject the 'Designer' and whose 'science' is constantly being superseded by 'new' discoveries which prove previous 'discoveries' were incorrect.

[29] The secret things belong to Yahweh our God; but the things that are revealed (to the 'few') belong to us and to our children forever, that we may do (respect and be obedient to) all the words of this law. Deuteronomy 29:29

The 'Sons of God' – their power, who are they and what do they do?

One word for 'God' in the Hebrew language is the plural word 'Elohim'. When the Word created all the spirit beings, some of them had the powerful status of the 'Sons of God'. They were 'lesser Elohim' but still a type of God rank. Very few people are even aware that such spirit beings exist. However they do, and they were and are part of God's Spirit Kingdom, like angels who have responsibilities to care for and watch over humans.

In the early days, as human beings began to grow in numbers some of these spirit beings who were 'Sons of God' could manifest, or 'morph' themselves into human form and have sexual relations with women. Some of the powerful spirit 'Sons of God' lusted after the beautiful daughters of men and they chose to have them as wives who bore them children. In doing so, clearly they had departed from obedience to God's service and had become associated with Satan in his work of leading the people further away from Yahweh.

The children of these 'mixed' marriages were different from others.

4 "There were giants in the Earth in those days because when the 'Sons of God' married the daughters of men, the children they bore to them became 'mighty men of renown'". Genesis 6:4

The human children of the wives of the Sons of God had considerably more powers than children born of two humans. These 'mighty men' were 'renowned' for what? They were powerful tyrants who oppressed the people, and lead their minds away from Yahweh. One such 'mighty man' was Nimrod who rose to great power, who set himself up in opposition to Yahweh as a 'god', and commanded that he be worshipped by the people.

[8] And Cush begat Nimrod: he began to be a mighty one in the earth. [9] He was a mighty hunter before (Strong's 6440 against) the Lord: wherefore it is said, Even as Nimrod the mighty hunter before (Strong's 6440 against) the Lord. [10] And the beginning of his kingdom was Babel… Genesis 10:8-10

Strong's {6440} µynip; — paniym, paw-neem'; the Hebrew can have many meanings, but here it is the face (as the part that turns); against, anger towards…

The last record of a giant in the Bible was Goliath, who was over nine feet (2.73 metres) tall. With God's help, David killed him with his sling, and cut his head off.

Many of the 'Sons of God' defected to Satan's perverted way of thinking, and they became the unseen pantheon of gods that then had influence over those who ruled over the nations of the world and who still do so to this day. So Yahweh passed judgement on some of the 'Sons of God', and told them because of their actions, they would die like men, but not all of them 'died'.

[6] I (God) said, "You are gods all of you (who) are Sons of the Most High. 7 Nevertheless you shall die like men, and fall like one of the rulers." Psalm 82:6-7

It was these rebellious 'Sons of God' that actually became the 'gods' that history records were worshipped by the nations through the centuries. The gods of Egypt, Isis, Osiris, Horus, Ra; the Canaanites, Ashtoreth, Baal, Chemosh; the Philistines, Dagon the fish god, a symbol of Dagon continues to this day with the 'fish' like hats of the church hierarchy; Greece, Zeus, Poseidon, Athena, Apollo; the Romans, Jupiter, Juno and Minerva. All these may well have been the actual 'Sons of God' who could manifest themselves in human form, but also remain invisible as they held humans under their sway.

Were the magicians of Egypt 'Sons of God', or men working under their influence? Able to turn their staffs into snakes, produced a plague of frogs, and turned the river into blood? They clearly possessed superhuman or supernatural powers to be able to mimic the miracles performed by God the Word through Moses.

These 'Sons of God' had rebelled against Yahweh, and gone over to Satan's adversarial activities. Many of them were destroyed by Yahweh, and died like men because of their rebellion, but others retained positions of authority under Satan to continue to influence human beings to serve the devil rather than Yahweh.

Some 'Sons of God' are very active now in our era, both those who are still faithful to Yahweh and those who are not. Some can, an no doubt do, influence human rulers for good, and some for evil.

Conspiracy theorists think that covert groups of powerful people hold sway over the events in this world. They undoubtedly do, but not entirely in their own strength, they are given superhuman powers of control, supported by and influenced by the unseen fallen 'Sons of God' who are doing Satan's bidding. Can some of them still manifest or 'morph' themselves as human advisers of the 'Nimrods' of this present age? Perhaps. Are they the 'ones' inspiring the tyrants of this evil world? Very probably. Are others exerting a positive influence on some of the leaders of this world? Undoubtedly.

Today the 'gods' people worship have different names. The manner of the lower nature of human beings today is to 'worship' almost anything they can think up or manufacture, money, wealth, cars, yachts, jets. People even worship people as in the whole celebrity thing, sports 'heroes'. In fact in many religions, people can and do 'worship' any and everything except the worship of the true God, and the result of this idolatry is very ugly.

The Flood of Noah did happen, but why?

Adam and Eve had children, and their children had more children, and sadly they were all tarred with the same Satanic brush, by giving in to the part of their own human nature that is enmity to Yahweh. Dreadful wickedness both moral, physical and Spiritual became epidemic, then pandemic, until God wearied of seeing the idolatrous way His Children were behaving.

In 2369 B.C, or only 1656 years man years after the Creation of Adam, Yahweh came to regret having created man, changes His mind, and decides to destroy all humans, and the fauna, the animals that breathed on the Earth with the flood.

Yahweh was not at all happy to strive with the human race and especially the actions of the Sons of God, and warns of the flood to come, and that in one hundred and twenty years, God would destroy all but eight of them.

[3] Yahweh said, "My Spirit will not strive with man forever, because he also is flesh; so his days will be one hundred twenty years (until the flood)." Genesis 6:3

Just one man had followed God's ways, and because of him, he and his family, eight in all, were miraculously saved in the Ark which Noah built under God's direction.

[7] Yahweh said, "I will destroy man whom I have created from the surface of the ground, man, along with animals, creeping things, and birds of the sky for I am sorry (deeply regret) that I have made them." [8] But Noah found favour in Yahweh's eyes. Genesis 6:7-8

From these eight people, from Noah's three sons and their wives the whole Earth was overspread. Shem gave rise to the white people, Ham to the brown and black people, and Japheth was the father of all the oriental people on Earth today. Which reveals how that happens, because it was built into the DNA of those six people that we came to have the three main different racial groups today.

[26] He made from one blood every nation of men to dwell on all the surface of the earth, having determined appointed seasons, and the boundaries of their dwellings, Acts 17:26

So how is the story of the Flood relevant today? It is a warning for everyone today, right now in this era, we who indeed appear to be approaching the ends of this world as we know it, to learn from. Nobody listened to the warnings of Noah, they thought he was insane, so took no notice. The situation seems to be being repeated in our era, and the population of the world is in for a shock.

All the chaos in the world, serious climate change which if unchecked will destroy the eco system of the earth in just a few years; unprecedented pollution of the Earth and its oceans; the renewed discussions for the further proliferation of nuclear weapons and the constant threat of the possibility of nuclear war; all these factors certainly indicate that things are getting much worse and not better. Could we be once again headed for the almost complete annihilation of the human race? This time not initially as a result of God's intervention in human affairs, but now entirely due to reckless aberrant human behaviour. This is emphatically not 'fake news', 'media lies' or 'doom and gloom' talk, it is pure realism.

The 'birth' of universal rebellion against God

The human race increased in numbers over the next few hundred years, until it is thought to be around 2354 years after the birth of humankind, when humanity made another choice. Their activities and behaviour were universally against Yahweh's wishes. The Earth's population was not interested in living under an Invisible God they could not see, they wanted a 'god' they could see, touch and feel. So at the instigation of Nimrod the tyrant who wanted all to worship him, they built a tower which reached 'up to heaven' to represent their 'god'.

At that time, all the people of the Earth spoke the same language. God could see that this would only assist and empower the entire population of the time to speed up further rebellion against Him. So at the Tower of Babel, God divided tribes into nations God confused their language so that could not understand each other.

[8] So Yahweh scattered them abroad from there over the surface of all the earth. They stopped building the city. [9] Therefore its name was called Babel, because there Yahweh confused the language (a babble) of all the earth. From there, Yahweh scattered them abroad over the surface of all the earth. Genesis 11:8-9

We have the word 'babble' in the English language. Yahweh's Divine Fiat was the origin of all foreign languages. Up until the time of Babel, Yahweh had been working with humans, but this is when God is 'giving up' on the nations, and giving them what they wanted which was a 'god' of their own.

Then Yahweh began His Work of developing His chosen Family through Abraham, Isaac, and Jacob who became Israel. The twelve tribes of Israel escaped slavery in Egypt through God's use of miracles.

Due to their rebellious attitude, Moses led the Israelites through the Sinai desert for forty years until they all died before their children were allowed into the 'Promised Land'. Then followed centuries of Yahweh pleading with Israel to love Him and obey His laws, but they did not.

Yahweh sent his Prophets for centuries to warn them and to reinforce His message to human beings, but the Israelites still did not listen.

The history of the world's human beings ever since the Tower of Babel in 2354 A.M. or 1670 B.C. continued through the centuries. Finally, in 6 B.C. Yahweh sent His Son into the world to provide His children with a different way to love and approach God, and to live a more obedient life.

Since Christ was born, humankind has continued on its same path of rebellion against God and His Laws to this day.

Now in our era, we are undoubtedly approaching the end of the age and the world as we know it as conditions and behaviours go from bad to worse. Yahweh is very specific as He has Paul to write to Timothy the way things will be in the last days.

[1] But know this: that in the last days, grievous times will come. [2] For men will be lovers of self, lovers of money, boastful, arrogant, blasphemers, disobedient to parents, unthankful, unholy, [3] without natural affection, unforgiving, slanderers, without self-control, fierce, not lovers of good, [4] traitors, headstrong, conceited, lovers of pleasure rather than lovers of God, [5] holding a form of godliness (churchianity), but having denied its power. Timothy 3:1-5

This is largely due to the activities of Satan, who is more than ever influencing the carnal minds of human being that are enmity to Yahweh to sink deeper into immorality and godlessness.

[12b] ...Woe to the earth and to the sea, because the devil has gone down to you, having great wrath, knowing that he has but a short time. Revelation 12:12b

It is ever more important now than ever that we strive with all our might to live the 'Way of Life' with Christ's Help through each day.

The next chapter reveals the incredible story of how the Word gave up His position with the Father to become a man and save us from certain death from our sins.

CHAPTER 5

GOD THE 'WORD' BECAME CHRIST, THE ONLY HUMAN BEGOTTEN SON OF THE FATHER

1 In the beginning was the Word, and the Word was with
God, and the Word was God. 2 The same was in the
beginning with God. 3 All things were made through him.
Without him, nothing was made that has been made.
4 In him was life, and the life was the light of men... 14
The Word became flesh, and lived among us. We saw
his glory, such glory as of the one and only Son of the
Father, full of grace and truth. 15 John testified about
him. He cried out, saying, "This was he of whom I said,
'He who comes after me has surpassed me, for he was
before me.'" John 1:1-4, 14-15

The disciples saw Christ's Glory in vision on the Mount of Transfiguration, Matthew 17. Christ had existed as the Word aeons before John the Baptist who testified to that fact.

Around between 6-3 B.C., the time had come when God would move to save humankind from themselves and the death penalty for their sins. Yahweh loved his potential Family, and wanted them all to have the opportunity to 'live', and God the Father, Yahweh, and His Son were prepared to pay an awesome price to achieve Their Plan. As decided, Yahweh's Plan was for the Word to relinquish his Power and position with the Father in Heaven and become a man.

God the Father, Yahweh, had caused His Son to form the 'first Adam' made from the elements in the red earth, 'earthy', as it says in 1 Corinthians 15.

[47] The first man is of the earth, earthy; the second man is the Lord from heaven. [48] As is the earthy, such are they also that are earthy: and as is the heavenly, such are they also that are heavenly. 1 Corinthians 15:47, 48

Now God the Father, Yahweh, took the Spirit Matter of which the Word was made and converted it into an embryo made of human flesh and blood. This human embryo God placed into the womb of Mary where it would grow for nine months, be born, and become Christ the Messiah the 'second Adam'.

When the Word relinquished his position as Co-Creator with the Father, He became Yah'Shua the human being born to Mary when she was still a virgin, and became the first and only human to become the 'Only Begotten Son of the Father'. (John 1:18; 3:16)

It is an astonishing fact that among the billions of human beings on this earth who have some connection to thousands of versions of 'Christianity', that only the very 'few' have any understanding of the true origin of the 'Christ' they imagine they worship. That 'personage' with long hair is actually an image of the pagan god Zeus that is pictured and formed into statues in their churches. God writes through Paul in 1 Corinthians:

[14] Does not even nature itself teach you, that, if a man has long hair, it is a shame to him? 1 Corinthians 11:14

So it is highly unlikely that Christ the Messiah had long hair. Most in 'Churchianity' know little or nothing of the origin of the real Christ, or what the real 'sacrifice' entailed that He and God the Father made for Him to become their 'Saviour'.

Christ, was the Word who Created the Universe

The plain teaching of Yahweh, through Christ, through the apostle Paul in Hebrews chapters 1 and 2 who gives very clear understanding of how it was that the Word was the One (under the power and auspices of Yahweh His Father, and our Father) who brought into existence the physical universe that we observe around us (both the heavens and the earth) and became Christ the Messiah.

Yahweh through Paul called Christ by the term "God" and said He was the divine personage being referred to in Psalm 45 (where a heavenly scene is depicted with heavenly geography that has names similar to our geography on earth). Paul said:

[1] God, having in the past spoken to the fathers through the prophets at many times and in various ways, [2] has at the end of these days spoken to us by his Son, whom he appointed heir of all things, through whom also he made the worlds... [8] "But unto the Son he [God the Father] says, 'Your throne, O God [Christ, Yah'Shua the Messiah, here is also called "God"], is for ever and ever [the age of the age]: a sceptre of righteousness is the sceptre of your kingdom. [9] You have loved righteousness, and hated iniquity; therefore God, even your God, has anointed you with the oil of gladness above your fellows (the other

Sons of God). [10] And you, Lord [Christ, Yah'Shua the Messiah, is called by Paul "Lord" (the "Lord", the "Rock" of the Old Testament)], in the beginning have laid the foundation of the earth; and the heavens are the work of your hands.'" Hebrews 1:1-2, 8–10

It states twice above in the book of Hebrews that the universe is the work of Christ's hands.

In the clearest of language the apostle Paul (under divine inspiration) states that it was Christ (Yah'Shua who had the rank of "God" on Him) who under God the Father created the heavens and the earth. This means that (Yah'Shua as Emmanuel –God with us) had a history of living existence that goes back ***before*** the heavens and the earth ever came into existence. Indeed, it was Yah'Shua in His former state as the Word, the Logos, who was with God the Father during the 'planning stage', and later when the Word created the heavens and the earth.

In the Book of Colossians, The Father through Paul stated (again in plain and simple language) that the first thing created by God the Father was Christ. Then God the Father gave power to Christ Yah'Shua the Messiah to create all the heavenly host of spirit beings, the lesser Sons of God who are His 'fellows', and then the entire heavens and the earth.

"Who [Christ - Yah'Shua] is the image of the invisible God [God the Father], the firstborn of every creature [Greek: creation]. For by Him [Christ - Yah'Shua] were all things created, that are in heaven, and that are in earth

[precisely as Paul wrote in Hebrews 1:8–10, and this interprets the prepositions of Colossians correctly], visible and invisible, whether they be thrones, or dominions, or principalities, or powers: all things were created by Him [by the hand of Christ - Yah'Shua], and for Him: and He is before all things and by Him all things consist." Colossians 1:15–17

The teaching of Christ (Yah'Shua) through the Apostle Paul stresses in the above section of Scripture that Christ (Yah'Shua) was ***"before* all things."** This clearly means that in matters of time and space, Christ (Yah'Shua) came BEFORE them all. Indeed, Christ (Yah'Shua) had to be BEFORE them all in time and space because God through Paul said that the FIRST CREATION of all things in the creation by God the Father was the Word who became CHRIST (Yah'Shua) HIMSELF.

This means that Christ (Yah'Shua) was a created being, so He is not to be reckoned as having an eternal existence, but He came into existence as the first creative act of God the Father, Yahweh created all things, even before "Wisdom" was created, as recorded in Proverbs 8:22–31. Please study all of the Proverbs Chapter 8, it is very inspiring.

The Word became God (like the Father) by being the first created of the Father. Those who claim that Christ (Yah'Shua) only came into a living existence at His birth in Bethlehem are as far off from the truth as they can get. Indeed, it was the Word/Christ who (under the authority of the Father) created the heavens and the earth. Christ (Yah'Shua was (and is) a part of the single "Godhead" called Elohim. Christ (Yah'Shua) was equal in every way with God the Father, as it says in Philippians, only that the Father, Yahweh, was and always will be God the Father of the Divine Family of God.

And what did the very Creator of heaven and earth, Christ (Yah'Shua) do some 2000 years ago? It was in the plan of God the Father, Yahweh, from before the Creation and Foundation of the world, for His Son to become a human being, and to experience the life of a human being, in order eventually to save and finally exalt the totality of the human race into a position of divine "Godhood" that both He and the Father now enjoy.

Few if any appreciate this aspect of the amazing extent of the sacrifice of the Word and Christ. Yah'Shua gave up being God to become a human being for us. This is incredible, but true.

The Father, Yahweh, through the apostle Paul explains this in Philippians in the clearest of ways.

3 *Let nothing be done through strife or vainglory; but*
in lowliness of mind let each esteem other better than
themselves. 4 *Look not every man on his own things,*
but every man also on the things of others. 5 *Let this*
mind be in you, which was also in Christ the Messiah: 6
Who, being in the form of God, thought it not robbery to
be **equal** *with God:* 7 *But made himself of no reputation,*
and took upon him the form of a servant, and was made
in the likeness of men: 8 *And being found in fashion as*
a man, he humbled himself, and became obedient unto
death, even the death of the cross. 9 *Wherefore God (the*

Father, Yahweh) also hath highly exalted him, and given him a name which is above every name: 10 That at the name of Yah'Shua every knee should bow, of things in heaven and things in earth, and things under the earth; 11 And that every tongue should confess that Christ is Lord, to the glory of God the Father. Philippians 2:3–11

So do not be led astray by any incorrect teaching that Christ, Yah'Shua the Messiah came into existence only 2000 years ago. Truthfully, Christ is the Logos, the Word, and the God Creator of the universe.

GOD the WORD became the man, Yah'Shua the Christ.

(Christ: (5547) Cristo>v, khris-tos'; from (5548) (cri>w); anointed, with oil, consecrated, i.e. the Messiah, Christ.)

So, the Word *(Logos)* came into the world and the world did not recognize Him

10 He was in the world, and the world was made by him, and the world knew him not. 11 He came unto his own, and his own received him not. 12 But as many as received him, to them gave he power (potentially) to become the (Spiritual and Eternal) sons of God (Yahweh), even to them that believe on his name: (John 1:10-12).

But John the Baptist finally became aware of who He was. He pointed Him out to the world and said *that Christ, Yah'Shua, was a person who* ***"is preferred before me: for he was before me" (John 1:15).*** *Also,* ***"for he was before me"*** *(John 1:30).* John the Baptist meant *"before me* IN TIME."

Indeed, not only did Christ have a history preceding that of John the Baptist, we read again in the same Gospel of John that Christ had an existence even before the patriarch Abraham (John 8:58).

[57] "Then said the Jews unto him, 'You are not yet fifty years old, and have you seen Abraham?' Christ, Yah'Shua the Messiah said unto them, [58] 'Verily, verily, I say unto you, before Abraham was, I am." [Exodus 3:14] John 8:57–58

Note: 'I AM' is one of the names of God, Yahweh and this infuriated the Jews.

Just Who Was (and Is) Yah'Shua?

The Father, through the apostle Paul reinforced the teaching of the pre-existence of Christ the Messiah (Yah'Shua) as a living personality with the rank of "God" when he told the Corinthians that the God of the Old Testament was actually Christ (Yah'Shua), the 'Rock'.

[4] "And [Israel] did all drink the same spiritual drink [at the time of the Exodus from Egypt]: for they drank of that spiritual Rock that followed them: and that Rock was Christ (Yah'Shua)." 1 Corinthians 10:4

Who was it standing before John the Baptist and the Jewish authorities in his day that was called *Emmanuel* **("God with us")** at his birth? The Book of Revelation adds some pertinent information: Note the clear teaching of the Scripture.

In most Bibles, the heading of the book of Revelation states 'The Revelation of St. John the Divine'. This is not so: Because Christ said in verse 1:

[1] *The Revelation which God (Yahweh the Father) gave unto him Christ, to shew unto his servants things which must shortly come to pass; and he sent and signified it by his angel unto his servant John: Revelation 1:1*

[8] *"I am Alpha and Omega, the beginning and the ending,' says the Lord, which is, and which was, and which is to come, the Almighty." Revelation 1:8*

This same personage is described in physical detail in the rest of chapter 1 of Revelation. He is also depicted as [11] the *"Alpha and Omega, the first and the last" (Revelation 1:11) and as the One [18] "that lives, and was dead"; and, behold, I am alive for evermore, Amen; and have the keys of hades and death." Revelation 1:18*

It is clear that He, the 'Alpha and Omega' the Beginning and the End is Christ (Yah'Shua) the same person who is described as associated with God the Father around the throne of the universe in Revelation chapter 5.

This 'GOD' is shown specifically to be the One who "was slain, and has redeemed us [humankind] to God by your blood" (Revelation 5:9) who is called "the Lamb of God" (verse 13)

Christ (Yah'Shua) is also the One unto whom the Father has committed all judgment of humanity. [22] *"For the Father judges no man, but has committed all judgment unto the Son" (John 5:22),* so when the time of judgment comes we find Christ (Yah'Shua) sitting on His throne of judgment with the absolute Power of God on His person.

[5] *"And he that sat on the throne [in judgment] said, 'Behold, I make all things new.' And he said unto me, 'Write: for these words are true and faithful.' And said unto me, 'It is done. I am Alpha and Omega, the beginning and the end. I will give unto him that is athirst of the fountain of the water of life freely. He that overcomes shall inherit all things; and I will be his God, and he shall be my son.'" Revelation 21:5–7*

In the Day of Judgment mentioned in the Book of Revelation, it is Christ (Yah'Shua) who bears in His person the Rank of God. Christ (Yah'Shua) also bears the name YHVH (Yahweh) in the prophecy of Zechariah 14:3–9.

As explained above, when the Word relinquished His position with the Father, Yahweh transformed the Spirit Matter of the Word into human flesh to form the embryo of Christ (Yah'Shua Kristos) the man, and placed it in Mary's womb.

God the Father, Yahweh, had caused His Son to form the first Adam who was made of the Earth, Earthy, from the physical elements of the soil.

Strong's (2424) Ælhsou~v, ee-ay-sooce'; of Hebrew origin [Hebrew {3091} (Yehowshuwa`)]. Yah'Shua the name of our Lord as a man. Christ: (5547) Cristo>v, khris-tos'; from (5548) (cri>w); anointed, with oil, consecrated, i.e. the Messiah, Christ.) the 'Second Adam'.

When the Word gave up His position with the Father, and became the human being Christ (Yah'Shua) born to the Virgin Mary, He became the first and only human ever to become the 'Begotten Son' of the Father.

It is an astonishing fact that among the billions of people who have some sort of connection or allegiance to the over 30,000 versions of 'Christianity' only a very 'few' understand the true origin of the Christ they worship. How many of them know and understand the true Nature of the false 'Christ' they worship? They speak of the 'sacrifice' of 'Christ' their 'Saviour', but do they have any real appreciation of just what that 'sacrifice' entailed?

The Word was the True Origin and Nature of Christ (Yah'Shua Kristos the Messiah)

The truth revealed in God's Word about the nature of God's Son who became our Saviour is astoundingly different from the world's view of Christ. The Universe, the Sun the Moon and the Planets of our system are all maintained and upheld continuously ever since His death and resurrection by the Power of Christ who Created it all in accordance with, and at the direction of the Father, Yahweh. The record in Hebrews repeated for emphasis.

1 God, who at sundry times and in divers manners
spoke in time past unto the fathers by the prophets, 2
Hath in these last days spoken unto us by his Son, whom he hath appointed heir of all things, by whom also he made the worlds; 3 Who being the brightness of his glory, and the express image of his person, and upholding all things by the word of his power, when he had by himself

purged our sins, sat down on the right hand of the Majesty on high: Hebrews 1:1-3

The awesome origin of the man Christ (Yah'Shua Kristos) is amazing. He was the God the Word, the Creator of all things. The true heritage and nature of the risen and Glorified Christ (who then became YahwehShua) who is 'currently upholding all things' is hardly ever represented as such in the world of Christendom.

Had all those religious people throughout history honoured Yahweh's commandment which forbids the making of graven images or the likeness of anything in connection with the worship of God, the images, statues and stained glass windows displayed in so many churches would not exist; but they do.

The night before Christ (Yah'Shua) was crucified by the Romans and stoned to death by the Jews, he prayed to His Father that He would restore Him to the Glory He once had with the Father. Christ (Yah'Shua) clearly knew about His origin.

4 I have glorified thee on the earth: I have finished the work which thou gave me to do. 5 And now, O Father, glorify thou me with thine own self with the glory which I had with thee before the world was. John 17:4-5.

As Christ (Yah'Shua) suffered the unbelievably cruel double form of torture of crucifixion by the Romans, and the stoning by the Jews that resulted in His death, He became sin personified as He took on the entire sin of all humans who had ever lived.

46 And about the ninth hour Christ, Yah'Shua the Messiah cried with a loud voice, saying, Eli, Eli, ~~lama sabachthani~~? That is to say, My God, my God, Matthew 27:46

These crossed out words 'lama sabachthani' are not a correct translation of the phrase in Aramaic. For two thousand years, 'scholars' have argued about the correct meaning of that phrase, but the truth of it can be found,

The King James Version has many errors injected by the translators at the insistence of the King who was not an honourable man, but power hungry and perverted. It is still one of the best translations, so long as the Christian student relies on God to help them in the process of checking the original texts whenever there is doubt about the meaning of any word or verse.

The meaning of 'lama sabachthani' offered by experts in Aramaic that resonates with the author of this book is:

"My God, My God, for this I was kept [this was My destiny - I was born for this purpose, to bring Salvation to all God's Children]."

Yah'Shua was crying out to those who were murdering Him that He was dying for them.

The awesome penalty of both the God the Father watching, as the Son (Yah'Shua) paid the penalty for the sin of all humankind was profound beyond our understanding.

As Christ (Yah'Shua) died, his human spirit returned to God. At the end of three days and three nights in the tomb, God the Father restored His human spirit, and resurrected His only begotten Son (Yah'Shua) to physical human life.

Christ (Yah'Shua) the Messiah did not allow anyone to touch Him until after He had been carried up to Heaven, cleansed God's Temple in Heaven with His blood on the Altar, at which time His physical body 'died', was changed, and He was clothed with Immortality. He returned to Earth to show Himself to His disciples and to thousands of witnesses to His resurrection.

The testimony of those terrible events shows us that Yahweh and His Son so loved the humans of the world, that the Godhead were willing to go through all that pain in order that their children would not perish, but would ultimately have eternal life as part of the Family of God.

[16] For God so loved the world, that he gave his one and only Son, that whoever believes in him should not perish, but have eternal life. [17] For God didn't send his Son into the world to judge the world, but that the world should be saved through him. John 3:16-17

Human beings are destined to be heirs together with Christ our Elder Brother the heir of all things. What an incredible future we are promised.

God is now working through Christ (Yah'Shua) the 'Second Adam

There is an even deeper meaning by implication in the Hebrew word 'Yatsar' used in the Bible when God was 'forming' Adam. It actually embraces the entire plan of God for His children. In 'forming' Adam physically so carefully from the red clay earth, moulding and shaping his whole body, and inserting human nature into his mind, Yahweh was also working with him spiritually. God much later in the story 'forms' the 'second' Adam, Christ who when resurrected and again back with the Father, is now working with all humans 'forming' them spiritually through the power of God's Holy Spirit.

Where do God and His Son live now in this age?

God's Energy, in all its Forms, is 'Everywhere' in the Universe. He stretches out the heavens as a curtain, and spreads them out as a tent to live in, and especially here near our Earthly home.

[22] It is he that sits upon the circle of the earth, and the inhabitants thereof are as grasshoppers; that stretches out the heavens as a curtain, and spreads them out as a tent to dwell in: Isaiah 40:22

God's 'Home' is not 'afar off'. He is right here with us, close to this Earth. God sits upon 'the circle of the Earth'.

God the Father and God the Son fill the Invisible Spiritual 'Heaven' which surrounds this Earth where the Father has His Throne and the Son sits with Him on the right hand of God, and the Earth is figuratively their 'footstool'.

Christ tells us not to 'swear by heaven; for it is God's throne, nor by the Earth; for it is his 'footstool'. What a lovely analogy.

[34] but I tell you, don't swear at all: neither by heaven, for it is the throne of God; [35] nor by the earth, for it is the

footstool of his feet; nor by Jerusalem, for it is the city of the great King. Matthew 5:34-35

The Father and the only Begotten Son are One God. God now lives close by our Earth surrounded by His Invisible Heaven. In all the vast expanse of the still expanding universe, this is the area where God has chosen to live. This is where God will ultimately rule all that there is when “All is in All”.

That Invisible ‘Cloud’ of God’s Energy that surrounds our Earth is a type of ‘womb’ within which God is nurturing and nourishing His human children with both visible physical things and spiritual energies. So that humans:

[27] *that they should seek the Lord, if perhaps they might reach out for him and find him, though he is not far from each one of us.* [28] *‘For in him we live, move, and have our being.’ As some of your own poets have said, ‘For we are also his offspring.’ Acts 17:27-28*

They (God) have their ‘eyes’ on every human being on Earth, watching over everything that is done here. God in His Heaven is watching over His children throughout the Earth for people who have given themselves completely to him whose hearts are completely committed to Him. He wants to strengthen them in their journey and He does. The Power of God’s Holy Spirit is Present everywhere. Especially with those who are ‘the called’.

[9b] *For Yahweh’s eyes run back and forth throughout the whole earth, to show himself strong in the behalf of them whose heart is perfect toward him. 2 Chronicles 16:9*

The True story of the Birth of Christ, Yah'Shua the Messiah, written by God the Word

Everything the 'world' believes about the birth of Christ are fables made up by humans, and are incorrect. God the Word wrote the Bible by inspiring men to write what He wanted to say, and the Bible is Truth and is correct.

[18] Now the birth of Christ the Messiah was on this wise: Matthew 1:18

So here, the Father is inspiring Matthew to write the true story of the virgin birth of Christ (Yah'Shua Kristos the Messiah) and how it came about according to God's Word, the Bible.

[14] Therefore the Lord himself will give you a sign. Behold, the virgin will conceive, and bear a son, and shall call his name Immanuel. Isaiah 7:14

It is astonishing that Christ (Yah'Shua Kristos) 'Immanuel', which means God with us, would be born to a virgin was prophesied by the Word, who became Christ (Kristos), hundreds of years previously.

[18a] When as his mother Mary was espoused (engaged to be married) to Joseph, **before they came together,** *Matthew 1:18a*

What does this mean "before they came together"? It means exactly what it would mean if it was said today. Before Mary and Joseph had sexual intercourse. Sex before marriage was strictly forbidden at that time.

Matthew 1:18b 'she was found with child of the Holy Ghost. (Incorrect translation, should be 'Spirit') Spirit.

Mary was found to be with child of God the Father, by means of His Holy ~~Ghost~~ (Incorrect rendering, actually) the Holy Spirit of God.

The first man Adam whose flesh was made of the 'dust of the ground', was of the earth, earthy. The second 'Adam' Christ's flesh was made by God the Father out of the Spirit Substance of His Son the Word, who willingly gave up His position as God's Son to become a human being to die for us.

Yahweh through Christ the Word inspired Paul to write in 1 Corinthians 15:

[45] And so it is written, the first man Adam was made a living soul; the last Adam was made a quickening spirit. [46] Howbeit that was not first which is spiritual, but that which is natural; and afterward that which is spiritual. [47] The first man is of the earth, earthy; the second man is the Lord from heaven. 1 Corinthians 15:45-47

When the Word willingly gave up His position as the Creator Son of God (a monumental sacrifice beyond imagination), God the Father converted the Spirit Substance of the Word into a human embryo which He placed into the womb of Mary who thus became Christ's surrogate mother. So Christ *(Yah'Shua Kristos)* was **literally** the Son of God the Father.

If the embryo of Christ (Kristos Yah'Shua) had been the result of Joseph's sperm and an ovum of Mary, He would not have been God's Son, but the physical son of Mary and Joseph. The embryo in Mary's womb was placed there by God the Father, Yahweh, who created it from His own Spirit Essence used to form the Word, so Christ (Yah'Shua Kristos) was literally the created Son of God.

However, as far as the 'world' was concerned, Mary and Joseph were officially and legally the parents of Christ (Yah'Shua Kristos) and as such, Christ (Kristos - Messiah) was a 'Son of David', since both Mary and Joseph were of royal descent of the line of David.

[42] Has not the scripture said, That Christ came of the seed of David, and out of the town of Bethlehem, where David was? John 7:42

[19] Then Joseph her husband, being a just man, and not willing to make her a public example, was minded to put her away privily (privately). Matthew 1:19

Joseph was an upright, God-fearing, law abiding respectable man of royal rank who did not want his espoused partner to be exposed to ridicule and contempt for being involved in premarital sex which broke the Law of God and attracted the death penalty by stoning. So he decided to take Mary away to somewhere where they were not known. But Joseph need not to have worried, God sent an angel to explain the situation to him.

[20] But while he (Joseph) thought on these things (he went to sleep), behold, the angel of the Lord appeared unto him in a <u>dream</u>, saying, Joseph, thou son of David, fear not to take unto thee Mary thy <u>wife</u>: for that which is conceived in her is of the Holy Spirit. Matthew 1:20

In the Bible, God always repeats things that are important and that example is also followed in this book.

In this case that the child Mary was pregnant with and was bearing, was indeed conceived as a result of the Holy Spirit of God the Father placing an embryo in her womb. Joseph knew full well that he and Mary had never had sexual intercourse as will be seen.

[21] And she (Mary) shall bring forth a son, and you shall call his name Yah'Shua the Messiah: for he shall save his people from their sins. Matthew 1:21

So Joseph learned that the name of the child was to be 'Yah'Shua' which means 'God our Saviour'. Not only that, the angel goes on to explain that this was prophesied hundreds of years previously in the book of Isaiah which Joseph would have known well.

[22] Now all this was done, that it might be fulfilled which was spoken of the Lord by the prophet (Isaiah 7:14), saying, [23] Behold, a <u>virgin</u> shall be with child, and shall bring forth a son, and they shall call his name Emmanuel, which being interpreted is, God with us. Matthew 1:22-23

So, this confirms and authenticates the fact that Isaiah 7:14, written in 600 B.C., the manuscript guarded very carefully by the top Jewish authorities for hundreds of years before Christ was born, is talking prophetically in great detail about Christ the Messiah to come.

Prophecy fulfilled like this is another of the solid proofs that God exists. No human can foretell the future at all, let alone with such pinpoint accuracy. God explains this to us in no uncertain terms. "Come on", God says, "let your 'gods' show us the future and tell us about things to come. Let them make something happen, good or evil", God says sarcastically, "and make us dismayed if you can". Of course they cannot. God throws down the challenge:

[21] "Produce your cause," says Yahweh (God the Word). "Bring out your strong reasons!" says the King of Jacob. [22] "Let them announce and declare to us what will happen! Declare the former things, what they are, that we may consider them, and know the latter end of them; or show us things to come. [23] Declare the things that are to come hereafter, that we may know that you are gods. Yes, do good, or do evil, that we may be dismayed, and see it together. Isaiah 41:21-23

People back then relied on their 'gods' a great deal like the billions do in our era, they just worship different 'gods' now. Now the 'gods' of politics, war, materialism, power, pseudo-science, medical 'science', and illicit sex and pleasure occupy most people's minds and time.

To continue in Matthew, it not only states that Christ was coming, but God's Word reaffirms that Mary was a virgin, that word is by definition a young woman who had not ever had sexual intercourse, and whose hymen was still intact.

[24] Then Joseph being raised from sleep did as the angel of the Lord had bidden him, and took unto him his wife: Matthew 1:24

It says in verse 24 that Joseph 'took' unto him his 'wife', so at some time during this period, Joseph and Mary had got married. However this 'took' did not mean in a sexual sense, and we know that because it makes that clear in the next verse.

[25] *And knew her not **till** she had brought forth her firstborn son: and he called his name [mistranslation] 'Yah'Shua'. Matthew 1:25*

And what does it mean "and knew her not"? Exactly the same as it did in verse 18. Mary and Joseph did not have sexual intercourse ***until*** Mary had given birth to Christ ('Yah'Shua' Kristos). That plain statement in the inspired Word of God, all of which is Truth, and is clear enough.

So when exactly was the Birth of Christ ('Yah'Shua' Kristos)?

The Inspired Word of God, the Bible, actually provides a great deal of evidence regarding the exact time, date and place of the birth of Christ (Kristos 'Yah'Shua').

Satan has the whole world believing a fictional story of the time of the birth of Christ ('Yah'Shua' Kristos) based on Pagan ideas and is completely wrong.

[1] *Now when ('Yah'Shua') was born in Bethlehem of Judaea in the days of Herod the king, behold, there came wise men from the east to Jerusalem, Matthew 2:1*

It is useful to notice that this verse is saying that Christ was born during the reign of Herod the King, but it does not say 'when' in his reign. The story about the visit of the 'wise men' that follows shows that it is referring to a time about two years after Christ was actually born in the stable in Bethlehem.

This fact is important because it highlights the fact that the popular fable believed by billions around the world about the birth of Christ (Yah'Shua Kristos) is inaccurate in so many ways. The 'wise men' were not present in the stall where the baby Yah'Shua the Messiah lay in the manger, and so they did not give Him gifts of 'gold, frankincense and myrrh' at that time.

So it is necessary to wind back the clock to the time and the day of the birth of Christ (Yah'Shua Kristos).

The Birth of Christ ('Kristos') - the real story: Christ (Kristos – Messiah) the Lamb was born on Nisan 1

The 'world' thinks that Christ (Kristos) was born on December 25. A close look at the Biblical record gives the clues to many facts that make this impossible. Christ (Kristos) was born in the Springtime, on Nisan 1 on the Hebrew Calendar.

Why were Joseph and Mary in Bethlehem?

1 *And it came to pass in those days, that there went*
out a decree from Caesar Augustus that all the world
should be taxed (and also subjected to a census). 2 *And*
this taxing was first made when Cyrenius was governor
of Syria. 3 *And all went to be taxed, every one into*
his own city.

4 *And Joseph also went up from Galilee, out of the city*
of Nazareth, into Judaea, unto the city of David, which
is called Bethlehem; (because he was of the house and
lineage of David:) 5 *To (enrol himself and) be taxed with*

Mary his espoused (engaged to become his) wife, being great with child. Luke 2:1-5

Note well that this is clear verifiable historical evidence that this event occurred at sometime around 6-3B.C.E.

Why no other accommodation available apart from a stable?

There was none because so many people had converged on Bethlehem from miles around to pay their taxes and enrol for the census.

[26] *And in the sixth month the angel Gabriel was sent from God unto a city of Galilee, named Nazareth,* [27] *to a virgin espoused to a man whose name was Joseph, of the house of David; and the virgin's name was Mary.* [28] *And the angel came in unto her, and said, Hail, thou that art highly favoured, the Lord is with thee: blessed art thou among women. Luke 1:26-28*

God would not have sent the angel Gabriel to Mary with such high praise if she and Joseph had committed fornication. God sent Gabriel to reassure Mary that she was faultless in that regard.

[7] *And she brought forth her firstborn son, and wrapped him in swaddling clothes, and laid him in a manger; because there was no room for them in the inn.* [8] *And there were in the same country shepherds abiding in the field, keeping watch over their flock by night. Luke 2:7-8*

Joseph and Mary were both of royal birth and were not poor.

Why were there shepherds living out in the fields at night?

Because it was Springtime which was the lambing season in Israel then, the shepherds had to be there to assist the ewes who were giving birth to lambs. Lambs in Israel were only born naturally then in the Springtime March/April the month of Nisan in the Jewish calendar.

This could not have been during the time of the Feast of Tabernacles, because all devout Jewish males would have to be in Jerusalem to attend the feast or would otherwise be breaking the Law. Law abiding Joseph would not have done that. God was making sure that even the parents of Christ (Yah'Shua Kristos), and therefore the baby would keep the Law perfectly.

[29] The next day, he (John the Baptist) saw 'Yah'Shua' coming to him, and said, "Behold the Lamb of God, who takes away the sin of the world! John 1:29

The celebration of the Passover was during the lambing season since the sacrificial lambs for this feast had to be exactly one year old (Exodus 12:5). It is not surprising that the *Lamb of God* (John 1:29) would be born during the lambing season, right before Passover (based on Luke 2:8), in Bethlehem (Matthew 2:1).

What was the significance of their being in Bethlehem

Historically the lambs for the Temple Passover sacrifice were kept in Bethlehem near the Tower of the flock mentioned as Rachel's burial place in Bethlehem mentioned in Genesis 35:19-21

Since these lambs were special and could not be hurt or damaged in order to be pure for the sacrifice, the shepherds who kept them were specifically trained for this task. They had to make sure nothing happened to the sacrificial lambs. These were the men who came to witness the birth of the *Lamb of God.*

This 'tower of the flock' in Bethlehem is also part of a prophecy by Micah hundreds of years previously:

[8] And you, O tower of the flock (Hebrew: Migdal Eder), hill of the daughter of Zion, to you shall it come, the former dominion shall come, kingship for the daughter of Jerusalem. Micah 4:8

[2] But you, O Bethlehem Ephrathah, who are too little to be among the clans of Judah, from you shall come forth for me one who is to be ruler in Israel, whose coming forth is from of old, from ancient days. Micah 5:2

The conditions regarding the Passover Lamb were set out in the Mosaic Law in Exodus 12.

[1] Yahweh spoke to Moses and Aaron in the land of Egypt, saying, [2] "This month (Nisan, in the Spring) shall be to you the beginning of months. It shall be the first month of the year to you. [3] Speak to all the congregation of Israel, saying, 'On the tenth day (Nisan 10 is Palm Sunday) of this month, they shall take (or accept) to them every man a lamb, according to their fathers' houses, a lamb for a household; Exodus 12:1-3

All of the significant days in the life of Christ (Yah'Shua Kristos) took place on God's Hebrew or 'Jewish' Holy Days.

Palm Sunday was on Nisan 10, and was the day when Christ (Yah'Shua) entered the city on a donkey in peace.

The Passover occurred on Thursday the 14th Nisan at the full moon when Christ (Kristos – Messiah) was born, and it was also the day on which He was crucified thirty-three years later.

Christ was raised up and ascended to heaven forty days after His resurrection from the grave on the Feast of First fruits. Ten days later on the day of Pentecost (which means 'count fifty') He sent the Power of Holy Spirit, the Comforter to His believers.

Christ will return in Power on a white horse at the time of the Feast of Tabernacles, the Day of Trumpets (Autumn, September time, year as yet unknown!) when Christ the King returns to 'Tabernacle' (which means to reside or dwell) with His children for evermore.

So which day was Christ ('Yah'Shua') actually born?

He was born on the 1st day of the beginning of the Hebrew New Year – Nisan 1. Christ, the Lamb of God, was the 'New Beginning' for all humankind, and He was born on the day of new beginnings, Nisan 1 in the March/April Springtime of the year during the 'lambing' season.

The evidence of Christ's ('Yah'Shua's) birth is an absolute historic fact. His birth, word, death and resurrection resulted in the whole calendar of the world being changed by the Roman Caesar from Before 'Christ', B.C. to After Christ, A.D. (Anno Domini Latin for

Day of the Lord). This was no small event. The whole world of that time was awed at those historic events.

The Hebrew calendar is based on the Moon, we have the word 'Month'. All months of that calendar begin with a 'New Moon'. When Christ died on the Passover, 14th Nisan, it was again the time of the full moon.

Experts have also looked to the stars to find that there were indications of the Birth of Christ in the planets which the astronomers of that age could recognise. Astrology is a mystical 'religious' theory that has its problems, and is not for Christians, but the astronomical signs of the Zodiac are Biblical.

The Magi of Zoroastrianism of that time in Persia used much true astronomical knowledge. The visit of the Magi recorded in the Bible, not just three of them but a large multitude, came about because they had observed the conjunction of planets in 6 B.C. which gave signs of a Royal Birth in the heavens. The visit of the Magi with their insightful gifts was prophesied hundreds of years before in the book of Isaiah.

[1] "Arise, shine; for your light has come, and Yahweh's glory has risen on you… [5b] The wealth of the nations will come to you. [6] A multitude of camels will cover you, the dromedaries of Midian and Ephah. All from Sheba will come. They will bring gold and frankincense, and will proclaim the praises of Yahweh. Isaiah 60:1, 5b-6

Matthew 2 tells of the visit of the Magi.

[1] Now when Yah'Shua the Messiah was born in Bethlehem of Judaea in the days of Herod the king,

behold, there came wise men from the east to Jerusalem,
[2] Saying, Where is he that is born King of the Jews? For we have seen his star in the east, and are come to worship him. Matthew 2:1-2

No star in the heavens can 'move', so what were they seeing?

Herod died in 4 B.C. and we know that Christ was born about two years before Herod died which helps to provide us with the date of the birth of Christ as 6 B.C.

Daniel the Prophet was in Babylon and he was appointed the chief over all the wise men or magi of Persia.

[48] Then the king made Daniel great, and gave him many great gifts, and made him rule over the whole province of Babylon, and to be chief governor over all the wise men (Magi of Persia) of Babylon. Daniel 2:48

Around 6 B.C., in the Spring time, there was a conjunction of Jupiter, Saturn, and Venus, converging into one part of the sky beginning on April 17th. Astronomers know that his only happens rarely. Jupiter was linked in their thinking to the 'King', and this convergence arrived in the part of the Zodiac which was Aries that was associated with Judea. The conclusion of the Magi was without doubt inspired of God.

Here is another important clue in the Bible as to the time when this event occurred. Priests had a 'rota', divisions or a 'course' for their time of service in the Temple so they knew in advance when they had to devote themselves to Temple duties.

[5] There was in the days of Herod, the king of Judea, a certain priest named Zacharias, of the priestly division of Abijah… [8] Now while he executed the priest's office before God in the order of his division [9] according to the custom of the priest's office, his lot was to enter into the temple of the Lord and burn incense…[11] An angel of the Lord appeared to him, standing on the right side of the altar of incense. [12] Zacharias was troubled when he saw him, and fear fell upon him. [13] But the angel said to him, "Don't be afraid, Zacharias, because your request has been heard. Your wife, Elizabeth, will bear you a son, and you shall call his name John. Luke 1:5, 8, 11-13

This record in Luke identifies the time that John the Baptist was born which was six months before Christ.

The 'courses' or 'lots' of the priests by weeks are listed in 1 Chronicles 24, and the 'course' of Abijah was number eight. We need to know when these listed 'courses' began and that information was discovered in the Dead Sea Scrolls. When a shepherd threw a rock into a grave, he broke a pot which contained scrolls of parts of the oldest Bible in history and also a Hebrew calendar of the 'courses'.

This calendar was not just for a year, but was for three years and then it would repeat itself. The scrolls gives astronomical details which make it clear that the calendar begins at the Equinox and on a Wednesday. An Equinox occurs twice each year around 20 March and 23 September. It is the moment at when the centre of the visible Sun is directly above the equator.

This information is confirmed by another evidence contained in the Talmud where it says that the Temple was destroyed in 70 A.D. on a Sunday and gives the name of the priest who was officiating on that day. If the data in the Dead Sea Scroll calendar is wound forward, and the Talmud record wound backwards they match, and leads to March 20th 6 B.C. which is Nisan 1.

In the hidden vaults of the Vatican there are writings by Hippolytus in the 2nd Century A.D., who had said the birth of Christ was the 25th December, but this is redacted or edited out, and replaced with the fact that Christ was born on Nisan 1. So His birth date is known by scholars.

What is the first shadow or inkling of God the Word, the 'Messiah' living among us in the Old Testament? It is the Tabernacle because it is when God came to 'live' in it. John 1 says that the Word became flesh and dwelt or 'tabernacled' with us. The first Tabernacle was a tent built in Sinai which took nine months to complete. What was the date that the Tabernacle was finished?

[17] In the first month (Nisan) in the second year, on the first day of the month, the tabernacle was raised up. Exodus 40:17

Nisan 1 is the day that everything becomes new. The Power of the presence of God, and then the Messiah makes everything new. All the time, and every day we acknowledge God, everything becomes 'new' in our lives. New Spirit, New Forgiveness, new measure of His Spirit.

In that sense, for Christians, every day is Nisan 1. We walk in the newness of life.

For all this to be true, everything had to happen according to God's Plan which it did. This is also the case with Christ's return, everything, EVERYTHING, **EVERYTHING** has always, and is still working exactly according to God's Timing and His plan.

Christmas Myth - The Pagan godless Winter Solstice of the Sun

So Christ ('Yah'Shua') was not born in December at all. So all the festivities that occupy the attention of perhaps the majority of people in the world for now nearly two months each year notwithstanding, they have got their date wrong. How did that Christmas tradition start and dominate the minds of so many people?

Millennia before the birth of Christ ('Yah'Shua'), Pagans, country people and heathens worshipped many 'gods' and most were involved in Sun worship as well. They mourned the death of the Sun at its lowest point, and celebrated its 'rebirth' as it began to rise in the sky again. The Sun of course does not move, it is the earth that moves in an orbit around it, but it appears to earth's inhabitants to move.

Pagans celebrated December the 22nd -26th because it is the time of the Winter Solstice when the Sun, as we view it in the Northern Hemisphere, reaches its lowest point and the shortest day and was thought to have died'; and then the days begin to lengthen and the Sun, reborn, appears to rise higher in the sky. Sun worship was deeply rooted in Pagan thinking, so when Christ ('Yah'Shua') was born, they absorbed His name and part of His message into their celebrations, and it became known as the 'Christ-mas' period. All the trappings of the Winter Solstice became the way to celebrate the birth of Christ ('Yah'Shua').

If anyone cares to go onto the Internet, and put 'Winter Solstice' in the Middle East, here is what comes up.

"In modern times Christians all over the world celebrate the birth of Christ on Christmas Day, which falls on December 25. Christmas is also referred to as Yule, which is derived from the Norse word jól, referring to the pre-Christian winter solstice festival".

'Nativity plays' held in and around places of worship are so completely wrong in the way the birth of Christ (Kristos – Messiah) is represented. Mary and Joseph were of royal descent and were certainly not poor. The reason they finished up in a stable was because at that time everyone had to attend a census and be taxed in the area, so there was no other accommodation available.

The shepherds would certainly **not** have been in the fields at night in December in Israel, as all the sheep were brought down from the hills long before the winter cold set in in the Middle East. Yet the Bible states that they were living in the hills and tending their sheep when they heard about the birth of Christ from an angel, in the evening, and came straight down to worship Him, and then went back to their flocks.

[8] *And there were in the same country shepherds abiding (living, not visiting) in the field, keeping watch over their flock by night …*[20] *And the shepherds returned, glorifying and praising God for all the things that they had heard and seen, as it was told unto them. Luke 2:8*

Notice, as soon as they had been told of the event by the angel, the shepherds came to see Christ in the stable in the evening after dark. Christ was actually born in the early evening.

The 'wise men' were not present in the stable at the time of Christ's birth. That is a complete fabrication. It really does show that virtually nobody reads what the Bible has to say about 'wise men' or when they actually visited Yah'Shua the Messiah. The story is very clear in the second chapter of Matthew.

[9] *When they (the 'wise men', and there were many of them, not three, who had travelled a long way from the 'East' for months, perhaps from Persia) had heard the king (Herod), they departed; and, lo, the star (probably Jupiter which appeared to move in relation to other stars), which they saw in the east, went before them, till it came and stood over (Jupiter apparently stopped moving East then) where <u>the young child</u> was.* [10] *When they saw the star, they rejoiced with exceeding great joy.* [11] *And when they were come <u>into the house</u> (not the stable), they saw <u>the young child</u> (not the baby) with Mary his mother, and fell down, and worshipped him: and when they had opened their treasures, they presented unto him gifts; gold, and frankincense and myrrh.* [12] *And being warned of God in a dream that they should not return to*

Herod, they departed into their own country another way. Matthew 2:9-12

The next part of the Biblical record shows the true time frame when after the wise men had observed the sign in the heavens, they had travelled many months from Persia and arrived in Israel, and Christ was now a toddler of about two.

[16] Then Herod, when he saw that he was mocked of the wise men, was exceeding wroth, and sent forth, and slew all the children that were in Bethlehem, and in all the coasts thereof, from two years old and under, according to the time which he had diligently inquired of the wise men. Matthew 2:16

To repeat: God wrote the Bible through men, and His record is true.

Christmas is satanic, 'Santa' is an anagram of Satan.

Satan, ('Santa' is an anagram of Satan), has the entire world mesmerised with the whole Christmas story into worshipping a false Christ at the wrong time of the year. What was originally a three day festival now takes up two months of everyone's time, and still has all the trappings of thousands of years of paganism, Xmas trees with little lights, Yule logs, Wreaths for the Sun, and everyone focussed on material things. The whole situation is best avoided and shunned by true Christians.

The next chapter will present the historic evidence that testifies to the fact that the Holy Bible is God's Word.

CHAPTER 6

ABSOLUTE PROOFS TESTIFY THAT THE HOLY BIBLE WAS WRITTEN BY GOD THROUGH MEN

Solid irrefutable evidence that proves that God exists, is real, and Created the Universe have been presented in this book.

Since God created the universe, life itself, DNA, the heart and mind of human beings, and the different instincts of every creature. How difficult would it be for Him to produce a book through men that was totally accurate, and exactly as He determined He wanted it to be?

In the light of all the evidence presented so far in this book, this is not really a good question to ask. Because of all the solid evidence, testimony and proof that the Bible contains, it is not reasonable for an open honest mind to doubt the veracity of God's existence, or the Truth of the Bible.

It is so very important that anyone who wants to have a proper relationship with God does not rely on any human religion, or any person, minister or priest to learn the truth...

[27] *But the anointing which you have (or will have) received of him abides in you, and ye need not that any*

man teach you: but as the same anointing teaches you ***of*** *all things, and is truth, and is no lie, and even as it hath taught you, ye shall abide in him.1 John 2:27*

But instead, each person needs to prove to themselves, for themselves, that God, the Awesome Mind and Power really does exist, and that His Word, the Bible is His Word, and is the Truth we need to know.

THE BIBLE IS GOD'S OPERATIONAL MANUAL FOR HUMAN LIFE

So how can we even begin to learn more about Who and What God **Is?** God actually wrote His 'manual' that tells us all we need to know about Him and everything in this life that we ***cannot*** find out for ourselves.

The Creator God wrote, through His servants, that all time 'best-seller called the Bible. More Bibles have been printed than any other book ever published, by far. It is the only Book that explains in detail how the Earth and the Universe was Created, by the Creator.

How did God write the Bible?

God dictated it to men, by inspiring them His servants to write down word for word each of the books the Bible contains. They were to be painstakingly spelled out on the original texts exactly as He wanted them to be written.

As already mentioned, each page was then checked by specialist professional 'counters' who counted every letter of every page, and if just one letter was missing or incorrect, the page was destroyed. God wanted His book exactly the way He planned it to be, and the original manuscripts are just that.

All translations by men or women contain inaccuracies and errors – the original manuscripts do not, as will be shown

Men have made hundreds of different translations and they all contain errors, because each one includes human fallible ideas about God. But that fact does not need overly to concern anyone who really wants to learn the 'truth'. God can make sure that a diligent student will learn what He wants them to know at any given time in their lives.

Many say that the Bible is impossible to understand. They say it is full of unbelievable stories, and contains many contradictions. As long as anyone thinks that way they will never even begin to understand its deeper meanings. Interesting, many who express this type of opinion have never actually read the Book.

Strange to relate, it is also a fact that the Bible was not written with the intention for it to be read and understood like any other book. The Holy Bible is not just another book, it is the unique 'Book of Truth' written by the Creator God that contains the truths we need to know, and are here to learn in order to make a physical and spiritual success of this life. It is the most complex Book in the world, written over centuries by many different people, but it all fits together like one huge jigsaw puzzle. There are no contradictions.

FIRST: ASK OUR HEAVENLY FATHER FOR HIS HELP TO UNDERSTAND HIS WORD BEFORE BEGINNING ANY STUDY

So if we truly want to learn about God, we have to read and study the Book He wrote very carefully, **and with His help.** Without asking for and receiving that 'help', the Bible appears to make no sense to the human mind and is even inexplicable. So much of the Book appears to be nonsense to the unbelieving reader.

Repeated for emphasis, this is explained in the Bible by Christ through Paul.

14 "Now the natural (carnal) man (with a human spirit) doesn't (cannot) receive the things of God's Spirit, for they are foolishness to him, and he can't know them, because they are Spiritually discerned". 1 Corinthians 2:14

It is said that 'seeing is believing' although in spiritual matters, 'believing IS seeing'. So with God's help and the right attitude, a person can begin to learn a lot more about Him, and how to live His Way from the Bible.

God's Word is for instruction in righteousness, or how to keep God's law, and for our teaching, and it can 'cut to the quick' as it shows us how far from God we are and what we need to do to please Him.

12 For the word of God is quick, and powerful, and sharper than any two-edged sword, piercing even to the dividing asunder of soul and spirit, and of the joints and marrow, and is a discerner of the thoughts and intents of the heart. Hebrews 4:12

EVIDENCE THAT PROVES GOD EXISTS AND THAT THE BIBLE IS HIS WORD

Before the beginning of everything we know of, GOD was a living Spirit Being. He had no beginning, has always 'been' and always 'will be'. The nearest English word to describe Him is ETERNAL.

The Bible is the only Book that quotes God speaking to us His children in the First Person.

[10] "You are my witnesses," says Yahweh (the Hebrew word for God), "With my servant whom I have chosen; that you may know and believe me, and understand that I am He, Before me there was no God formed, neither will there be after me.[11] I myself am Yahweh. Besides me, there is no Saviour". Isaiah 43:10-11

And in Isaiah again.

[5] "I am Yahweh, and there is no one else. Besides me, there is no God. I will strengthen you, though you have not known me, [6] that they may know from the rising of the sun, and from the west, that there is no one besides me. I am Yahweh, and there is no one else. [7] I form the light and create darkness. I make peace and create calamity. I am Yahweh who does all these things". Isaiah 45:5-7

[11] "He has made everything beautiful in its time. He has also set eternity in their hearts, yet so that man can't find out the work that God has done from the beginning even to the end". Ecclesiastes 3:11

[17] "Then I saw all the work of God that man can't find out the work that is done under the sun, because however much a man labours to seek it out, yet he won't find it.

Yes even though a wise man thinks he can comprehend it, he won't be able to find it". Ecclesiastes 8:17

These quotes from the Bible, His Word, show that God has set definite limits on the abilities of His children especially when it comes to Spiritual matters.

It is a really tragic fact that most human beings are so unwilling to observe the Mind and Hand of God and His unfathomable Powers in everything we know about. It is really exciting to meditate on the Creative Powers of the One who made us. We are His offspring, His children, and when we fail to acknowledge this, we limit ourselves.

The mind and ways of God are so far above and beyond human comprehension.

[8] *"For my thoughts are not your thoughts, and your ways are not my ways," says Yahweh.* [9] *"For as the heavens are higher than the earth, so are my ways higher than your ways, and my thoughts than your thoughts." Isaiah 55:8-9*

It is a tragedy that although the human mind has expanded to an enormous extent over the last few decades, that development and all its achievements appears to have taken humans further from any sincere appreci ation of their Creator.

The human order of the day is to take personal credit for all their amazing discoveries, or give credit to other frankly insane notions like everything coming from nothing, instead of giving praise and thanks to the Almighty for their abilities. There is a word for this attitude, and it is 'sacrilege' which literally means 'stealing from God.

So how can we learn about 'Who and What God Is'?

Study carefully the Book God Wrote we call the Bible. It tells us that God is made of Spirit Matter and Spirit Essence which is invisible and indestructible, as are all His many Powers which extend everywhere, and are Om nipresent. The ONE God, the father and the Son is the Origin of Creation.

[15] Study to show yourself approved unto God, a workman that needs not to be ashamed, rightly dividing the word of truth. 2 Timothy 2:15

The information in this book will help you to 'rightly divide' or study effectively the Word of Truth. It is very important to know exactly how the Bible came into existence.

When God first decided to create a Family, He began by creating His Son, the Word. The two Beings were One God, and the plural is used when the Father and the Son are being referred to. As They developed their plans for a human family, They foresaw the need for there to be an 'Instruction Manual'. It would have to provide human beings with all the necessary information about what God expected of them that they could not find out for themselves. The Holy Bible is that manual, and there is no other.

So after the Creation of the Heavens and the earth and the first man and woman, Adam and Eve, and succeeding generations were born, God formed personal relationships with those with whom He wished to work. Over more than two thousand years God appointed and inspired certain individuals and families beginning first with Job then Moses who became His servants, to write down at His dictation, information about Himself, the history of man, and the lessons that would need to be learned by His children as time progressed.

This is why the Bible is totally accurate and true, because every word that became the Holy Scriptures came from God. However it is true that when men translated these manuscripts into other languages, they made human errors all to the sincere and diligent student of the Bible, as there simple ways, with some work, to solve this situation, which will be covered in this book.

The Bibles we have now are made up of 66 books, 39 in the Old Testament and 27 in the New Testament. Interestingly, the number 6 is the number of man. However this is not the number of books that God designed to be included in His Bible. This will become clear.

Bible study is pointless unless the reader is absolutely, utterly and totally convinced that it is truly the Word of the Almighty God.

Armed with that conviction and God's help, any and all doubts will evaporate, apparent contradictions will be readily resolved, and the knowledge, understanding and wisdom otherwise hidden from the casual reader, or the average 'churchgoer', will flood into the mind of the earnest student.

The next section contains 'keys' to enable careful diligent study which will 'unlock' the spiritual secrets the Bible contains. Study takes work.

Here is an example of an approach to careful study.

16 All scripture is given by inspiration of God, and is profitable for doctrine, for reproof, for correction, for instruction in righteousness: 2 Timothy 3:16

Many know this verse by heart. Any time we think we know a verse so well that we have it memorised, a proper approach to Bible study will involve our checking whether we truly understand what it is actually saying to us or not.

***Key Study Aid:** Use a concordance, like Strong's, to check the significant words in the passage in the original Hebrew or Greek text that is translated into English. It will often reveal more meaning.

2 Timothy 3:16 begins, "**All Scripture** is given by inspiration of God..."

The word 'scripture' in the original text is translated from the Greek word 'grafay' which means 'writings' or 'documents', the base of the word 'graphic'.

Strong's (1124) grafh>, *graf-ay';* from (1125) (gra>fw); a document, i.e. holy *Writ* (or its contents or a statement in it): — scripture that means 'writings'.

Is 'all Scripture' inspired of God – is 'all Scripture' part of the Bible? We definitely know that not all of the thousands or even millions of ancient 'writings' discovered by archaeologists are inspired of God. So what does **'all** scripture' mean here?

Do we have the Book that God wants us to have? Yes, absolutely, we definitely do. Are there errors in translations? Yes, all of the many translations from the original texts do contain errors of translation. But this does not need to be a problem to the careful student. All translators do make errors, or do not perhaps choose the ideal meaning where there is a choice in the wording of the original language, but we can be sure that the original manuscripts do contains the inspired 'truth'. Yes we can, but how?

So how can we rely on what we read in God's Word? Whenever in doubt, check the word in the original text using a concordance. A 'concordance' is an alphabetical list of the words contained in a text or texts, together with the explanation of the meanings in English of those words in the original language they were written in. This enhances clarity and understanding.

This verse in the New Testament, 2 Timothy 3:16 actually means that we can know, and be sure, that **all** the books that are included in the Bible we have, are inspired.

Here is that verse and the following verse in 2 Timothy 3 explains the reason why serious Christians should study God's Word.

[16] Every (canonised) Scripture is God-breathed and profitable for teaching, for reproof, for correction, and for instruction in righteousness, [17] that each person who

belongs to God may be complete, (and is) thoroughly equipped for every good work. 2 Timothy 3:16-17

As anyone develops in the Christian way, their study will result in being properly equipped to 'grow in grace and knowledge'.

Is there evidence that provides solid proof that the Bible is correct?

Yes there is a vast amount of evidence. How can we know for certain that the Bible we have does actually include all the correct books? It is very important to understand how it happened that the books in the Bible are those that God wanted it to contain, no more, and no less. Each person needs to have the solid evidence of that fact in their armoury. That evidence is contained in the exacting procedure that was used to put the books of the Bible together. That procedure, mentioned briefly earlier, is called 'Canonisation'.

All the Books in the Bible were 'Canonised' by men under God's Inspiration

What does "Canonised' mean? A dictionary may give us its definition, but in this case, the word 'Canon' actually means "a rule or law," or in classical Latin, "a standard of excellence."

***Study Key: Practise the 'dictionary habit'. Whenever in doubt as to the meaning of any word, check**

it with a dictionary or an etymological dictionary. They are free to use online.

According to one dictionary: *"A biblical canon or canon of scripture is a set of texts (scrolls or 'books') which a particular religious community regards as authoritative scripture".* We repeat, this is not a true definition of the Holy Bible. Not all dictionaries give correct definitions, and it is necessary to be aware of the publisher's 'opinions'. The content of the original manuscripts was determined by God, not by human beings or any religious body.

It is logically and statistically impossible according to the Laws of Probability, that any man or group of men and women could have assembled the Old and New Testament collection of books from the many thousands of manuscripts written by the Prophets and Apostles and other secular historians over a period of thousands of years.

It is important for us to come to appreciate that the precise choice of books and their order was controlled specifically by The Almighty God as He Inspired and Oversaw the work done to collate them by His servants the Prophets.

The Bible consists of the Old Testament which was assembled and Canonised in God's Holy Temple under God's direct supervision to a very high standard of excellence. It was meticulously checked by God's servants, the Jewish Authorities under God's Divine direction, so there could be no possible room for error, and then kept under armed guard.

The New Testament was 'Canonised' and 'sealed' at the end of the first century by Peter, James and John who were eyewitness of all the acts of Christ. These Scriptures were carefully protected by those of His sound minded servants that God caused to perform that task. To resolve any questions, the student refers to these manuscripts in the original language. All this work is already done by people who have made concordances and dictionaries of the original languages.

Those who study the Bible earnestly with God's help with receive the same sound mindedness that those who Canonised them were given.

[7] For God hath not given us the spirit of fear; but of power, and of love, and of a sound mind. 2 Timothy 1:7

It is all these solid facts that testify to the accuracy and purity of the Bible.

The Old Testament

The Old Testament is the most accurate historical record of people and events that exists on the earth. Whenever historians and archaeologists think or consider that the Bible is at fault, they are incorrect. The Bible, inspired to be written by God is the true standard they should trust.

The Old Testament of the Bible in common use now consists of 39 books, but this is not how the Old Testament was intended to be structured. Originally,the Old Testament consisted of 22 books, one for each letter of the Hebrew alphabet, and they were Canonised by Ezra, the Priest and Prophet of God under God's direction about 445 years before Christ.

The Priest/Historian Josephus recorded Jewish history, with special emphasis on the first century 66–70

A.D. His writings confirm that the books of the Holy Scriptures were deposited in God's Temple in the care of the Chief Priests and those who had prophetic rank. This was not only to show them respect but for their preservation, and also as a sign of the great authority and honour that these 22 books were accorded by the top Jewish authorities. It is important to bear in mind that God and Christ are in charge of the whole process.

Josephus was certainly speaking about the sacred books of the Holy Scriptures when he said that these documents were preserved in the Temple under armed guard.

Canonisation – a legal, strict and detailed procedure

When the Old Testament was compiled, the Word who became Christ, inspired the Priest and Prophet Ezra, whose name was also Malachi, to select and assemble only the books He wanted the Testament to contain, and then to bind them up and seal the entire work. God the Word says through Isaiah:

16 "Bind up the testimony, seal the law among my disciples". Isaiah 8:16

There was a very strict procedure that had to be adhered to when the 'manuscripts', which literally means 'handwritten' documents, were being copied. Only those Scribes who were highly trained were authorised to make copies of the original books that were to be included in the 'Canon'. Those Scribes who did the actual copying were strictly overseen by the Jewish authorities.

If any unauthorised person did make a copy, they committed a capital crime, and when caught would have been instantly executed by the armed Jewish guards in the Temple. Anyone unauthorised person to enter the Temple would have met the same fate.

It was Ezra the Priest Prophet who then placed the copies of the 22 books into the hands of the 'Sopherim', those who checked the copies made by the Scribes. The 'Sopherim' were highly trained skilled priests who performed their specialised functions in the Temple in Jerusalem. It is very important to understand the function of the 'Sopherim' who were called the 'counters'.

The 'Sopherim', the 'Counters', were people who examined each letter, each word, each line of each page of the completed copy. If there was any error at all, even one letter, that page was destroyed under supervision, and the Scribe had to make a new one.

This procedure shows that the statements of unlearned critics who question or refute the authenticity of the 22 books of the original Old Testament are absolute nonsense.

The book of Nehemiah, in chapter eight gives a lot of detail about how Ezra opened up the completed Book of the Law, showed it to the people, and the whole assembly stood up in respect and admiration. Chapter 8 goes on to state that Ezra read the book in such a way as to make the sense and meaning clear so that everyone understood what they were hearing.

Christ inspired Isaiah to write:

[16] Bind up the testimony, seal the law among my disciples…[20] To the law and to the testimony: if they speak not according to this word, it is because there is no light in them. Isaiah 8:16, 20

From these passages in Isaiah repeated for emphasis, we can rely on the fact that only those who God was inspiring and guiding were involved in the canonisations.

Once complete, the Old Testament 'Canon' was 'sealed' under the Word's (who became Christ) supervision, and was carefully guarded, and was never to be changed.

Of what practical use is the Old Testament to Christians today?

The Old Testament is an accurate history, indeed it is the most truthful history we have in this world because God 'wrote' it. Men always add their own spin onto histories that they write. For instance, a history of the American civil war written by a person from the North is so completely different from a history written by someone from the South, one might think they were about different wars. Human histories are always biased and inaccurate. So of what value to us are all the stories in the Old Testament today? They are absolutely accurate, and all contain valuable lessons for us to learn from.

[11] Now all these things happened unto them (all humans then) for examples: and they are written for our admonition (to warn and teach us vital principles for living today), upon whom the ends of the world (age – now?) are come. 1 Corinthians 10:11

The Old Testament was written through the ages by many different people who were specifically inspired by God to write down each word, but it is also written especially for us today. There are physical and Spiritual lessons to be learned from every part of God's Word. Above and behind all the stories about physical events, there are profound Spiritual meanings. The most important lesson for us is that we should obey God and His commandments in every detail that applies to us today, and obey and practice only those doctrines that do apply now in this era.

The Old Testament, all inspired by God, contains the book of Isaiah one of God's Prophets, and these next quoted words were written thousands of years ago, yet in his writings, Isaiah mentions truths that have only been discovered by scientists in the last few decades. Isaiah who quotes God speaking in the First Person tells of the heavens 'stretching out' and there is also a word in the Hebrew that describes the 'spiral' nature of galaxies in the universe.

[2] Who covers yourself with light as with a garment: who stretches out the heavens like a curtain: Psalm 104:2

Astro physicists have only relatively recently been able to observe that indeed the universe is stretching outwards, yet this was written in the Bible over two thousand years ago. They also know now that a main characteristic of the design of the universe is the spiral shape that may be also observed replicated in the shape of some sea shells, and both RNA and DNA which are the foundation of all life.

The New Testament Canon

The New Testament Canon was assembled by James, Peter and John late in the first century A.D. under the inspiration of the risen Christ at the Right hand of the Father. There is no doubt that Christ the Son of God oversaw the selection of the choice of the 27 books of which the New Testament consists and ensured that they were included, no more and no less. There is a warning in the book of the Revelation of Yahweh the Father, through the risen Christ (YahwehShua) not to add or detract from the canon of the Bible.

[18] For I (YahwehShua) testify unto every man that hears the words of the prophecy of this book, If any man shall add unto these things, God shall add unto him the plagues that are written in this book 19 And if any man shall take away from the words of the book of this prophecy, God (Yahweh) shall take away his part out of the book of life, and out of the holy city, and from the things which are written in this book. Revelation 22:18-19

The amazing structure of God's Word

God, Yahweh, has written the Bible in His own language, in His own style, and it is structured in a most remarkable way. Once we understand the nature of its unique structure, we are able to investigate the parts of each concept that are contained in the immediate context, or indeed we may also find many other parts of the Bible that help us build up a more complete picture of the subject.

God's special Book contains unique information vital to our ability to live a successful and fulfilled life. There is no other book on earth like it.

God tells us twice for emphasis how the Bible is constructed, and how its teachings and doctrines are presented in a number of discrete parts, and that it is necessary to consider each part that contributes to a given topic in order to get the whole 'picture' of that part.

[28] To whom shall he (God) teach knowledge? and whom shall he make to understand doctrine? Them ('the called') that are weaned from the milk (of God's Word), and drawn from the breasts. [10] For precept must be upon precept, precept upon precept; line upon line, line upon line; here a little, and there a little: [11] For with stammering lips and another tongue will he speak to this people. Isaiah 28:9-11

Verse 10 uses the word 'precept' here three times, and it is of extreme importance that we understand the complete meaning of this word as it applies to the whole of God's Word, our Maker's instruction book and guide that tells us how to live this wonderful life. We may think we 'know' roughly what 'precept' means, but a dictionary definition, and synonyms can supply much greater understanding:

Precept: *"a commandment or direction given as a rule of action or conduct. An injunction as to moral conduct; maxim, a procedural directive or rule, as for the performance or conduct of any activity or operation. Law, a writ or warrant".*

Synonyms: "axiom, canon, commandment, doctrine, dogma, edict, bidding, command, decree, fundamental, guideline, instruction, law, mandate, maxim, order, ordinance, principle, regulation, rule, saying, statute".

If ever the 'dictionary habit' paid off, it certainly did on this occasion. Our million piece 'jigsaw puzzle', God's Word, is made up of interlocking 'concepts' or 'precepts' and all that word means and implies, which together make up one amazing 'picture' of God's Plan for his human children on earth now, and for their eternal future. Enough new information to bring tears of joy into one's eyes?

Verse 11 uses the analogies of 'stammering', someone who stammers is not always easy to understand, and requires patience; and 'another tongue' means that the Bible is written in a different type of 'language' from other books which makes it hard to understand.

The teachings of the Bible are written by God piece by piece, a concept here, and a thought there, the pieces of the 'puzzle' not necessarily or apparently related to each other, but they are interwoven. The way God's Book is structured is very different from the way human being normally use language. But why is that the case? Two verses later, in verse 13, more explanation is provided.

Precept is used 3x previously and 4x here 3 + 4 = 7 the perfect number for a word so important.

13 *But the word of the Lord was unto them precept upon precept, precept upon precept; line upon line, line upon line; here a little, and there a little; (so) that they might go, and fall backward, and be broken, and snared, and taken. Isaiah 28:13*

To fall backwards is usually as a result of the action of evil spirits. The Bible is written so that those who are not yet ready to be given the gift of understanding are 'broken' and 'snared' in their attempts to understand God's Word. This is to protect them from learning things which will ultimately make them even more guilty of not obeying God

Notice, the original Bible, as constructed under the guidance of the Word who became Christ, contained 49 books, a perfect number in God's eyes being 7x7 = 49 books.

Bibles printed in our era have 39 books in the Old Testament, and 27 in the New Testament making a total of 66 books. This is interesting because the number 6 is the number of 'man', so 66 is totally the imprint of human interference of the Book God caused to be assembled. Not only is that the case, but the original order of the books is also jumbled up. How confusing would that be if that was done to any other book?

The chart reproduced here shows how wonderfully amazing is the Word of God. What balance and beauty there is in its original symmetrical perfection! Now we

Chart of the original structure of the Bible

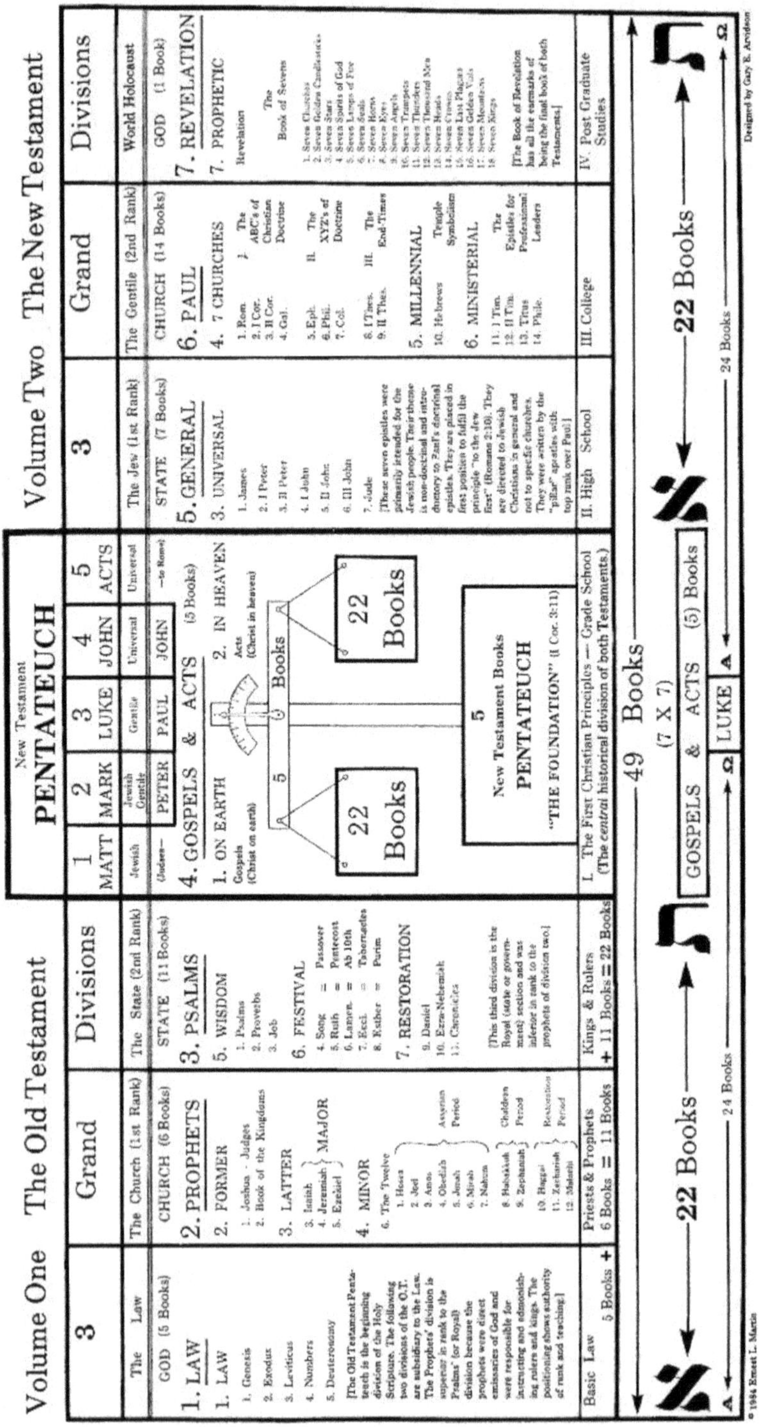

Volume One — The Old Testament

3 Grand Divisions

The Law

GOD (5 Books)

1. LAW

1. LAW
   1. Genesis
   2. Exodus
   3. Leviticus
   4. Numbers
   5. Deuteronomy

[The Old Testament Pentateuch is the beginning division of the Holy Scripture. The following two divisions of the O.T. are subsidiary to the Law. The Prophets' division is superior in rank to the Psalms' (or Royal) division because the prophets were direct emissaries of God and were responsible for instructing and admonishing rulers and kings. The positioning shows authority of rank and teaching.]

Basic Law — 5 Books +

The Church (1st Rank)

CHURCH (6 Books)

2. PROPHETS

2. FORMER
   1. Joshua - Judges
   2. Book of the Kingdoms

3. LATTER
   3. Isaiah, 4. Jeremiah, 5. Ezekiel — MAJOR

4. MINOR
   6. The Twelve
   - 1. Hosea, 2. Joel, 3. Amos, 4. Obadiah, 5. Jonah, 6. Micah, 7. Nahum — Assyrian Period
   - 8. Habakkuk, 9. Zephaniah — Chaldean Period
   - 10. Haggai, 11. Zechariah, 12. Malachi — Restoration Period

Priests & Prophets — 6 Books = 11 Books

The State (2nd Rank)

STATE (11 Books)

3. PSALMS

5. WISDOM
   1. Psalms
   2. Proverbs
   3. Job

6. FESTIVAL
   4. Song = Passover
   5. Ruth = Pentecost
   6. Lamen. = Ab 10th
   7. Eccl. = Tabernacles
   8. Esther = Purim

7. RESTORATION
   9. Daniel
   10. Ezra-Nehemiah
   11. Chronicles

[This third division is the Royal (state or government) section and was inferior in rank to the prophets of division two.]

Kings & Rulers — + 11 Books = 22 Books

New Testament PENTATEUCH

1 MATT	2 MARK	3 LUKE	4 JOHN	5 ACTS
Jewish	Jewish Gentile	Gentile	Universal	Universal
(Judaea—	PETER	PAUL	JOHN	—to Rome)

4. GOSPELS & ACTS (5 Books)

1. ON EARTH — Gospels (Christ on earth)
2. IN HEAVEN — Acts (Christ in heaven)

22 Books — 5 Books — 22 Books

5 New Testament Books PENTATEUCH "THE FOUNDATION" (I Cor. 3:11)

I. The First Christian Principles — Grade School (The *central* historical division of both Testaments.)

Volume Two — The New Testament

3 Grand Divisions

The Jew (1st Rank)

STATE (7 Books)

5. GENERAL

3. UNIVERSAL
   1. James
   2. I Peter
   3. II Peter
   4. I John
   5. II John
   6. III John
   7. Jude

[These seven epistles were primarily intended for the Jewish people. Their theme is non-doctrinal and introductory to Paul's doctrinal epistles. They are placed in first position to fulfil the principle "to the Jew first" (Romans 2:10). They are directed to Jewish Christians in general and not to specific churches. They were written by the "pillar" apostles with top rank over Paul.]

II. High School

The Gentile (2nd Rank)

CHURCH (14 Books)

6. PAUL

4. 7 CHURCHES
   - 1. Rom., 2. I Cor., 3. II Cor., 4. Gal. — I. The ABC's of Christian Doctrine
   - 5. Eph., 6. Phil., 7. Col. — II. The XYZ's of Doctrine
   - 8. I Thes., 9. II Thes. — III. The End-Times

5. MILLENNIAL
   - 10. Hebrews — Temple Symbolism

6. MINISTERIAL
   - 11. I Tim., 12. II Tim., 13. Titus, 14. Phile. — The Epistles for Professional Leaders

III. College

World Holocaust

GOD (1 Book)

7. REVELATION

7. PROPHETIC
   Revelation

The Book of Sevens

1. Seven Churches
2. Seven Golden Candlesticks
3. Seven Stars
4. Seven Spirits of God
5. Seven Lamps of Fire
6. Seven Seals
7. Seven Horns
8. Seven Eyes
9. Seven Angels
10. Seven Trumpets
11. Seven Thunders
12. Seven Thousand Men
13. Seven Heads
14. Seven Crowns
15. Seven Last Plagues
16. Seven Golden Vials
17. Seven Mountains
18. Seven Kings

[The Book of Revelation has all the earmarks of being the final book of both Testaments.]

IV. Post Graduate Studies

←— 49 Books (7 X 7) —→

א ← 22 Books → ת | GOSPELS & ACTS (5) Books | א ← 22 Books → ת

A ← 24 Books → Ω | LUKE | A ← 24 Books → Ω

Designed by Gary E. Arvidson

have solid irrefutable evidence of the inspired structure of the entire Bible and how it was put together and Canonised by God. We also have the evidence of so many instances of fulfilled prophecy which could not have been 'dreamed up' by people, and mathematically, the statistics of improbability of the number of details are staggering.

This should give us absolute confidence that when God says His Word is Truth we can rely upon that fact completely and absolutely.

It is also very interesting to note that the Old Law consisted of 5 books, Genesis, Exodus, Leviticus, Numbers and Deuteronomy.

The New Law also consists of 5 books, Matthew, Mark, Luke, John and Acts which are in the exact centre of the original Bible and would be today if the Bible was printed and presented still in its original order as shown in this chart by Gary Arvidson, which is reproduced here by the kind permission of the Association of Scriptural Knowledge. A.S.K. A copy for personal study may be requested from the author's website. Fill out the "Request Information" form. www.ernestworkman.com.

Scoffers, who deny the authenticity of the Bible are the ignorant fools referred to by Christ through Paul in Romans, who have not the slightest inkling of God's hand in it.

[21] *Because that, when they (scoffers) knew (about) God, they glorified him not as God, neither were thankful; but became vain (empty, futile, pointless) in their*

imaginations, and their foolish heart (Psalm 14:1 The fool hath said in his heart, There is no God.) They are corrupt, they have done abominable works, there is none that does good was darkened.[22] Professing themselves to be wise, they (these very intelligent, highly educated but ignorant men) became fools, Romans 1:21-22

So when we apply ourselves to the ardent study of God's Word, we can have the absolute total confidence that we are actually studying the Book that Our Father, the Almighty God wrote, not some random set of writings that some ignorant humans put together.

[2] Give unto the Lord the glory due unto his name; worship the Lord in the beauty of (His) holiness. Psalm 29:2

PROGRESSIVE REVELATION is the vital key to a proper understanding of the whole Bible

Without this **KEY** it is virtually impossible to unlock the progressive storyline, or see the big picture of what God wants us to get from His Book the Bible.

Most of the billions of people who have a Bible think that everything within its pages is sacrosanct, that every part of it can be used to support their ideas and teachings, and that everything in it applies to us today, and to them in particular. This simply is not the case. Very far from it.

Ignorance of the nature of God's 'Progressive Revelation' of essential information is part of the reason why there are so many thousands of different groups of people, denominations, 'churches' each with their own interpretation of what the Bible means. Each group has different ideas of what God requires of us in this era, each has their own doctrines or set of teachings, and even their own ideas of what they insist is the way Christians should conduct themselves.

Yes, every word of the Bible is true, but if anyone picks it up and uses it like a dictionary, or a cookbook or a DIY manual, and takes information at random and applies it in some way that they feel is right and that suits their agenda, they are going to be part of the total confusion that exists in all the branches of 'Churchianity' that exist today.

Yes, and everything certainly does have some relevance and teaching for us today, but not every detail of the 'law' applies to us in this era. The way God deals with His children, and what He expects of them, has been progressive and has changed dramatically over thousands of years. It takes detailed study to learn to appreciate and apply this information. People do not usually take the necessary time or make the required effort. True Christianity is not for the hobbyist, or the casual 'believer', God expects us to work at it.

The Bible, from Genesis to Revelation, contains information that begins with a simple story with the most basic of Laws. However, the more we study the seemingly simple story of the 'beginning' in Genesis chapters 1 and 2, the more profound we realise it is, and how much more information there is 'hidden in plain sight' within its simplicity. In fact those two chapters contain much more detailed information of such critical importance that is lost in the English translations from the Hebrew that they certainly merit more than a casual reading.

Progressive Revelation applies in two ways, Biblically and Personally

Biblically. Failure to understand the principle of 'Progressive Revelation' leads to massive confusion in the minds of those who study the Bible. Ignorance of this vital principle leads many people to think that everything in the Bible is to be heeded and obeyed by all people at all times. This is definitely not the case. Also some English translations often obscure rather than clarify the meaning of the original language.

One verse in the Bible that appears to be universally misunderstood by people in Churchianity, and applies to everything Christ (Yah'Shua) the Word says and does. It states that God does not change. This understanding is incorrect. It is important to know this in connection with 'Progressive Revelation'. It is also typical of how many misunderstandings can occur due to familiarity with what we think, or have been told the Bible is saying, when it is not.

[8] Christ (Yah'Shua Kristos) the same yesterday, and today and for ever. Hebrews 13:8

This verse in the King James Version of the Bible seems to be very clear in stating that Christ (the Word - Yah'Shua Kristos) does not change and is always the same, but in fact this verse does not mean that at all. King James was not a 'saint' by any means. He was a power hungry king who wanted to maintain absolute control of his 'church', the renegade Church of England which had seceded from the Catholic or universal church run by the Pope, because King Henry the VIII wanted to marry against the wishes of the Pope, and who later went on to murder more wives.

Hebrews 13:8 is misunderstood for two reasons. Firstly, the Greek word translated 'same' actually means 'self' or 'himself'. So when it says 'Christ the same' it actually means 'Christ (Kristos) is Himself...' and secondly: 'today and forever', actually means 'always will be 'Himself', the Son of God, the Word.

Another verse that is used to insist that God does not change is Malachi 3:6

For I am the Lord, I change not, Malachi 3:6

When the words in this one verse are taken out of context, it denies all the evidence in the entire Bible from Genesis to Revelation that God does indeed change. God does change His mind, He does repent or change His decisions about certain actions, He changes His Laws as often as He thinks fit, and of course He is absolutely entitled to do so.

The revelation of the Plan of God, His Laws, His teachings, and the responses He requires of His human children are **progressive** over centuries of time.

Revelation of God's requirements of His children started in Genesis 1, when God gave Laws to Adam and Eve. Then He gave different laws to Noah at the time of the flood. At the time of the Exodus, God gave the Israelites a complete expanded set of intricate laws to live by as they travelled for forty years in the Sinai desert, and then a very different set of regulations when they are settled in towns and cities in the Promised Land. Revelation continues to develop progressively throughout the Old Testament, when at times, some laws are quite dramatically changed.

A dramatic example that God does change His Laws

Deuteronomy was written in 1451 B.C., and in chapter five God, through Moses, is reminding Israel of all the commandments they were given by God through him initially in Sinai in 1491, forty years earlier, with some modifications. Moses is telling the children of the Israelites who died in the desert, that when they enter the Promised Land they must be sure to keep this new version of the commandments.

[5] Thou shalt not bow down thyself to them, nor serve them: for I the Lord thy God am a jealous God, visiting the iniquity of the fathers upon the children unto the third and fourth generation of them that hate me; Exodus 20:5

This important commandment was repeated later in Exodus 34:

[7] Keeping mercy for thousands, forgiving iniquity and transgression and sin, and that will by no means clear the guilty; visiting the iniquity of the fathers upon the children, and upon the children's children, unto the third and to the fourth generation. Exodus 34:7

There is no doubt that God wanted successive generation to honour Him and keep His Laws. Also it is likely that had God hoped that fathers who knew that the result of their transgressions would drastically affect their children, and their children to the third and fourth generation, they would consider this and be more likely to be respectful of God's Laws and keep them. Sadly this does not seem to be the case.

Then, while the Children of Israel were captives in Egypt, God wrote in Deuteronomy a change in this law.

[16] Parents are not to be put to death for their children, nor children put to death for their parents; each will die for their own sin. Deuteronomy 24:16 NIV

After hundreds of years had elapsed from 1451 A.D., nearly a thousand years later, in B.C.593 God inspired Ezekiel by the Word to update the law in respect of the father's sin's and repeats the dramatic change that the effect will not be passed on.

The result of the father's sins going forward are no longer to be inherited or be suffered by later generations.

[18] As for his father, because he cruelly oppressed, spoiled his brother by violence, and did that which is not good among his people, lo, even he shall die in his iniquity. [19] Yet say you, Why? Does not the son bear the iniquity of the father? When the son has done that which is lawful and right, and has kept all my statutes, and has done them, he shall surely live. [20] The soul that sins, it shall die. The son shall not bear the iniquity of the father, neither shall the father bear the iniquity of the son:

the righteousness of the righteous shall be upon him, and the wickedness of the wicked shall be upon him. Ezekiel 18:18-20

At this time, God also changes His Law in respect of the 'wicked', they shall pay the penalty for their own sin, and God introduces the life-saving possibility of a repentant attitude.

[21] But if the wicked will turn from (and repent of) all his sins that he has committed, and keep all my statutes, and do that which is lawful and right, he shall surely live, he shall not die. [22] All his transgressions that he has committed, they shall not be mentioned unto him: in his righteousness that he has done he shall live. Ezekiel 18:21-22

So clearly, the interpretation in 'Churchianity' of Malachi 3:6, "For I am the Lord, I change not; [6] therefore ye sons of Jacob are not consumed.

God does not change His character, and yes, He DOES CHANGE His conditions and rules for His children whenever He chooses.

God the Father continued introducing vast changes to His Laws when His Son, the Word, relinquished His Glory and Power with the Father to become our Lord and Saviour Christ, Yah'Shua the Messiah, the man.

When Christ came, He kept perfectly and thus 'fulfilled' and completed the Old Law, and when He died, He abolished it, as its function was no longer needed and it passed into history. Christ during His ministry, began to reveal some aspects of the New 'upgraded'

Mental/Spiritual Law which made even thinking badly of someone, being angry with them, or imagining illicit sex, and so on, were all sin.

After His death and resurrection in 33 A.D., Christ sent the Holy Spirit on the Day of Pentecost fifty days after He ascended to the Father, this was the most momentous change ever for all God's human children.

The Father gave Christ (Yah'Shua) further inspired revelations and instructions and commissions to His disciples. Then yet more to Paul in Acts and his epistles, and then later in 63 A.D. when the Father through Christ (Yah'Shua) revealed the secret of the Mystery of the Gentiles and Universal Salvation.

'Progressive revelation' is a continuous thread which runs through the whole Bible. It finishes in Revelation 22 with the instruction which forbids anyone to add to the Bible in any way or detract from it.

If a person does not understand and appreciate that God's Plan for His children is progressively revealed throughout His Word, that person will never truly come to a mature knowledge of the Truth, or frankly how to live as a true Christian in this present era.

This knowledge of the nature of 'Progressive Revelation' is very rarely understood, and then only by a very few people. Churchianity is virtually completely unaware of this principle which God reveals to the 'few' that He is calling at this time.

Progressive revelation also applies on a Personal level. God has a specific personal plan for each one of His human children. God reveals His plan for that person progressively throughout their life. God has a very carefully managed educational program for each individual that leads them, at the appropriate time in their lives, progressively to a greater and expanded knowledge, understanding, and wisdom, and an ever closer relationship with God and His Son.

In the time since Adam, millions and now billions have been born and died who have not yet even begun their Spiritual journey. Most of those alive today will have to wait until they are resurrected out of their graves to begin their true Spiritual journey. Timing for each human being's Spiritual development and relationship with God is in His hands.

The next chapter expands on the phrase "give us this day our daily bread" in the model prayer that Christ gave us.

CHAPTER 7

GIVE US THIS DAY OUR 'DAILY BREAD'

How to get fresh Spiritual nourishment every day.

Daily Bread

Everyone needs physical 'bread' or food every day or we get hungry. Huge numbers of the world's population are hungry, many even starving.

Not everyone realises that we also need 'spiritual bread' daily as well. Billions are spiritually starving due to the lack of that type of 'bread'.

Christ's words in the Bible are that 'Spiritual Bread'. Christ says that He is the 'Bread of Life'. And that we need to eat of Him figuratively or starve spiritually.

So how do we eat of that spiritual bread? By making sure that we study God's Word daily.

Global starvation of the True 'Daily Bread' of Life

Billions around the world do not get enough food to eat. Other billions are obsessed with food, eat too much and fall prey to the pandemic epidemic of obesity. Overeating is a quick way to fall prey to many diseases and an earlier death.

Decades ago, one would never see anyone walking along the road eating, it was just 'not done' by respectable people. Oh yes, perhaps an ice cream on the promenade when on holiday, but certainly not 'takeaways' or huge 'whopper' type burgers which did not exist! The physical act of eating nourishes the body, and mind, but not necessarily the spirit. There are literally hundreds of cooking shows on television, in fact it is difficult to turn the TV on at any time without seeing more than one on the guide. Satan has been hard at work to ruin the health of God's children by putting so much emphasis on physical foods, especially those that are not conducive to a healthy way of life.

Our daily Spiritual 'Bread' is gained from the study of His Word

It is by daily 'eating the bread' by reading the Scriptures that we accumulate our 'treasures' in Heaven. As we do so, that work produces permanent changes in our minds and hearts that will exist as a basis for more learning for eternity.

28 They said therefore to him, "What must we do, that
we may work the works of God" 29 Yah'Shua the Messiah
answered them, "This is the work of God, that you believe
in him whom he has sent." 30 They said therefore to him,
"What then do you do for a sign, that we may see and
believe you? What work do you do? 31 Our fathers ate the
manna in the wilderness. As it is written, 'He gave them
bread out of heaven to eat.'" 32 Yah'Shua the Messiah
therefore said to them, "Most certainly, I tell you, it wasn't
Moses who gave you the bread out of heaven, but my

Father gives you the true bread out of heaven. [33] For the bread of God is that which comes down out of heaven, and gives life to the world." [34] They said therefore to him, "Lord, always give us this bread." John 6:28-34

Christ then tells His disciples, and the crowd that were listening, how they can have free access to this 'bread'.

[35] Yah'Shua the Messiah said to them, "I am .the bread of life. Whoever comes to me will not be hungry, and whoever believes in me will never be thirsty. [36] But I told you that you have seen me, and yet you don't believe. [37] All those whom the Father gives me will come to me. He who comes to me I will in no way throw out. [38] For I have come down from heaven, not to do my own will, but the will of him who sent me. [39] This is the will of my Father who sent me, that of all he has given to me I should lose nobody, but should raise him up at the last day. [40] This is the will of the one who sent me that everyone who sees the Son, and believes in him, should have eternal life; and I will raise him up at the last day." John 6:35-40

There were disbelieving Jews in the crowd who objected strongly to Christ's words. Here is a warning to us all that if we talk about the things of God in His Word, we may well attract trouble to ourselves we do not want. Our job is to be a light, and lights are silent, they just give out light. By living and doing the Christian 'works' we are to be silent 'lights' exemplifying the 'Way' to others. However, we are also to be ready to answer (briefly without 'preaching') anyone who may ask us about our beliefs.

*[15] But sanctify the Lord God in your hearts: and **be ready always to give an answer to every man that asks you a reason of the hope that is in you with meekness and fear** 1 Peter 3:15*

But some religious Jews were after His blood.

[41] The Jews then murmured at him, because he said, I am the bread which came down from heaven. [42] And they said, Is not this Yah'Shua the Messiah, the son of Joseph, whose father and mother we know? How is it then that he says, I came down from heaven? [43] Yah'Shua the Messiah therefore answered and said unto them, Murmur not among yourselves. John 6:41-43

This passage offers a most important lesson for anyone who feels they should or would like to 'spread the word' and proselytise, and preach the gospel to others to try to get them saved. But does the Word not say, "Preach the Gospel and heal the sick"? Yes, but to whom were those instructions directed? The disciples then, not necessarily to anyone today.

Only the Father does the 'calling', and it seems that at this time, 'few' there be indeed that He does call. Our job as believers, as Christians, is to be a silent light to the world. The 'light' others see in us is when we are actually living the life God wants us to, loving Him and loving our fellow humans with all our might.

Truly most of the time, preaching to or at others, has the opposite effect to that which we might think. The average person's heart and mind are not favourably disposed towards God, in fact have a degree of hostility to him.

[7] Because the carnal (human) mind is enmity (an enemy at war) against God: for it is not subject to the law of God, neither indeed can be. Romans 8:7

Surely not? Most people might think that is an outrageous thing to say, and it happens to be the truth. Look at the behaviour of the vast majority of the seven, nearly eight billion on earth today. Is it not very clear that the love of God is very far from their minds and hearts? Believe what Christ says to us through His Word

[44] No man can come to me, except the Father which hath sent me draw him: and I will raise him up at the last day. John 6:44

All the preaching and evangelising by sincere preachers notwithstanding, only those who God draws to Him will be called. Men cannot get anyone 'called'.

[45] It is written in the prophets, 'They will all be taught by God.' (Isaiah 54:13) Therefore everyone who hears from the Father and has learned, comes to me. John 6:45

Being 'called' is only when someone 'hears from the Father' and God's Spirit moves in a person's mind, and opens it to His Word, and starts the teaching process.

[46] Not that anyone has seen the Father, except he who is from God. He has seen the Father. [47] Most certainly, I tell you, he who believes in me has (the prospect of) eternal life. [48] I am the bread of life. [49] Your fathers ate the manna in the wilderness and they died. [50] This is the bread which comes down out of heaven that anyone may eat of it and not die (permanently). [51] I am the living bread which came down out of heaven. If anyone eats of

this bread, he will live forever. Yes, the bread which I will give for the life of the world is (the sacrifice of) my flesh." John 6:46-51

Christ knew full well that He was dealing with physical carnal minds who were not capable of understanding that Christ was speaking metaphorically and figuratively, not literally.

[53] Yah'Shua the Messiah therefore said to them, "Most certainly I tell you, unless you (figuratively) eat the flesh of the Son of Man and (figuratively) drink his blood, you don't have life in yourselves. John 6:53

It is important to note that the essence, the spirit of life, is in the blood. If a person loses too much of their lifeblood, they die, we know that for a fact, it happens to some people every day. (For the life of the flesh is in the blood Leviticus 17:11)

[54] He who (figuratively) eats my flesh and (figuratively) drinks my blood has eternal life, and I will raise him up at the last day. [55] For my flesh is (spiritual) food indeed, and my blood is (spiritual) drink indeed. [56] He who (figuratively) eats my flesh and (figuratively) drinks my blood lives in me, and I in him. [57] As the living Father sent me, and I live because of the Father; so he who feeds on me, he will also live because of me. [58] This is the bread which came down out of heaven not as our fathers ate the manna, and died. He who eats this bread will live forever. John 6:54-58

***Key Study Aid: There is a Spiritual component in everything Physical**

Here Christ explains a very important principle which can open up a completely new way of thinking about the life we have. There is a Spiritual component in everything Physical because everything Physical is made of and is part of God's Secret Spiritual powers. God is All in All. Bible study is physical with Spiritual rewards.

[61] But Yah'Shua the Messiah knowing in himself that his disciples murmured at this, said to them, "Does this cause you to stumble? [62] Then what if you would see the Son of Man ascending to (Heaven) where he was before? [63] It is the spirit who gives life. The flesh profits nothing. The words that I speak to you are spirit, and are life. John 6:61-63

It is important to bear in mind that few people are open to true spirituality, and most are completely unaware of the Spirit of God, and His Spiritual Laws. An important principle in this regard, is only to give information to those who specifically ask, and even then to be minimal in the answer, and avoid getting into a 'preachy' mode. It will only put people off if they are 'preached at', and it may even cause friction. We are advised not to offer our valuable pearls of truth before swine, or 'pigs' who cannot appreciate them.

[6] Give not that which is holy unto the dogs (false ministers or irreligious people), neither cast ye your pearls before swine (those who do not appreciate God's Word), lest they trample them under their feet, and turn again and rend you. Matthew 7:6

What about our spiritual 'Daily Bread'

Our Spiritual 'Daily Bread' does not appear miraculously as did the 'manna' appear every morning to feed the Children of Israel in the Sinai desert. Feeding on God's Word is 'work'. The physical act of figuratively eating 'the bread that comes down from heaven' nourishes the mind, the spirit, yes, and it also nourishes the health of the physical body, and leads to spiritual rewards for eternity.

13 And no man has ascended up to heaven, but he that came down from heaven, even the Son of man which is in heaven. John 3:13

Christ, Yah-Shua, through the beloved John clearly says: ***No man has ascended up to heaven,*** this verse among many others, confirms that human beings do not go to heaven when they die.

33 For the bread of God is he (the Word, Christ, Yah'Shua the Messiah) which came down from heaven, and gives life unto the world. John 6:33

Figuratively speaking, Christ the Word, our Lord, Master, Elder Brother and Saviour is the 'Bread of God'.

Many who use the 'Lord's Prayer' as a model often repeat:

11Give us this day our daily bread. Matthew 6:11

What does this verse, that many repeat every day in their prayers, mean in terms of our everyday Christian life? This next section will offer some in-depth thoughts, concepts and exciting ideas about what it can mean for each of us.

[44] But he (Christ) answered (the devil) and said, It is written (in Deuteronomy 8:3), Man shall not live by bread alone, but by every word that proceeds out of the mouth of God. Matthew 4:44

The fifth book in the Bible is Deuteronomy, it is mainly a restatement of the Laws of God and a historical record from which we can learn a lot more about God.

Deuteronomy Chapter 8 is about the refusal of the Children of Israel to go into Canaan the Promised Land, and the result of their rebellion was that they all died in the Sinai Desert. Here are some salient but edited quotes for brevity, but of course the whole chapter and the entire book make fascinating reading

When the children of Israel had escaped from Egypt they complained to Moses (and God) that they had no food. So God provided quails so they could eat meat in the evening and in the morning they had 'manna'. This word 'manna' actually means 'what is it'? They had never seen anything like it before.

[1] You shall observe to do all the commandments which I command you today, that you may live, and multiply, and go in and possess the land which Yahweh swore to your fathers. [2] You shall remember all the way which Yahweh your God has led you these forty years in the wilderness, that he might humble you, to test you, to know what was in your heart, whether you would keep his commandments or not. [3] He humbled you, allowed you to be hungry, and fed you with manna, which you didn't know, neither did your fathers know, that ***he might teach***

you that man does not live by bread only, but man lives by every word that proceeds out of Yahweh's, God's mouth. *Deuteronomy 8:1-3*

The purpose of the 'manna' was to feed the Israelites but also to emphasise the principle of living by the instructions of the Word of God, but they did not listen.

They were also totally incapable of understanding the Spiritual aspect of Law.

The Children of Israel had heard that the people of the new land were ferocious warriors and they allowed themselves to be afraid. God said through Moses, "You do not have to be at all concerned about them, I will fight for you". They did not listen.

The Children of Israel rebelled, and refused to obey or trust God and enter the Promised Land as they were told by God to do.

So God told Moses to send men to spy out the land, and they returned with very positive reports confirming that Canaan was a good land with wonderful crops and foods to delight them, but the Children of Israel were still afraid although God had promised to protect them.

[26] Notwithstanding you would not go up, but rebelled against the commandment of the Lord your God: Deuteronomy 1:26

God through Moses told them to gather so much manna according to the size of their families, no more and no less. They did not listen. Some who gathered more saw that they only had their 'ration', and those who gathered less still had their full 'ration', another miracle.

God through Moses had told them not to keep any overnight, and of course they did not listen, but some of them left of it until the morning, and it bred worms, and stank

God also used 'manna' to teach the children of Israel to observe the Sabbath Day. We know now that to observe the physical Sabbath is actually impossible, and is no longer a requirement for Spiritual Christians. Even any attempt by anyone to do so in the twenty-first century actually denies the sacrifice of Christ.

So on the sixth day they gathered twice as much manna, and it would keep well overnight so they could rest on the Sabbath. Some defied God and still went out on the Sabbath, and of course there was none.

Miracle after miracle, yet the Israelites just did not get it. They were physical people, completely unaware of the spiritual implications of what they were doing, or their need to obey God. The Israelites still continued throughout history to rebel against Moses and therefore against God. This is a big lesson for us.

The Bible is the 'Maker's Instruction Book'

God wrote His unique Special 'Instruction Book' by dictating what He wanted to include in the Book to many of His servants the Prophets and the Apostles and Disciples of Christ to write down. It took a period of over two thousand five hundred years to complete the 49 books. No human or group of humans could have done this.

God wrote this Book for His children so they could learn about their Father, and how to live a successful and fulfilled life. It contains all the exclusive information human beings need to be able to please their Father, and cannot fathom or work out for themselves. There is no other book on earth like it.

Clear EVIDENCE PROVES that the Bible really is the Word of God

The Bible contains history, prophecies, moral law and spiritual information that could not possibly have been written by, or assembled by carnal human beings.

It was written by God through men, and it is perfect in every detail. It is an absolutely accurate legal document full of legal testimony and proofs of its authenticity.

There are no contradictions, and no errors. God does not 'do' errors.

Since you are reading this, you probably have no problem believing that the Bible is God's Word, but are you sure? How sure are you? What is your 'belief' based on? If you are to base your present and your Eternal life on this book, you will want and need to be completely sure that it is truly God's Word.

Many 'ordinary' people, some 'scientists', and even a few 'theologians' scoff at the Bible, and say it is full of errors and contradictions. That can be unsettling to those who want to believe, and need to have complete confidence that it is really God's Word. 'Confidence' means to have full trust or reliance and that it is faithful. We can trust God that He is most certainly Faithful and True.

[17] *Sanctify them (the called) through thy truth: thy word is truth. John 17:17*

Many people try to read the Bible, but give up because it is not an 'easy read'. It is not meant to be easy for everyone to read. God's help is required.

Here are some vital 'keys' to help you understand God's Word in a more mature and much deeper way than is possible by just reading it.

Have you been deceived before? Are you deceived now?

How can you know? When Christ was answering the question that the disciples had posed in Matthew 24:3 *"tell us what shall be the sign of your coming, and the end of the age?"* Christ gave a **very** strong warning.

Christ answered and the **first** thing He did was to warn them: [4]*"Take heed that no man* **deceive** *you."* Matthew 24:4

If you have discovered that you have been deceived before, how do you know that you are not being deceived now? How can you tell? The awful answer is, YOU CAN'T, at least, not without God's help. Why can that be? Because part of God's plan for this period of human existence is to allow Satan to deceive the whole world, with the exception of a very 'few' whose minds He protects. Are you one of them?

[9] *And the great dragon was cast out, that old serpent, called the Devil, and Satan, which deceives the whole world: Revelation 12:9*

Absolute truth: Anyone who is deceived does not know they are deceived!

Everyone that does come to realise that they were once deceived has a lot to 'unlearn', and has a very great deal more to learn about God's Truth.

So even if you 'think' you are not deceived, you may be to some extent even now, and not know it. Pray that you are not, and that God will open your mind to more of His Truth. Ask and you shall receive. God's Spirit will flood into your mind, and you will see where you have been deceived, and be enlightened.

We may think that we know what we know. But do we? Might it be an idea to question those things we have long thought to be true, and look into ideas we cherish, a lot more closely? Chances are, the person who is willing to do this may be surprised, or even get something of a shock. Another true maxim:

Self-deceit is an inherent human trait

When we deceive ourselves, we are not aware of that either. When study is done prayerfully, we get help to see where we have allowed ourselves to be deceived, and given the strength to accept new truth.

What we do not know, we do not know, or are aware that we do not know

We are not aware of 'not knowing' the things we know nothing about. This can also be thought provoking, and might lead us to examine more carefully what we currently hold to be true.

BEWARE: The deadly deceptive 'Counterfeit' principle. What is the definition of a counterfeit? ***"To make a copy of, imitate without authority or right, especially with a view to deceive or defraud."***

How deceptive are 'counterfeits'? There are many kinds of 'counterfeit' in this present world. It is virtually impossible for the average person, or even an expert, to be able to detect a 'counterfeit' from the genuine article. In the art world and in the financial world of currency, 'counterfeiters' have become so clever, that they can even fool the most knowledgeable experts.

Virtually all the religions of this world contain 'counterfeit' teachings that look and sound authentic, but when compared very carefully with God's Word, they are not, so be warned.

All human religions and ideas about God incorporate deceptions

How can you be sure that you have not been, and are not deceived now to some degree about matters in God's Word? You have to ask for God's protection, and also put a lot of time and energy into checking carefully what you may have accepted without investigation, simply because most people believe it or you were told by some religious person that it was so.

People say jokingly, “How do you know when a politician is lying or being deceitful”? Answer: “When his lips move and you hear words”. The same is sadly true of many ministers, priests, and religious people among all the thousands of denominations of ‘Churchianity’ that exist on this earth. Does that mean that they are not sincere? Not at all. They may be the most sincere, dedicated, earnest, and apparently God-fearing people you meet. However...

Christ also warned us about how religious people may appear to be ‘good’.

[15] Beware of false prophets (priests and ministers of all types), which come to you in sheep's clothing, but inwardly they are ravening wolves. [16] You shall know them by their fruits. Do men gather grapes of thorns, or figs of thistles? Matthew 7:15-16

Hardly a day goes by without some religious figure or another being accused of corrupt, morally debased activities among those to whom they minister. “You shall know them by their fruits.” It is sometimes so hard to believe it of them, but more evidence comes to light almost every day.

[7] Be not deceived; God is not mocked: for whatsoever a man sows, that shall he also (will eventually) reap. [8] For he that sows to his flesh shall of the flesh reap corruption; but he that sows to the Spirit shall of the Spirit reap life everlasting. Galatians 6:7-8

False ministers, preachers, priests, rabbis can even appear 'angelic'.

[13] For such are false apostles, deceitful workers, trans- forming themselves into the apostles of Christ. [14] And no marvel; for Satan himself is transformed into an angel of light. [15] Therefore it is no great thing if his ministers also be transformed as the ministers of righteousness; whose end shall be according to their works. 2 Corinthians 11:13-15

Almost all these types of people 'dress up' in some garb to impress and control others. Almost everything that Satan does 'looks good' and can be superficially attractive.

[1] But there were false prophets also among the people, even as there shall be false teachers among you, who cunningly shall bring in damnable heresies (like keeping the Old Law, tithing etc.,), even denying the Lord that bought them, and bring upon themselves swift destruction. 2 Peter 2:1

Many damnable heresies like insisting on obedience to the Old Law God gave to Moses which was then, and still is impossible, and is even a sin to try, as it denies the sacrifice of Christ. Some also exercise the calculated 'merchandising' of followers by using the now illegal principle of tithing for their own profit, and profligate lifestyles. Tithing ended with the destruction of the Temple and the cessation of the Levitical priesthood.

WHY do we need to study God's Holy Bible?

Because it is the 'Maker's Instruction Book' for human being's. It contains the information that is nowhere else available that everyone needs to operate and run their lives according to God's Will for each of us. In everyday matters, if we do not operate any product in accordance with the maker's instructions we risk many things. Our ignorance of the correct operation may lead to damaging the product irreparably, and we may put ourselves at risk of physical injury, even death. That is true of life too.

The main point of, and the reason for the detailed study of the Scriptures is not to learn a lot of complex doctrinal matters, or to be able to 'parrot' verses, but to extract from its pages the practical 'tools' we need to live by each moment of every day of our lives in a way that will benefit us and please our Creator.

Theologians and ministers of the many religions that base their ideas on the Bible, all too often fall into the trap of minutely examining each 'jot and tittle', each minute technical part of doctrinal teaching, while missing the simple essential points which God wants us appreciate that show us how to live in every aspect of our lives.

[20] For I fear, lest, when I come, I shall not find you such as I would, and that I shall be found unto you such as you would not: that there be debates, envyings, wraths, strifes, backbitings, whisperings, swellings (of ego), tumults: 2 Corinthians 12:20

The Word of God should never be 'debated' because it gives rise to 'strife' and arguments between people. On the contrary, each person should apply themselves to a personal understanding of the Scriptures with the help of our Father, the Author of the Book.

[3] If any man teach otherwise, and consent not to wholesome words, even the words of our Lord, Christ, Yah'Shua the Messiah, and to the doctrine (teaching) which is according to godliness; [4] He is proud, knowing nothing, but doting about questions and strifes of words, whereof comes envy, strife, railings, evil surmisings, [5] Perverse disputings of men of corrupt minds, and destitute of the truth, supposing that gain is godliness: from such withdraw yourself. 1 Timothy 6:3-5

The despicable actions of corrupt minds in the world's denominations are in the news daily.

[23] But foolish and unlearned questions avoid, knowing that they do engender strifes. 2 Timothy 2:23

The top ministers of different religions, and many 'theologians' spend a lot of their time 'doting about questions', 'nit-picking' and debating technical matters in the Scriptures, when they would be better occupied studying the words of Christ whose teachings are Godly.

[7] Ever learning, and never able to come to the knowledge of the truth. 2 Timothy 3:7

Because the minds of their ministers are blinded.

[4] Neither give heed to fables and endless genealogies, which minister questions, rather than godly edifying which is in faith: so do. 1 Timothy 1:4

The evil origin of the word 'Church' almost nobody knows

The denominations of 'Christianity' are all tainted with fables and riddled with paganism and idolatry. The word 'church' should never have been allowed to be translated in the Bible as the English word was derived from the Greek 'ekklesia' which means 'group' or 'assembly'. 'Ekklesia' does NOT mean a building, nor a system of control which most religious organisations have become.

The origin of the word 'church' is actually disturbing, unpleasant and even horrific. It is an adaptation of the name of an ancient Greek 'goddess', **CIRCE,** pronounced 'Kirky'. Welsh and Scottish places of worship are often called 'Kirks' to this day. So what is wrong with that? All words have meaning, and it is important to know the derivation of any word that is used in connection with the worship of God.

'Circe' was a sexually promiscuous witch, who claimed to use hallucinating drugs and other devices to turn humans into animals. Certainly 'Circe' is not a figure or a word that should be associated with Christian worship.

There are architectural features of almost all churches that would horrify those who attended them if they knew what they picture and mean. Here is a story that lists of some of the wrong practices and disgusting aspects that may be seen in churches all over the world. Please do not dismiss this next section as being an extreme view. A short time doing some research about the subject on the Internet will make it clear that this information is actually well known by those who are willing to look at the subject objectively.

A 'story' which could well be true, that is a warning to 'churchgoers'

In the last book of the Bible, Revelation, Christ tell us that Satan has deceived the whole world.

The great dragon was thrown down, the old serpent, he who is called the devil and **Satan,** the deceiver of the whole world. Revelation 12:9

This means the entire world! Satan's master stroke of deception is to get almost all of humanity to think that he does not exist. But he most certainly does. Here is a present day scenario which could be happening as you read this book. It is an example built on a past event mentioned in the book of Job in the Old Testament which is the oldest book in the Bible, written long before Genesis.

When God in this era calls a council in heaven (which He does) of the 'Sons of God', angels, and including Satan the Devil, they all have a dialogue with one another. This story uses a similar scenario to when Satan and some of the 'Sons of God' came to God's heavenly council in the time of Job

[6] Now on the day when God's sons came to present themselves before Yahweh, Satan also came among them. [7] Yahweh said to Satan, "Where have you come from?" Then Satan answered Yahweh, and said, "From going back and forth in the earth, and from walking up and down in it." [8] Yahweh said to Satan, "Have you

considered my servant, Job? For there is no one like him in the earth, a blameless and an upright man, one who fears God, and turns away from evil." Job 1:6-8 (also Job 2:1-6).

God no doubt still asks Satan on such occasions where he has been recently. Satan would probably tell God he had been going throughout the earth as he did in Job's time. God would ask Satan if he noticed the humans on earth who were His human sons and daughters who were 'churchgoers'.

Here is what Satan might say in his answer God in our era:

"Yes, I have been witnessing the people you call your so-called sons and daughters and they are so ignorant and stupid that I have got them into worshipping You in the most disgusting ways imaginable. I have them all meeting in "churches" which are named after the Great Whore of Revelation.

I have them assembling in their 'churches' where in, on and around their churches they can observe sexual representations of male and female organs in every part of their structure including steeples, obelisks which are pillars, and monuments all of which are images of upright and erect penises used in pagan worship for thousands of years. Even the entrances of many of their impressive cathedrals and abbeys symbolise the female vulva. They will see but not realise my influence in the gargoyles with demonic features.

And when they go in their churches, I have them seeing pictures and images in prominent positions of the pagan god Zeus with his long-hair, and I get them to call this image of Zeus by the name of "Jesus" despite the fact that you say in your Word that it is a shame for a man to have long hair, and that using images of any kind is forbidden.

I have them teaching the doctrine of the 'Immortality of the Soul' spawned thousands of years ago in Egypt which you have stated in your Bible is completely false, because you make plain that when humans are dead, they are completely dead and have no consciousness.

I have them worshipping You with their false doctrine of the 'Trinity'.

I have them congregating on the pagan days of the ancient world which they now call Easter and Christmas (and other heathen days and customs they now call "Christian festivals") when you have said clearly not to learn the way of the heathen. ("So said the Lord, Learn not the way of the heathen, and be not dismayed at the signs of heaven; for the heathen are dismayed (or afraid) of them". Jeremiah 10:2)

I have given them religious ceremonies that they call 'Christian worship' which originated with the pagans that you have always condemned and told them not to use.

I have them also reading from their Bibles which are printed in an order of the biblical books completely different from your original manuscript design which came from the Apostles, and this false design brings them into utter confusion and prevents them from understanding true biblical story and teachings.

They think they are worshipping You, God, but in reality they are worshipping me. That is what I, Satan, have got your so-called sons and daughters doing who are supposed to be going to become Spirit members of your divine Family. I have done all this deceit."

Is that all a far-fetched ridiculous story? Any honest, sincere person would at least want to look .into what is said above to be facts about their current places of worship, and the teachings of 'Christianity' and verify them for themselves. That is the challenge being presented here. Please do not react emotionally and dismiss what you have just read.

Check it out. There is nothing above that is not easily accessible to anyone willing to spend an hour or two on the Internet doing the research.

The Bible is not intended to be easily understood by everyone

So as hard as it is to believe, accept or understand, God did not write the Bible for the average person or the masses to understand. Only those who God selects at any given time will be able fully to understand its message, let alone appreciate the deeper spiritual meanings of the Scriptures.

Why did Christ talk to the crowds in parables?

When His disciples asked Him about the reason He spoke in parables, Christ told them plainly, the bottom line is that it was not their time to understand. He did not want them to be healed of their sin at that time. Parables are not simple stories used to illustrate, they actually mask the deeper spiritual meaning. Those who now have the Holy Spirit will be able to discern that.

The disciples did not have the Holy Spirit, and they always had a problem with what Christ was teaching, they just could not understand Him. This is clear through the whole New Testament. It was not their time, they would have had to wait until after the death, resurrection and ascension of Christ, Yah-Shua for the day of Pentecost and the coming of the Comforter for them to begin to have a clear understanding of what Christ taught.

10 The disciples came, and said to him, "Why do you
speak to them in parables?" 11 He answered them, "To
you it is given to know (some of) the mysteries of the
Kingdom of Heaven, but it is not given to them. 12 For
whoever has (the gift of understanding), to him will be given, and he will have abundance; but whoever doesn't have (the gift of understanding), from him will be taken
away even that which he (thinks he) has. 13 Therefore I
speak to them in parables, because seeing they don't see, and hearing, they don't hear, neither do they
understand. 14 In them the prophecy of Isaiah (written 400 years earlier) is fulfilled, which says, 'By hearing you will hear, and will in no way understand; Seeing you will see, and will in no way perceive (or understand);
15 for this people's heart has grown callous, their ears are dull of hearing, and ***they have closed their eyes;*** *or else otherwise they might perceive with their eyes,*

hear with their ears, understand with their heart, and would turn again, and I would heal them. (Isaiah 6:9-10) [16] *"But blessed are your eyes, for they see; and your ears, for they hear.* [17] *For most certainly I tell you that many prophets and righteous men desired to see the things which you see, and didn't see them; and to hear the things which you hear, and didn't hear them. Matthew 13:10-17*

Christ's disciples still did not 'get it', they had to ask Him what it meant in verse 36:

[36] *Then Yah'Shua the Messiah sent the multitude away, and went into the house: and his disciples came unto him, saying, Declare unto us the parable of the tares of the field* [37] *He answered and said unto them, He that sows the good seed is the Son of man;... Matthew 13:36-37*

The 'average' person does not want 'to know about God', let alone 'be converted', or to do anything else they would regard as 'religious'. There is an inbuilt resistance and enmity towards the true 'God' in human nature. This is easy to observe in the world we live in. Almost everyone it seems, uses blasphemous, disrespectful words or symbols in virtually every sentence, OMG (Oh My God!), 'Christ', 'God knows', 'Jesus!" etc., and even far worse blasphemous epithets using that name which will not be quoted here. This profanity is more prolific among irreligious people, than it is used incorrectly by those in Christendom when they say at every occasion, "In the name of Jesus". 'Jesus is NOT the name of God's son, it is 'Yah'Shua'.

God selects the people whose minds and hearts He is opening, and they will be 'converted' and healed at the most appropriate time for them. The 'few', 'the called' at any given time, are those who are given understanding of the true Gospel, and the deeper spiritual 'secret' meanings of the Scriptures.

Christ came to reveal information which had been hidden since before the foundation of the world, this important fact is repeated in verse 34. We who do understand what the Bible is all about are indeed very blessed. Billions do not have this 'Gift' and so do not get the blessings.

[34] Yah'Shua the Messiah spoke all these things in parables to the multitudes; and without a parable, he didn't speak to them, [35] that it might be fulfilled which was spoken through the prophet, saying, [2] "I will open my mouth in parables; I will utter things hidden from the foundation of the world. (Psalm 78:2) [36a] Then Yah'Shua the Messiah sent the multitudes away, and went into the house. Matthew 13:34-36

Christ's disciples still did not understand the parables. *[36b] His disciples came to him, saying, "Explain to us the parable of the weeds of the field."* So Christ explained it to them after the crowds had left.

***Key Study Reminder:** When studying God's Word, it is essential to ask God for the Author's help to understand the complete concept in any part we are studying. It may be necessary to look at a verse or verses before the one we are reading, or after it, or both, and in other places in the Bible in order to understand the concept in its entire context and arrive at its real meaning.

Fresh 'Bread' every day

Where we are able to have access to fresh bread every day it is part of the way to live and enjoy the good life. Stale bread is not a delight. Not that the 'bread' we are talking about goes stale, exactly the opposite. But we need to get this 'bread' by feeding on God's Word fresh every day too.

[27] Labour not for the meat (food) which perishes, but for that meat (spiritual food) which endures unto everlasting life, which the Son of man shall give unto you: for him has God the Father sealed. John 6:27

When we consider the words of Christ about laying up spiritual treasures in heaven as opposed to storing up physical treasures on earth, we can learn that the treasures we learn from His Word of Knowledge, Understanding and Wisdom are those which hold eternal value for us.

What are the 'Treasures in Heaven' compared to in physical terms?

[44] The kingdom of heaven is like a very precious treasure hidden in a field, which a man found and hid again; then in his joy he goes and sells all he has and buys that field thus securing the treasure for himself. Matthew 13:44

[45] Again, the kingdom of heaven is like unto a merchant man, seeking goodly pearls: [46] Who, when he

had found one pearl of great price, went and sold all that he had, and bought it. Matthew 13:45-46

The examples here show that the kingdom of heaven is compared to earthly treasures of great value, and when a person finds a treasure, he makes a very large commitment to secure that treasure for himself. It becomes the intense focus of that person who pursues the treasure until they have it. These parables exemplify just how much commitment a person will make for earthly treasure. Just how much more should we eagerly pursue the 'Treasures in Heaven" that we glean from the Bible?

So exactly what are the 'Treasures in Heaven' Spiritually?

In the book of Proverbs, Spiritual treasures are mentioned first, then compared to the most valuable physical things.

Let the Bible explain itself, it is the best and really the only proper and safe way to correct understanding. Christ used parables about objects of high earthly value to show us the value of Spiritual treasures.

Solomon was the wisest man who had ever lived up to his time. Inspired by God, he assembled the book of Proverbs in the Bible, and it is indeed full of 'treasures' about how to live. The first ten chapters are attributed to Joseph who lived hundreds of years before Solomon. It is apparent that he had greater wisdom than any other person, and also had the 'Spirit of God' with him.

[38] And Pharaoh said unto his servants, Can we find such a one as this is, a man in whom the Spirit of God is? [39] And Pharaoh said unto Joseph, Forasmuch as God

hath shewed thee all this, there is none so discreet and wise as thou art: [40] *Thou shalt be over my house, and according unto thy word shall all my people be ruled: only in the throne will I be greater than thou.* [41] *And Pharaoh said unto Joseph, See, I have set thee over all the land of Egypt. Genesis 41:38-40*

This is another really beautiful example of just how poetic and figurative the Old Testament can be.

[1] *My son, if thou wilt receive my words, and hide (keep hidden within you like treasure) my commandments with thee;* [2] *So that thou incline thine ear (Listen!) unto* **wisdom**, *and apply thine heart (work at it) to* ***understanding;*** [3] *Yea, if thou criest after* ***knowledge,*** *and lift up thy voice (pray) for* ***understanding;*** [4] *If thou* ***seek her*** *(Wisdom has female connotations) as silver, and* ***search*** *for* ***her*** *as (in the same way as you would) for hidden treasures;* [5] ***Then*** *shalt thou understand* ***the fear of (or respect for) the Lord,*** *and find* ***the knowledge of God.*** [6] ***For the Lord*** *giveth* ***wisdom****: out of his mouth cometh* ***knowledge*** *and* ***understanding.*** *Proverbs 2:1-6*

The 'treasures in heaven' we are to seek earnestly and search for so diligently are: Knowledge, Understanding and Wisdom, and a deep respect for God and His Knowledge and the knowledge of Him.

Repetition is God's way of getting His point across, the Bible is full of it.

[13] *Happy is the man (and woman of course) that finds wisdom, and the man that gets understanding.* [14] *For the merchandise of it (wisdom) is better than the*

merchandise of silver, and the gain thereof than fine gold. [15] She (Wisdom) is more precious than rubies: and all the things you can desire are not to be compared unto her. [16] Length of days is in her right hand; and in her left hand riches and honour. [17] Her way are ways of pleasantness, and all her paths are peace. [18] She (Wisdom) is a tree of life to them that lay hold upon her: and happy is every one that retains her (Wisdom). Proverbs 3:13-18

'Wisdom' is of infinitely greater permanent value than any amount of silver, gold, and even highly priced and sought after rubies, or physical wealth in any form.

The Word, the Son of God who became Christ created all things for the Father with Wisdom, Understanding and Knowledge

[19] The Lord by wisdom, by understanding hath he established the heavens. [20] By his knowledge the depths are broken up, and the clouds drop down the dew. [21] My son, let not them depart from your eyes: keep sound wisdom and discretion: [22] So shall they be life unto your soul, and grace (like a stunningly beautiful necklace) to your neck. Proverbs 3:19-22

Wisdom brings life and health both physically and Spiritually to our very being.

[10] Receive my instruction, and not silver; and knowledge rather than choice gold. [11] For wisdom is better than rubies; and all the things that may be desired are not to be compared to it. Proverbs 8:10-11

[16] Better is little with the fear of the Lord than great treasure and trouble therewith. Proverbs 15:16

[16] How much better is it to get wisdom than gold! and to get understanding rather to be chosen than silver! Proverbs 16:16

[15] There is gold, and a multitude of rubies: but the lips (words) of (God's) knowledge are a precious jewel. Proverbs 20:15

The Father gave Christ (Yah'Shua) words that inspired Paul to write:

[4] In whom the god of this world (Satan) has blinded the minds of them which believe not (It is not their time), lest the light of the glorious gospel of Christ, who is the image of God, should shine unto them. [5] For we preach not ourselves, but Christ Yah'Shua the Messiah, the Lord; and ourselves your servants for' sake. [6] For God, who commanded the light to shine out of darkness, has shined in our hearts, to give the light of the knowledge of the glory of God in the face of Christ. (Yah'Shua Kristos) [7] But we have this treasure (the Knowledge of God, of the Kingdom, of Wisdom and Understanding) in earthen vessels (our bodies made of the dust of the earth), that the excellence of the power may be of God, and not of us. 2 Corinthians 4:4-7

We cannot seek these Spiritual treasures in our own strength.

[2] That their (our) hearts might be comforted, being knit together in love, and unto all riches of the full assurance of understanding, to the acknowledgement of the mystery of God, and of the Father, and of Christ; [3] In whom (Christ

and His Word) are hid all the treasures of wisdom and knowledge. Colossians 2:2-3

[34] *Then (when Christ returns) shall the King say unto them on his right hand… (to those who have sought His Wisdom in Christ)… 'Come, blessed of my Father, inherit the Kingdom prepared for you from the foundation of the world; Matthew 25:34*

And this verse in Isaiah amplifies the thought.

[6] *And wisdom and knowledge shall be the stability (based on the ROCK, Christ (Yah'Shua)) of thy times (of your life), and strength of salvation: the fear (respect) of the Lord is his treasure. Isaiah 33:6*

We have a figurative glimpse that we are already 'there' with Him:

[1] *If ye then be risen with Christ (Yah'Shua) [and figuratively believers are], seek those things which are above, where Christ is sitting (and living Christians are now) on the right hand of God.* [2] *Set your affection on things above, not on things on the earth. Colossians 3:1-2*

Personal Development

Many people attend 'personal growth' seminars in the hope that they will become more effective in their lives, and of course, some do get benefit, but there is little truly spiritual about the growth they may experience. Certainly honesty, reliability, punctuality, efficiency all have spiritual connotations, but they are on a human spirit level, but not necessarily on a God-plane level. God is timeless, but He runs His universe to a clock more accurate than anything a human being can construct. We feel our Quartz clocks are accurate, and our Atomic Clocks ever more accurate, but nothing that humans can make is as accurate as the perfect timeliness our Solar system runs on. God although timeless in Himself has a Plan which is, and always will be, exactly on schedule, upon that we can rely. So punctuality is definitely something we children of God should strive for in every way possible.

PUNCTUALITY

'Punctuality' is an extremely important Spiritual Christian function. In our modern world, punctuality, which used to be a highly prized character trait, has almost fallen into disuse. So many people will make all kinds of excuses why they are not on time, and in most cases, but not all, are frankly pathetic invalid reasons for not making the effort or having the character to be on time. Being late is discourteous, rude, and a waste of the life-time of the persons kept waiting.

Although the study of God's Word is a physical activity, the spiritual results of doing that activity on a daily basis has permanent benefit and an eternal potential. For emphasis Christ says again, that no human effort can cause a person to seek God unless the Father is calling him or her.

[65] And he (Christ) said, Therefore said I unto you, that no man can come unto me, except it were given unto him of my Father. John 6:65

Duration is not necessarily a required function of effective study.

One or two minutes of pondering on the meaning of a verse or two of God's Word can set us up for the day. Placing undue and unnecessary time conditions on our study time is truly pointless and only leads to frustration, disappointment in ourselves, and failed expectations. That is not what God wants us to do to ourselves. He wants us to be happy as much of the time as we can be.

Millions of people 'try' to read the Bible, not realising that it is not meant to be read like books written by humans, they find it all very difficult to understand, get discouraged, and often give up.

If we do ask for our 'Daily Bread' during our contact with 'Abba' our Father, it is a reminder for us to do the physical 'work' of planning to read the Word every day.

[36] He said, "Abba, Father, all things are possible to you. Please remove this cup from me. However, not what I desire, but what you desire." Mark 14:36

[14] For as many as are led by the Spirit of God, they are the sons of God. [15] For you have not received the Spirit of bondage again to fear; but have received the Spirit of adoption whereby we cry, Abba, Father. [16] The Spirit itself bears witness with our spirit, that we are the children of God. Romans 8:14-16

[5] that he might redeem those who were under the law, that we might receive the adoption as children. [6] And because you are children, God sent out the Spirit of his Son into your hearts, crying, "Abba, (Dad) Father!" [7] So

you are no longer a bondservant, but a son; and if a son, then an heir of God through Christ. Galatians 4:5-7

As we ask 'Abba', our 'Dad' daily for help to understand, we will become more skilled at 'rightly dividing' what we read. It helps us to 'partition' each concept off in our minds, and focus on it until we have extracted all the meaning and benefit from it that God wants us to have at that time. We do this before we move on to other verses that will further expand our understanding, and to deal with other different thoughts and concepts.

So as we read, or repeat memorised verses or Godly concepts silently in our minds, whether it be as we lie down to sleep, or during the wakeful night watches, or when we wake up in the morning, we receive spiritual energy and physical benefit from that activity.

[4] I will both lay me down in peace, and sleep: for You, Lord, only make me dwell in safety. Psalm 4:8

[24] When you lie down, you shalt not be afraid: yes, you shalt lie down, and your sleep shall be sweet. Proverbs 3:24

Sleep is partly a Spiritual Gift. It is wise to chew over thoroughly the meaning of any concept we learn about in God's Word, 'bite by bite', 'digest' it well, and extract all the nourishment possible.

Thankfulness

Thankfulness is an important spiritual activity. Gratitude leads to more joy and joyfulness, as when in a thankful frame of mind, our appreciation of what we are learning grows. When Christ fed the thousands, He gave thanks before they began to eat the food.

[36] And he took the seven loaves and the fishes, and gave thanks, and brake them, and gave to his disciples, and the disciples to the multitude. Mathew 15:36

[11]And Yah'Shua the Messiah took the loaves; and when he had given thanks, he distributed to the disciples, and the disciples to them that were sat down; and likewise of the fishes as much as they would. John 6:11

As a matter of important interest, Christ, Yah'Shua the God of our Salvation, ate meat (the Passover lamb), and fish, and provided a promised land of milk and honey to the children of Israel. Christ is our example of how to live, and it is clear that He was not a 'vegetarian' or a 'vegan'.

If living with the constraints of those belief systems is what a person wants to do, that choice is up to the individual. Unfortunately, some who practice these ways, sometimes attempt to put pressure on others to follow their example, and perhaps even give the impression, suggest, or even insist(!) that restricting what a person does in their diet in these ways makes them somewhat more 'spiritual' or more healthy. That notion is certainly not supported by, or true according to the Scriptures.

It is good to give thanks for the food we have to eat.

[35] When he (Paul) had said this, and had taken bread, he gave thanks to God in the presence of all, then he broke it and began to eat. Acts 27:35

[20] *Giving thanks always for all things unto God and the Father in the name of our Lord Christ (Yah'Shua Kristos) Ephesians 5:20*

We can and certainly should be very thankful that in most so-called civilised countries, we are in a position to be able to study God's Word without being persecuted, thrown in jail, beaten, or in any way harmed. We can and should pray daily to be delivered from such evil.

Thank God continuously for his gift of His knowledge and understanding, and ask for the Wisdom to put what we learn daily from His Word into practice in our lives.

The next chapter expands on the benefits of not merely just reading the Bible, but the use of the special tools that reveal the methodical 'HOW' of Bible study in order to extract everything God wants each individual to derive from their work.

CHAPTER 8

HOW TO STUDY THE BIBLE EFFECTIVELY

THE TOOLS GIVEN HERE ARE ON

HOW TO STUDY THE BIBLE EFFICIENTLY WITH DIRECT HELP FROM GOD

RATHER THAN USE IDEAS OR TEACHINGS FROM ANY HUMAN ORGANISATIONS

THESE TOOLS DO **NOT** TELL THE STUDENT

WHAT TO STUDY OR BELIEVE, BUT TO TRUST GOD TO INSPIRE THEM

***'Key Study Aids' will also be suggested as this section progresses.**

Why study the Bible? To get to know more about God and Christ (Yah'Shua)

The purpose of human life is to learn about God and His Son Christ so we can grow in spiritual knowledge and strive to be like Them. The more anyone knows about God and His Son, the more they are able to appreciate Who and What They Are, and what They want for their human family.

Start the study of God's Word simply, but also yearn to learn more.

Always begin by asking God for His direct help to understand His Word. Once God is working in your mind, study becomes progressively more interesting, even exciting. We become ever more eager and passionate about the increase in our Knowledge, Understanding and Wisdom.

[2] As newborn babes, desire the sincere milk of the word that you may grow thereby: 1 Peter 2:2

People who do not study earnestly cannot even understand what the 'milk' of the word is, let alone the 'meatier' parts with deeper meaning.

[2] I have fed you with milk, and not with (strong) meat: for previously you were not able to bear it, neither yet now are you able to. 1 Corinthians 3:2

A few readers may not be quite ready for some of the 'meat' suggested here. However, as anyone persists in their studies with God's help, they will find that they are able to digest more and more of the facts that provide the absolute evidence that prove the truth of the Word of God is True beyond all reasonable doubt, and grow in strength and conviction.

***Key Study Aid: Use a concordance, like Strong's, which gives the meanings of the Hebrew or Greek words from which the English word is translated.**

It is enlightening to check the significant words in the passage in the original Hebrew or Greek text as it will often reveal more depth of meaning. Strong's is available to download freely from some sites online.

How can we know if all Scripture is inspired of God?

Is all Scripture given by inspiration of God?

16 *All scripture is given by inspiration of God, and is profitable for doctrine, for reproof, for correction, for instruction in righteousness (obeying God's Law of Love): 2 Timothy 3:16*

Many have learned this verse by heart, and it is important to be clear about what it means. When it says 'all Scripture', the word translated 'Scripture' in the KJV is Strong's (1124) grafh>, — graf-ay'; from (1125) (gra>fw); a document, i.e. holy Writ (or its contents or a statement in it): — scripture or 'writings', English word 'graphic'

There are millions of ancient 'writings' (manu-scripts, literally handwritten) and this verse cannot mean that they are all inspired. We need to understand how the many specific 'writings' came to be included in the Old and New Testament, and that how only those documents God wanted included, were included by virtue of the God inspired and controlled mechanism of assembling of the Canon, explained briefly in chapter 6.

When it came to the end of the first century, the Apostles James, Peter and John, all eyewitnesses to Christ's work, death, His resurrection and ascension, were inspired by the risen Christ to assemble the Canon of the New Testament which consisted of 27 books.

[19] *And I will give unto thee the keys of the kingdom of heaven: and whatsoever thou shalt bind on earth shall be bound in heaven: and whatsoever thou shalt loose on earth shall be loosed in heaven. Matthew 16:19*

[18] *Verily I say unto you, Whatsoever ye shall bind on earth shall be bound in heaven: and whatsoever ye shall loose on earth shall be loosed in heaven. Matthew 18:18*

The Apostles had the powers of 'binding and loosing' in their day. We Christians in this era do not have this power, no human being does. To suggest anyone, or any human organisation, does have that power today, would indicate they do not understand the principle of "Progressive Revelation" explained in chapter 6.

The next verse in 2 Timothy 3 gives a wonderful, powerful reason why we should desire to study God's Word earnestly. It is so we can be well equipped to do the work of a true Christian.

[17] *That the man of God may be perfect, thoroughly furnished (equipped to apply themselves) unto all good works. (the works required of a Christian today, not in order to be saved which is a free gift, but to qualify for a position in the Kingdom when Christ returns.) 2 Timothy 3:17*

Thoroughly equipped to make the most of the teaching, the correction we need to progress, and the education in true righteousness.

An example of how to study God's Word effectively

***Key Study Aid: Study the concept of the thought and check the meaning of each of the significant words in it in a concordance or Bible dictionary.**

So what meaning does this verse in second Timothy hold for when it is looked at analytically?

> [15] *Study to shew thyself approved unto God, a workman that needs not to be ashamed, rightly dividing the word of truth. 2 Timothy 2:15*

The chances are that many may know this verse by heart, however...time spent on more understanding of the words that are underlined above will be profitable.

***Key Study Aid: Familiarity with a verse can be a trap, and hold us back.**

This is an important principle of diligent thorough study. When a person knows a verse by heart, it is highly possible that there is more to learn from it than may be obvious. Also someone who just reads a verse a few times, becomes familiar with it and thinks they 'know it', but may not appreciate its full meaning. Such familiarity can be a comfortable trap, and may lead to a lack of complete understanding, or to being open to learn more and grow in knowledge, or both.

***Key Study aid: Adopt the 'dictionary habit'.**

The 'dictionary habit' is a most useful aid to the study of anything. Check the actual meaning of words in a dictionary, even those with which one might be very familiar. And also sometimes to use an etymological dictionary, to see its synonyms, and perhaps even its antonyms, is usually mind expanding. It is surprising how often very commonly used words we think we know so well can contain and imply much more meaning that we might think. The more extensive our vocabulary, the more clearly and deeply we can think and use our minds.

***Key Study Aid: Check the meaning of every significant word in verses we think we know well.**

The first word in 2 Timothy 2:15 is 'study' to notice, pause and examine before we rush on to the rest of the verse we feel we know so well..

How are we to 'study'? To 'study' has a very different meaning than to 'read'. Here are some synonyms of a word we have known all our lives that will enhance the attitude of the one who 'studies' rather than just 'reads':

To study is to strive toward, devote oneself to, cultivate, apply oneself, show zeal for, to examine, eagerness, to be diligent, to strive after.

These synonyms indicate that to 'study' involves being energetic, eager, diligent, devoted, and more. This is a very different approach from than just simply reading a verse or verses, or even to memorise them.

The next words to notice are 'approved of God'. We want God to approve of our study, so how do we go about getting His approval?

Here is another vital principle that will help us to come to understand God's word in a thorough way:

Key Study Aid: The Bible interprets itself.

The earnest student does not need the opinions of religious men or women about what the Bible means. Apart that is, from being clear about the definitive meaning of specific words in the original texts, and how and whether they are correctly, appropriately, and meaningfully translated into English from the original language.

Approved of God, a 'workman' not to be 'ashamed'
This next part of the verse itself reveals to us the need to be 'approved of God'. True Christians want to be the type of 'workman' (or woman) that needs not to be ashamed, or think less of themselves.

So we could embark on a study of 'work', but here are a few verses about work and being a 'workman' which shows the attitude God wants us to adopt towards any type of labour we engage in. This is a useful example to see how we can use the Bible to interpret itself.

[6] Go to (look at) the ant, thou sluggard (lazy person); consider her ways, and be wise: [7] Which having no guide, overseer, or ruler, [8] Provides her meat in the summer, and gathers her food in the harvest. Proverbs 6:6-8

Anyone who has ever observed ants at work, they see that they are incredibly energetic and industrious. They just get on with whatever the task they are pursuing.

[23] In all hard work there is profit, but the talk of the lips leads only to poverty. Proverbs 14:23

Talk is cheap. Most group discussions about God's Word can often lead to 'poverty', poor understanding.

Participants tend to say things like “Well I think…”, or “I believe…” and everyone expresses their opinions, and little or nothing is gained. It is important not to ‘Lean on our own understanding’ or that of others, but trust that with God’s help in our personal study our work will be profitable.

5 Trust in Yahweh (God the Father and His Son Christ) with all your heart, and don’t lean on (or trust) your own understanding. 6 In all your ways acknowledge him, and he will make your paths straight. 7 Don’t be wise in your own eyes. Fear Yahweh, and depart from evil. 8 It will be health to your body, and nourishment to your bones. Proverbs 3:5-8

[10] Whatever work your hand finds to do, do it with your might; for there is no work, nor plan, nor knowledge, nor wisdom, in the grave where you are going. Ecclesiastes 9:10

This verse tells us that God wants us to apply ourselves diligently to any job or work we undertake with all our ‘might’, and that includes study. So out comes the online etymological dictionary, (https://www.etymonline. com/) we can find the synonyms of this key word ‘might’.

‘Might’ is the quality of being able, and have the ability to do or act with power, bodily strength, focus, authority, and self-control. The ‘work’ of study involves might, energy, effort, strength, and self-control.

That gives an entirely different sense than just ‘reading’ or casually looking things up. The Bible also helps us to understand how to avoid being **ashamed’**.

[20] O keep my soul, and deliver me: let me not be ashamed; for I put my trust in you. Psalm 25:20

[1] In you, O Lord, do I put my trust; let me never be ashamed: deliver me in thy righteousness. Psalm 31:1

[20] According to my earnest expectation and my hope, that in nothing I shall be ashamed, but that with all boldness, as always, so now also Christ shall be magnified in my body, whether it be by life, or by death. Philippians 1:20

When put our ***trust in God*** as we apply ourselves diligently to His Word, our earnest expectation and hope is that we shall have no need to be ashamed when our workmanlike attitude to study is approved of God.

The importance of 'rightly dividing' the word of truth. The next phrase in 2 Timothy 2:15 is 'rightly dividing', this word in the original text implies 'correctly partitioning'. The Word of God is not written like any other book, it is written by Him, dictated to men word for word, precept by precept, or concept by concept. It is very important to know how to look for and find the beginning and end of each concept in order to arrive at the best understanding.

*Key Study Aid: The chapter breaks and verse numbers in the Bible are not inspired.

The chapters and verses are often actually a very useful navigational tool for finding our way around the Scriptures, but they are not inspired, nor are they part of the original manuscripts. These two features of all translations can both help but also confuse, obscure or make difficult to understand the concepts that the Word, Christ wants us fully to understand from any part of His Word the Bible that He is leading us to study.

So it is best not be restricted by verses and chapters, but look carefully for the beginning and end of the subject we wish to understand. It may only be one verse, or several, and the whole thought may be split by a chapter heading. In most bibles a paragraph mark like this appears after a verse number as an indication that the verse begins another thought or subject. Helpful on occasions, but not to be relied upon. Seek carefully for yourself where thoughts and subjects begin and end. Careful practice makes perfect.

God wrote the Bible in His own 'style', and it is like no other book in the world. It is like a 'million piece jigsaw puzzle' of thoughts, notions, principles and concepts, but there is no 'picture' on the box to help us. However, every piece of the 'puzzle' contributes to the proper understanding of each part of the 'picture'.

***Key Study Aid: Take the whole context of the entire thought or teaching into account, it is crucial to be able to arrive at a thorough complete understanding.**

Whether it is only one or two verses, or spans before and after a chapter break, be careful to include the entire thought or concept of the whole context as our study proceeds.

There is a tendency to think that Biblical verses we learn contain complete thoughts on any subject. This may or may not be true. Here is an example.

Perhaps it is best to avoid religious discussion groups. The verse that follows 2 Timothy 2:15, contains a warning which is linked to this concept. There are as many ideas about what a verse or passage might mean as there are people willing to discuss or even ague about it. Groups that form to study the Bible often sadly descend into conflicts of opinion and debate. This was mentioned earlier. Each person tends to say, "Well I think so and so…" What 'they' think or say is not relevant to the true student. It is what the Bible actually says that is important, and what God reveals to you in your personal relationship with Him.

16 But shun profane (to desecrate or render unholy) and vain (empty, vanity filled, pointless) babblings: for they will increase unto more ungodliness. 2 Timothy 2:16

2 If any man teach otherwise, and consent not to wholesome words, even the words of our Lord Christ, Yah'Shua the Messiah, and to the doctrine which is according to godliness; 3 He is proud, knowing nothing, but doting about questions and strifes of words, whereof cometh envy, strife, railings, evil surmisings (uneducated guesses) 5 Perverse disputings of men of corrupt minds, and destitute of the truth, supposing that gain (of useless information) is godliness: from such withdraw thyself. 1 Timothy 6:2-5

A true Christian will avoid any form of 'debate' a form of discussion because it is one of the evil works of the flesh. The Word of God is not to be debated, but to be examined carefully and prayerfully, understood, and then used to live by every day.

Another example of the need to study carefully verses we think we know well.

A minister was asked if he knew Matthew 6:33 by heart. His immediate response was to say, “Of course, “But seek ye first the kingdom of God, and his righteousness; and all these things shall be added unto you”. I have known that verse for over forty years.” He was then asked, “What are ‘all these things’ that shall be added to you?” He replied, “Good question. I don’t know, I have never thought about it.”

This minister of forty years’ experience was so familiar with what he thought the verse represented, i.e., that we should seek first the Kingdom of God and obedience to God’s Law, and we would have ‘all these things’ added to us. But he had never thought to check and did not know what ‘all these things’ were. He had never examined the context of the complete thought or concept that Christ was explaining.

***Key Study Aid: The Bible explains the Bible.**

We do not need to guess what anything in the Bible means, or ask others what it might mean. There are always other verses which shed more light on the meaning we are looking for.

Matthew 6 plainly tells us what ‘these things’ are. Verse 25 begins the next subject of the concept that Christ was teaching. He introduces the subject of the whole section of the discourse which is being ‘anxious about life’, or worry about what we will eat or drink, or whether we have clothes to wear.

25 Therefore I tell you, don't be anxious for your life: what you will eat, or what you will drink; nor yet for your body, what you will wear. Isn't life more than food, and the body more than clothing? 26 See the birds of the sky, that they don't sow, neither do they reap, nor gather into barns. Your heavenly Father feeds them. Aren't you of much more value than they? Matthew 6:25-26

Look at the natural world, Christ says, they do not worry about 'these things'.

27 "Which of you by being anxious, can add one moment to his lifespan? 28 Why are you anxious about clothing? Consider the lilies of the field, how they grow. They don't toil, neither do they spin, 29 yet I tell you that even Solomon in all his glory was not dressed like one of these. 30 But if God so clothes the grass of the field, which today exists and tomorrow is thrown into the oven, won't he much more clothe you, you of little faith? Matthew 6:27-30

So here 'take no (anxious) thought' is the object lesson Christ is teaching us, is repeated again for emphasis in verse 31, is how **not** to think.

31 "Therefore don't be anxious, saying, 'What will we eat?', 'What will we drink?' or, 'With what will we be clothed?' 32 For the Gentiles seek after all these things; for your heavenly Father knows that you need all these things. Matthew 6:31-32

So don't worry about 'all these things', here is how God wants us to think.

33 But (instead) seek ye first the kingdom of God, and his righteousness; and all these things shall be added unto you. [34] Take therefore no (anxious) thought for the morrow: for the morrow shall take thought for the things (food, drink and clothes) of itself. Sufficient unto the day is the evil thereof. Matthew 6:33

The minister was astonished that in all those years he had never thought to examine more carefully what he thought the verse meant, especially as he knew very well the importance of using context to arrive at a proper understanding of any part of the 'jigsaw puzzle' in relation to other pieces.

A list of Bible 'Master Class' *Key Study Aids

Essential Keys to understand the Bible better and get to the 'meat' of the matter.

***Key Study Aid #1. First ask God for the help of Holy Spirit every time we study.**

***Key Study Aid #2. God has written His Book in His Language, Styles and Structure.**

God's language is not our language. His way of thinking is not our way.

***Key Study Aid #3 There is a Spiritual component to everything physical.**

***Key Study Aid #4. Use a reliable translation, the King James is good but has errors. All translations contain errors, but don't let that put you off! If ever in doubt about the meaning of any verse or passage.**

Check each word or phrase in the original manuscripts Hebrew, Greek or Aramaic using the appropriate resource.

Another translation in more colloquial English is the World English Bible (WEB) which has been used extensively in this book.

***Key Study Aid #5: Use a concordance, like Strong's, which gives the meanings of the Hebrew or Greek words from which the English word is translated.**

It is enlightening to check all the significant words in the passage in the original Hebrew or Greek text as it will often reveal more depth of meaning. Strong's is available to download freely from some sites online.

***Key Study Aid #6: Study the whole concept of the thought and check the meaning of the significant words in it in a concordance or Bible dictionary.**

This key is often important to arrive at a correct understanding of any Scripture.

***Key Study Aid #7: Familiarity with a verse can be a trap, and hold us back.**

Familiarity can be a comfortable trap, and may lead to a lack of complete understanding or to our not being open to learn more and grow in knowledge.

***Key Study Aid #8: Adopt the 'dictionary habit'.**

The 'dictionary habit' of checking even words that we think we know well is a most useful aid to the study of anything.

***Key Study Aid #9: Check the meaning of every significant word in verses we think we know well.**

We may think we know and understand the meaning of the verse, but check them in the etymological dictionary to be sure.

***Key Study Aid #10: The Bible interprets and explains itself.**

We do not need opinions of religious men or women about what the Bible means. We do not need to guess what anything in the Bible means, or ask others what it might mean. There are always other verses which shed more light on the meaning we are looking for.

***Key Study Aid #11: The chapter breaks and verse numbers in the Bible are not inspired.**

The chapters and verses are actually a very useful navigational tool for finding our way around the Scriptures, but they are not inspired, nor are they part of the original manuscripts. Use this information to look for, and find the complete concept.

***Key Study Aid #12: Take the whole context of the entire thought or teaching into account.**

It is crucial to be able to arrive at a thorough complete understanding. Whether the context is only one or two verses, or spans before and after a chapter break, be careful to include entire thought or concept of the whole context in your study.

***Key Study Aid #13 Check the grammatical syntax.**

Look out for words like 'if', 'because', 'but', 'before', 'after' 'then', 'now', they are often meaningful; and look also for interrogative adverbs like who, what, where, when, why, as these interrogative words sometimes reveal more much meaning when they are taken into account.

***Key Study Aid #14. Note the timing or chronology of the event if relevant.**

***Key Study Aid #15 Take account of the geography where relevant.**

***Key Study Aid #16 Use the Internet to navigate the Scriptures.**

The best way to navigate the Scriptures, to find words, verses, subjects etc., is to use the internet free resource to check any word, phrase, or text in the Bible instantly. https://www.biblegateway.com/ is a good source and there are others.

***Key Study Aid #17 Use a Concordance**

To gain more understanding of any topic in the Bible, look in a concordance for the first time a word is used and the last time it appears. Then check some of the other occurrences for a more complete understanding of how that word is used in the Bible, and in what contexts.

For example, the word 'learn'. The first occasion is in Deuteronomy 4:10 "Assemble the people to me, and I will make them hear my words, that they may learn to fear me all the days that they live on the earth, and that they may teach their children." The emphasis is to learn to fear to offend God and to respect Him and to teach our children to do so.

There are 61 occurrences in the Bible, each one will give a different aspect of what we are to learn and not to learn. The last occurrence in the Bible is in Revelation about the 144,000 being the only ones who can sing this particular song. It is not necessary to examine each use of the word, only to be aware of the principle that looking at other instances can help clarify any subject.

***Key Study Aid # 18 The King James, and many other versions of the Bible have a column of references in between the two main columns on each page.**

There are some that are numbered, which give alternative meanings for words; and others are lettered a, b, c, etc., and these sometimes, but not always, give useful links to other verses on the same subject, and where they appear. This is particularly useful where in the Old Testament pages, it gives references as to where the verse appears in the New Testament and vice versa. Another useful study aid to use when appropriate.

It is not necessary to use all these Key Study Aids every time you study. They are simply 'tools'.

When we are in a shed or workplace, we do not attempt to use every tool we have in our workshop, we just pick the ones that are appropriate to address the job at hand. It is the same when studying, the 'tools' are intended to make study more effective and productive, not to tie anyone down to a 'system'. So please enjoy using them to get more out of your study of God's Word.

The next chapter focusses on the actual **'work'** that is involved in being a Christian.

CHAPTER 9

IT TAKES **WORK** TO BE A TRUE CHRISTIAN

Eternal Life is a Free Gift from God the Father and His Son, no work or 'works' on our part are needed.

However, to be a true Christian takes a lot of hard work. It involves diligent work on ourselves, on our thoughts, attitudes, and our actions in order to live each day in accordance with the wishes and the demands of God our Father and Christ our Elder Brother. True Christianity is not just a belief system, it is a rigorous, exacting way of life.

What does it take to become a true Christian?

Can any person become a Christian? Yes and no. Yes if, and only if, God the Father calls that person at that time. No, if someone just decides they want to become a Christian, but God has not called them at that time.

God the Father inspired the entire Bible, word for word. Christ (Yah'Shua the Messiah) during His lifetime spoke only what the Father inspired Him to say.

*[44] No man (person) can come to me, **except the Father** which hath sent me **draw** him (that person): and I (YahwehShua) will raise him up at the last day John 6:44*

It is important to trust, heed and believe what Yah'Shua, the God of our Salvation tells us.

'Churchianity' will tell you that Salvation is a free gift and a Christian does not have to do any works to receive it, we cannot earn it. Ultimately that is absolutely true because every human being will be saved ultimately, but not necessarily in this lifetime.

Therefore to say, "We do not have to do anything at all to be saved." Is NOT true, it is a FALSE statement.

Salvation through history is only granted when a person firstly has God's Gifts of Faith, and Believes, and Repents of their own volition of all their sins. However, nobody can do these things unless or until God calls them and gives that person those spiritual gifts of 'Faith', 'Belief' and 'Repentance'. Then that person has to respond by action to that call.

*That **if** you shall confess with your mouth the Lord, Yah'Shua (the Messiah) and shall **believe** in your heart that God has raised him (or her) from the dead, you shall be **saved**. Romans 10:9*

Note the word **'IF'** in the above verse.

[1] *And they said, **Believe** on the Lord Christ the Messiah, and you shall be **saved**, and your house. Acts 16:1*

Also to be saved, eventually, when the time is right, God will grant a person another Gift, that of Humility.

[2] *And Jesus called a little child unto him, and sethim in the midst of them,* [3] *And said, Verily I say*

unto you, Except you be converted, and become as little children, you shall not enter into the kingdom of heaven. [4] *Whosoever therefore shall humble himself as this little child, the same is greatest in the kingdom of heaven. Matthew 18:2-4*

"Except you be converted" and "become as little children" these are **conditions** to entrance into God's Kingdom.

'Unconditional love' – is a Satanic myth.

Here is a basic truth:

> ***The greater the number of people who strongly believe something is true, the less likely it is to be true.***

"Unconditional love" is a very popular belief held by millions and millions of people… but it is not true. It is a myth, it does not exist.

If anyone searches the Internet on "Unconditional Love" they get 57 million responses in a quarter of a second. On any site, they may see hundreds or even thousands of cards, posters, poems, beautiful words, all 'worshipping' the untrue notion that there is such a thing as 'unconditional love'.

Many websites offer things like "20 ways to know someone loves you unconditionally", or "10 ways to love people unconditionally", "How to love your children unconditionally." They may all look very plausible and 'lovely', but the truth of the matter is that human 'love' is never unconditional, there is always an element of "I love you but..." or "If you did something bad enough, I wouldn't love you any more..."

Some think a dog or cat has "unconditional love" for its owner, but this is not so. People say that pets give their owners "unconditional love" no matter how badly the owner treats them. They might take a lot of harsh treatment, but like humans, if things get bad enough, even an animal's 'love' tends to get strained, and then turns on the offending person.

Shock! Horror!! Is this your reaction to reading this?

Then how about this?

God's love is Unlimited, but not unconditional

We are physical human beings with a very limited connection to God via the 'Silver Cord' which connects God to our 'Spirit in Man'. Limited, not because God is in any way limited, but because we humans are. God says:

[8] For my thoughts are not your thoughts, neither are your ways my ways, says the LORD. [9] For as the heavens are higher than the earth, so are my ways higher than your ways, and my thoughts than your thoughts. Isaiah 55:8-9

So how much 'higher' are God's thoughts than ours?

So high that we cannot even begin to comprehend.

God requires many things of His children, and if these requirements are not met, then there are always penalties. Is God's Love Unlimited? Of course it is. But it is CONDITIONAL upon each person's response to Him.

A brief list of some of the requirements God has for us are: Belief, Trust, Faith, Repentance, Obedience. Note each of these words is capitalised to indicate that these are all Gifts from God. Those same words when used of the human actions, are used in this book starting with a small letter.

If these requirements are not met, then our contact and relationship with Him will be limited. Note the word **'if'**, according to the eliyah.com concordance, it appears one thousand five hundred and ninety times (1,590) in the King James Version. The vast majority of these instances are in the context of God saying to us in effect:

"This is what I want you to do... and here is what will happen 'if" you do not comply."

The conditional word 'if' in God's Word

The word '**if'** occurs 1595 times in 1420 verses in the English KJV translation of the Bible. The word 'if' followed by any statement makes that statement conditional.

Most Christians assume that the promise of the gift of salvation, like all other promises in the Bible, is free. People are taught that salvation is a free gift from God with the usual comment "you cannot earn your way into Heaven". Doesn't John 8:36 say "*so if the Son sets you free, you will be free indeed*"? And doesn't Romans 6:23 say "*for the wages of sin is death, but the gift of God is eternal life in Christ Jesus our Lord*"?

Everyone thinks that God's gifts are free – without any attached strings – but is that true when we look at the many various promises in the Bible?

The primary Salvation promise is in John 3:16 which says:

[16] For God so loved the world that he gave his one and only Son, that whoever believes in him shall not perish but have eternal life. John 3:16

However, John 3:16 does not say that Salvation is a free gift without conditions because it contains an "if" statement – you will not perish and have eternal life **if** you believe in Yah'Shua the Messiah. So there is a condition to that gift, and that condition is that you must accept that Yah'Shua is Lord.

This is only a partial statement because just acknowledging that Christ is Lord the Messiah is not sufficient – even Satan acknowledges that Yah'Shua is Lord, but nobody would claim that Satan is saved at this time!

The John 3:16 statement is further clarified in the Word where it says that you must not only accept that Yah'Shua is Lord (the Messiah as foretold in the Old Testament, Khristos, Christ the Messiah in the New) but you must also submit yourself to Yahweh, God the Father (something that Satan does not do at this time!).

So God's promises are conditional, they are only "free" **if** you obey certain conditions. Around 1,500 verses in the Bible contain the word "if", and there are other promises Yahweh makes in Scripture that do not use the word "if" but still contain conditions.

"Unconditional love" would be love for something regardless of anything that person, animal, or object is, or does. Love without an 'object' of that love is meaningless.

"Unconditional love" does not exist in this world, either among human beings, or even from God the Father Yahweh, for us.

Human beings have Free Will and the Power of choice Everyone is free to think and act as they wish, but we are**forced** to choose.

Choice is not an option. Every thought we think and every action we take is as a result of making a conscious or subconscious choice. This human life is a continuous series of choices over a period of time for however long we live. We have to take responsibility for the choices we make.

There are only two basic choices. Either to live according to God's Laws of Love for Him and for everyone with whom we come into contact; or to disregard those Laws and live our lives according to our own whims and fancies.

God told the Children of Israel, the nation He had chosen to work with directly, that when they entered the Promised Land they faced a life of choices.

[19] I call heaven and earth to witness against you today that I have set before you the way of life and the way of death, the blessings (of a wonderful life for obedience)

and the curse (of misery and death, the inevitable result of disobedience). Therefore ***choose*** *(My Way of) life, that you may live, you and your descendants. Deuteronomy 30:19*

The Israelites were a physical people, they had the spirit in man, but they were not spiritually aware or receptive in any way, so God had to deal with them on a purely physical level, but they still could not comprehend how to respond obediently to God.

Christ (Yah'Shua Kristos) came to introduce the new Spiritual 'Way of life'.

He came to save us from the eventual ultimate consequence of our going our own way and for making the wrong choices, by offering us forgiveness and the free offer of eternal life.

5 Thomas said to him, "Lord, we don't know where you are going. How can we know the way?" 6 Yah'Shua the Messiah said to him, "I am the way, the truth, and the life. No one comes to the Father, except through me. 7 If you had known me, you would have known my Father also. Now you know him, and you have seen him." John 14:5-7

Christ (Yah'Shua) also said that He and the Father are One, but they did not understand it.

8 Philip said to him, "Lord, show us the Father, and that will be enough for us."

9 Yah'Shua the Messiah said to him, "Have I been with you such a long time, and do you not know me, Philip? He who has seen me has seen the Father. How do you say, 'Show us the Father?' [10] *Don't you believe that I am in the Father, and the Father in me? The words that I tell you, I speak not from myself; but the Father who lives in me does his works.* [11] *Believe me that I am in the Father, and the Father in me; or else believe me for the very works' sake. John 14:8-11*

There are two 'Ways' of life, one is much easier than the other.

[13] *"Enter in by the narrow gate (not easy); for the gate is wide and the way is broad (much easier) that leads to destruction, and there are many who enter in by it.*

[14] *Narrow is the gate (difficult by comparison) and the way is restricted (hard work) that leads to life! Few (the 'called') there are who find it. Matthew 7:14*

So there is a specific 'Way' for Christians to conduct their lives, and that 'Way' is explained in the Bible, another powerful reason to study it daily.

Human nature has two choices, the 'take' way, or the 'give' way

The world is run almost totally on the 'take' way, the way of the 'flesh', living by the lower nature which lusts for power over others, and greed, the root of them both is selfishness. Here is also a list of the 'take' traits of the 'flesh' in Galatians.

[19] *Now the deeds of the flesh are obvious, which are: adultery, sexual immorality, uncleanness, lustfulness,*
[20] *idolatry, sorcery, hatred, strife, jealousies, outbursts of anger, rivalries, divisions, heresies,* [21] *envy, murders,*

drunkenness, orgies, and things like these; of which I forewarn you, even as I also forewarned you, that those who practice such things will not inherit God's Kingdom. Galatians 5:19 -21

The wrong uses of sex, religious idolatry, the occult, hatred in every form, envy, murders, drunkenness and drug use, all the things that dominate the news media every hour of every day that are the 'take way' which is 'way' of the world.

The opposite traits and behaviours are the way of the Spirit.

[22] But the fruit of the Spirit is love, joy, peace, patience, kindness, goodness, faith, gentleness, and ***self-control****. Against such things there is no law. [24] Those who belong to Christ have crucified the flesh (carnal mind) with its passions and lusts. [25] If we live by the Spirit, let's also walk by the Spirit. Galatians 5:22-25*

The choices are very clear, and so is God's instruction to the Christian.

[16] But I say, walk by the Spirit, and you won't be involved with the lusts of the flesh. [17] For the flesh lusts against the Spirit, and the Spirit against the flesh; and these are contrary to one another, that you may not (be able to) do the things that you (i.e. your Spirit-led self really, truly) desire. Galatians 5:16-17

It is what Christians do that counts, not what they say Christians are called to be 'lights', only a light that is faulty makes a noise. The 'light' we show to others is when they observe that we behave differently from other people. Christians are to be more polite, more caring, more considerate, more tolerant, more kindly, friendlier, more helpful, and less selfish, to mention but a few characteristics.

[14] You are the light of the world. A city located on a hill can't be hidden. [15] Neither do you light a lamp and put it under a measuring basket, but on a stand; and it shines to all who are in the house. [16] Even so, let your light shine before men, that they may see your good works and glorify your Father who is in heaven. Matthew 5:14-16

Christians do not do what they do to be praised, or to be thought well of, but that hopefully when people see how you behave and react, they may come to realise that you have some sort of a relationship with a God of Love, and your conduct may lead them to praise and glorify Him.

'Walk' in the spirit, with God's help, all the time

To walk in the 'Spirit' is not an easy path, in fact it is totally impossible without inviting the help of the Father and His Son on a moment by moment basis. To control all our every thought and action takes His help, and vigilant work on our part.

[8] for by grace you have been saved through faith, and that not of yourselves; it is the gift of God, [9] not of works, that no one would boast. [10] For we are his workmanship, created in Christ Yah'Shua the Messiah for good works, which God prepared before that we would walk in them. Ephesians 2:8-10

When 'walking' in the Spirit, God is doing the 'good works' with and in us. Those 'works' of right thoughts and actions are those that God has prepared for us and helps us to perform.

Our minds, the special 'Godlike' way our human brains think and reason are our most precious possession. God holds us all responsible for the way we use our minds. We are exhorted to learn how to think like Christ thinks.

[5] Look not every man on his own things, but every man (person, look) also on the things of others. Let this mind be in you, which was also in Christ, Yah'Shua the Messiah: Philippians 2:5

It is important and fine to take good care of ourselves, and always to be thinking of the needs of others as well.

We do not have to strive to get Christ's mind, which is to keep our minds on God and the needs of others, because it is ours as a free gift for the asking.

But as we have already seen, it is inherent in our human nature to be resistant to change. While we might be emotionally 'in love' with God and His Gospel, AND we do still have a continual fight on our hands. Christ says through Paul,

[19] For the good that I would I do not: but the evil which I would not, that I do. [20] Now if I do that I would not, it is no more I that do it, but sin that dwells in me. [21] I find then a law, that, when I would do good, evil is present with me. Romans 7:19-21

Christ through Paul went on to say that the good things Paul really wants to do, he does not do; and the bad things he does not want to do, he does. Any struggling Christian knows what that is all about.

[22] For I delight in the law of God after the inward man: [23] But I see another law in my members, warring against the law of my mind, and bringing me into captivity to the law of sin which is (inherent) in my members or minds). Romans 7:22-23

This inbuilt 'law' affects our minds and bodies and indeed our whole being. Sad, but this is the experience of all who would be Christian, and we need constantly to ask for help to fight that tendency and to control our own nature.

Christians need to control their own human nature, not attempt to control other people. Satan's 'world' runs on controlling others

God's Word tells us in great detail how He wants His children to live. Although He could, God does not control His children. He wants each of them to be in control of their own lives, to choose of their own volition to love and worship Him, and live according to His wishes. The exercise of 'Self-Control' is possibly our most difficult task. Self-control is a Godly quality.

The human desire to control others is not Godly or Christian

Unfortunately the desire to control others is also part of our inbuilt human nature. The exercise of this desire is one of the root causes of all the strife in the world.

Whether between individuals, or where people are organised into groups, committees, religions, churches, political parties or governments, or in commerce, the element of the subtle control of others is always present.

In everyday conversation nobody is aware of, or realises, just how very controlling people are. There are words in constant use by everybody which have an unrecognised aspect of control. Listen to children at play as they are an absolute prime example. They are all ordering each other around. We learn to control early.

Sadly, it is all too easy to be blind to our own glaring faults, while we pick at the minute failings of others. This is certainly something Christians will want to eliminate from their conduct with other people.

[1] Don't judge (condemn), so that you won't be judged (condemned). [2] For with whatever judgment you judge, you will be judged; and with whatever measure you measure, it will be measured to you. [3] Why do you see the speck that is in your brother's eye, but don't consider the beam that is in your own eye? [4] Or how will you tell your brother, 'Let me remove the speck from your eye,' and look, the beam is in your own eye? [5] You hypocrite! First remove the beam out of your own eye, and then you can see clearly to remove the speck out of your brother's eye. Matthew 7:1-5

Christians will want to resist strongly any attempt to control others

When Christians observe that certain 'controlling' words are embedded in almost every conversation, once aware of them, and the damage they can do to relationships, they will want to avoid them. The use of them is so commonplace that unless we know what they are, notice them, and are cognisant of the harm they can do, we can slip into using them too. For instance, if the word 'you' is followed by 'should', 'could', 'ought', or 'must', this is a clear attempt to control the other person. It is not a good idea to tell others what to do.

Some have observed that many people spend quite a lot of time making a bit of a mess of their own lives, but they are so ready to tell others how they 'could', 'should', 'ought', or 'must' live their lives a certain way. That habit is certainly best avoided.

There are other words best avoided like the plague. Like **'why'** which calls the other person into question, and puts them in a defensive stance. Remember how you felt when you were a child, and anyone demanded of you to know 'why' you did something?

'Yes but' which completely denies what the other person has just said. You are lovely, kind, warm and friendly, **BUT**... We all know how that feels.

Telling people to **'try to'** is pointless, as it simply does not work because that word causes confusion in the mind. While anyone is **'trying'** to do anything they will never succeed. Tell someone to **'try'** to hold your hand, and they will immediately hold your hand. Then if you say, "I did not say 'hold my hand'. I said TRY to hold my hand." It will be easy to observe their puzzlement.

Popular 'soap operas' adored by millions are almost entirely built on characters that constantly use these words blatantly in attempts to control others. The resulting stress, arguments, and other attention-getting emotional parts of the script keep the viewers riveted, and of course there is always one character the audience is 'trained' to dislike. Once aware of this type of 'control' one can began to see the danger of it.

Unless our paid occupation involves being 'in charge' of people, all controlling words are best left out of any conversation. Any comments to others that constitute giving orders, commands, warnings, threats, moralising, preaching, advising, offering solutions, suggestions, teaching, lecturing, logical argument, judging, criticising, blaming, name-calling, interpreting, diagnosing, analysing, probing, interrogating, or making adverse personal comments are all best avoided and not used at all. Even 'bosses' need to be careful of the use of controlling words.

This is a lot to think about, but the common factor in all these words involves the factor of a degree of control. A powerful analogy from a famous poem might help.

> **"As an arrow loosed from the bow, so a word, once spoken, cannot be recalled".**

No matter how much we might want to 'take it back', we cannot. The damage is done, and cannot be undone.

Controlling what we say is not easy, it takes careful thought and consideration.

When anyone lets 'loose an arrow' and they see that it hits and hurts the 'mark', they immediately say, **"I was only joking."** They were not, it came from their heart, their inner being. He/she just does not want to take responsibility for their words. **What they said was not a "joke", it was actually a lie.** It is very important we do not do this, especially with children as they are growing up. This practice actually teaches them not to trust their parents. Then the kids do it, and the result is that nobody can trust what they say.

[34b] ... for out of the abundance of the heart the mouth speaks. Matthew 12:34b

Everything we say with any degree of emotion can be out of the bad side of human nature. So ponder on that.

[4] Look, the ships also, though they are so big and are driven by fierce winds, are yet guided by a very small rudder, wherever the pilot desires. [5] So the tongue is also a little member, and boasts great things. See how asmall fire can spread to a large forest! [6] And the tongue is a fire. James 3:4-6

Christians are urged to control the tongue, which is like the small rudder of a big ship. A tiny movement can have an enormous effect. Or produce a 'spark' that could ignite a disastrous 'fire' in a relationship.

The only 'control' we need to practice daily is **'self-control'**. To avoid using controlling words takesa lot of personal discipline, awareness, and careful attention moment by moment, as well as many years of thoughtful practice to perfect. Listen to yourself, and listen to others, and **strive** to avoid this practice.

Development of good character

A few decades ago, before the 'world' accelerated onto its current rapid slide into lawlessness, immorality and depravity, much emphasis was given to the importance of the development of good character traits. People who developed them earned respect from others and gained advancement in the path they chose in life.

We have to 'work' continuously on our minds that always have the tendency at some level to resist God and His ways of Love, and even be at enmity with Him, and at 'war' with His Spirit. It is only with the addition of and the help of God's Holy Spirit Power that we can even begin to do this very specialised 'work'.

We have to suppress our own carnal feelings like holding down a spring. A moment of inattention and our minds spring back and revert to the baser acts of carnality. No human can do this 'work' effectively without the presence and flow of God's Holy Spirit in their hearts and minds.

The first and most important 'work' God requires of us is to 'fear' to offend Him, and deeply to respect the Lord our God, to walk in all His ways, and to love him, and to serve the Lord God with all our heart and with all our soul (being), heart and mind.

God wants us to bear good 'fruit' like a 'fruitful' tree planted by rivers of water.

[1] Blessed is the man (person) who doesn't walk in the counsel of the wicked, nor stand on the path of sinners, nor sit in the seat of scoffers; [2] but his delight is in Yahweh's law. On his law he meditates day and night. [3] He will be like a tree planted by the streams of water, that produces its fruit in its season, whose leaf also does not wither. Whatever he does shall prosper. [4] The wicked (ungodly) are not so, but are like the chaff which the wind drives away. [5] Therefore the wicked shall not stand in the judgment, nor sinners in the congregation of the righteous. [6] For Yahweh knows the way of the righteous, but the way of the wicked shall perish. Psalm 1:1-6

The good 'fruit' we develop as we grow are spiritual 'fruit'. This requires us to be diligent in our 'work'. We need to ask God daily for more faith, and add to that Faith He gives us. We are to develop *'virtue'* whichembraces many Spiritual qualities of character.

Virtuousness includes: Godliness, truthfulness, honesty, reliability, politeness, integrity, gratitude, temperance, commitment, faithfulness, self-control, patience, fairness, generosity, bravery, courage, joyfulness, respect, level headedness, charitable-ness, friendliness, brotherly love, kindness, warmth, humour, and more.

***Key suggestion. Sometimes, perhaps check out the synonyms and antonyms of all these aspects of character. It is illuminating, revealing, and mind expanding.**

These listed above are just some of these qualities, and of course there are many more that we need to be 'working' on daily and developing with God's help. This 'work' will ensure that we will not be barren or unfruitful, but always producing good 'fruit' and growing in the Knowledge of our Lord Christ (Yah'Shua Kristos).

[7] And to godliness brotherly kindness; and to brotherly kindness charity. [8] For if these things be in you, and abound, they make you that ye shall neither be barren nor unfruitful in the knowledge of our Lord Christ, Yah'Shua the Messiah. 1 Peter 1:7-8

But 'sincere' people who lack these qualities, however religious, are blind, short-sighted and fail to see the need to develop them, and have lost sight that Christ expects them to pursue Christian works.

[9] For he who lacks these things is blind, seeing only what is near (under their noses), having forgotten they are cleansed from their old sins. [10] Therefore, brothers and sisters, be more diligent to make your calling and election sure. For if you do these things, you will never stumble. [11] For thus you will be richly supplied with entrance into the eternal Kingdom of our Lord and Saviour, Christ, Yah'Shua the Messiah. 1 Peter 1:9-11

The 'called', the 'ekklesia', our 'brothers and sisters' in Faith who really do give diligence to these things will never fall short, and can look forward to the promise of being in the everlasting kingdom of our Lord and Saviour Christ (Yah'Shua Kristos) at His coming.

So 'busy' there is no time for others?

We live in frenetic times and everyone is so 'busy'. It is one word that is grossly overused. It trips off the tongue. 'BUSY' happens to be an acronym of the phrase '**B**uried **U**nder **S**atan's **Y**oke'. This is Satan's world, and he has got 8 billion people rushing around like headless chickens. Time not only appears to be speeding up, it really does feel like it is. Of course there are still 168 hours in a week and twenty-four hours in a day but they appear to fly by at an ever increasing rate.

The Book of Job was written before Genesis, even then, some thought that time went by too fast.

[6] My days are swifter than a weaver's shuttle, and are spent without hope. Job 7:6

[25] Now my days are swifter than a post: they flee away, they see no good. [26] They are passed away as the swift ships: as the eagle that hastes to the prey. Job 9:25-26

We can exercise our God given Power of 'Choice', unless we are so caught up with frenetically 'doing, doing', doing' that there is no time to spare for anything or anyone. With thought and consideration, we can decide to ***choose*** how to spend each moment and not lose sight of, or forget, how to savour the moment. Here is a part of the poem, 'Leisure' by William Henry Davies.

"What is this life if full of care we have no time to stand and stare

No time to stand beneath the boughs and stare as long as sheep or cows?

A poor life this if full of care we have no time to stand and stare".

It really does feel like most people have little or no time for other people. In days gone by, with no radio or television and no mobile phones, life was different. People did have more time for each other. Observe any four people at a table anywhere, and the chances are they will not be interacting with each other much at all, but will all be staring into the little screens of their 'god' which voraciously eats up their time. Or when they walk along the street with earphones and eyes glued on their 'iphone'. Do they realise just how much they are missing? Sadly, probably not.

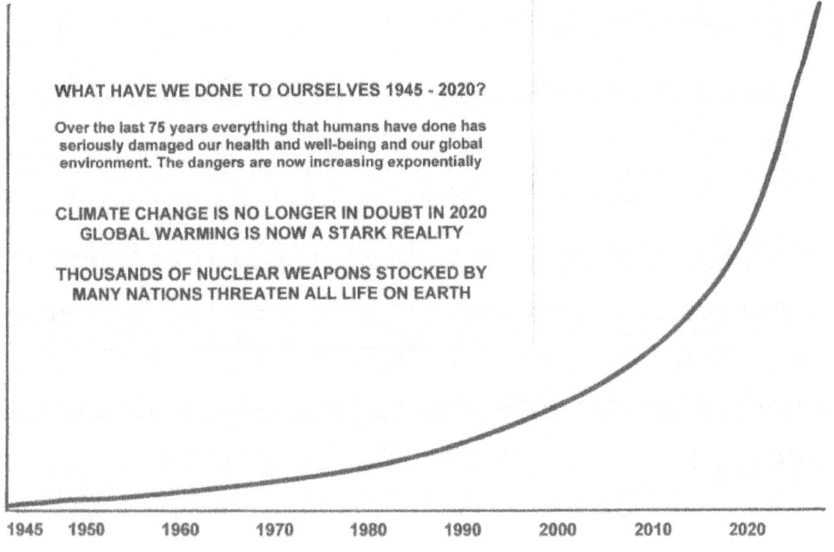

Take time to be with others

It is not at all easy to find people who are like-minded, because interest in God has waned dramatically and exponentially in the more than seventy-five years since He delivered us from World War I & II.

It now appears that there are very 'few' indeed that find the 'Way', but prayerfully we can always ask for God's help to find one or two. It is wonderful when that happens, as there is a promise when we do. Yes, this promise was given directly and specifically to Christ's disciples, and I choose to believe it applies to those who are earnestly seeking God in this age.

[20] *For where two or three are gathered together in my name, there I am in the middle of them." Matthew 18:20*

Certainly, one way to show love to others is to spend time with them.

[23] *This is his commandment, that we should believe in the name of his Son, Christ, Yah'Shua the Messiah, and love one another, even as he commanded. 1 John 3:23*

This phrase 'love one another' is one of the 'new' laws that Christ defined.

[34] *A new commandment I give to you, that you* ***love one another****. Just as I have* ***love****d you, you also* ***love one another****. By this everyone will know that you are my disciples, if you have* ***love*** *for* ***one another****." John 13:34-35*

The phrase also appears no fewer than twenty times in the New Testament.

On the other hand, Christians do have to be aware and careful of how closely we become involved with those who have little or no respect for God or His Word.

[14] Don't be unequally yoked (or be too involved) with unbelievers, for what fellowship do righteousness and iniquity (sin) have? Or what fellowship does light have with darkness? 2 Corinthians 6:14

That does not mean that we look down on or avoid others. On the contrary, we should exhibit all of the charateristics and fruits of the spirit towards everyone in our lives that we have anything to do with.

The foundation for our Christian life is Christ (Yah'Shua) the Rock, the Word.

There are about two billion people who call themselves Christian, but are they living their lives according to the wishes of their Leader Christ? (Yah'Shua Kristos) If they are not, Christ says to them:

[46] "Why do you call me, 'Lord, Lord,' and don't do the things which I say? Luke 6:46

The teachings and practices of almost all the thousands of denominations of Churchianity fall very short of the standards of thought and action required by Christ (Yah'Shua).

[47] Everyone who comes to me, and hears my words, and ***does*** *them, I will show you who he is like. [48] He is like a man building a house, who dug and went deep, and laid a foundation on the rock. Luke 6:47-48*

The earnest Christian student has to be a <u>doer</u>, not just a hearer. The called have the 'work' involved in building their Spiritual house on a strong Foundation.

[49] But he who hears, and doesn't do, is like a man who built a house on the earth (or sand) without a foundation, against which when the stream broke, and immediately it fell, and the ruin of that house was great." Luke 6:49

The 'Christianity' of 'Churchianity' is only partly built on the Rock of the Word, and much of it is built on the 'sand' of divisions, and the misapplication of the "wood, hay, and stubble" of incorrect human ideas and ungodly practices that makes it unstable and open to so much misunderstanding, and to be in so many fractured parts.

[11] For other foundation can no man lay than that is laid, which is Christ, Yah'Shua the Messiah. [12] Now if any man build upon this foundation (of) gold, silver, precious stones, (or) wood, hay, stubble; [13] each (the quality of every) man's work will (eventually) be revealed. 1 Corinthians 3:11-13

Our 'foundation' is the 'Rock' which is Christ (Yah'Shua), and our job is to build our Spiritual 'house' on that 'Rock' and with His help. We either build carelessly with 'wood, hay, and straw' by relying upon our own human ideas which are easily consumed by the 'fire' of trials or neglect; or we build with the spiritual treasures of gold, silver, and precious stones which are the jewels of knowledge, understanding and wisdom which have eternal value.

[3] And did all eat the same spiritual meat; [4] And did all drink the same spiritual drink: for they drank of that spiritual Rock that followed them: and that Rock was Christ. 1 Corinthians 10:3-4

We can be in touch daily with Christ, the 'Rock' the 'Builder', the 'Author and Finisher' of our Faith through prayer and the prayerful study of His Word.

[2] Looking unto Yah'Shua the Messiah the author and finisher of our faith; who for the joy that was set before him endured the cross, despising the shame, and is set down at the right hand of the throne of God. Hebrews 12:2

This book is about how to have and develop a direct personal relationship with God through the One and only Mediator He has given us, Christ, Yah'Shua the Messiah.

[5] For there is one God, and ***one*** *mediator between God and men, the man Christ, Yah'Shua the Messiah, 1 Timothy 2:5*

All man-made religions have those who claim to be 'mediators' between their members and God. Some even 'hear confessions', apportion penalties, and 'forgive sins'. No man can forgive or give 'absolution' for sin. There is only one Mediator, Christ, Yah'Shua the Messiah, and He is only the One who can forgive sin which He did for all by dying on the tree.

[18] For through him (Christ) we both have access by one Spirit unto the Father. [19] Now therefore you are no more strangers and foreigners, but fellowcitizens with the saints, and of the household of God; [20] And are built upon the foundation of the apostles and prophets, Christ, Yah'Shua the Messiah himself being the chief corner stone; [21] In whom all the building fitly framed together grow unto an holy temple in the Lord: [22] In whom you also

are builded together for an habitation of God through the Spirit. Ephesians 2:18-22

God, Christ, actually dwells in us, we who are collectively His Temple, He lives in us, in our physical bodies, in our minds and in our spirits; and true Christians are living their lives in His Son in his Heavenly Household. Those who have direct contact with God have a firm foundation which stands on Rock and has this seal,

[19] The Lord knows those who are his, and, "Let everyone who names the name of the Lord depart from unrighteousness. However God's firm foundation stands, having this seal, "The Lord knows those who are his and, let everyone who names the name of the Lord depart from unrighteousness (sin, breaking God's Laws)". 2 Timothy 2:19

As such, we have to be vigilant, resist sin, and trust that He presents us (present continuous) to the Father, spotless and without blame, with all our sins are forgiven.

[4] Whosoever commits sin transgresses (breaks) alsothe law: for sin (which is unrighteousness) is the transgression of the law. 1 John 3:4

Those who are 'in Christ' are in a state of continuous forgiveness, washed white as snow as far as God the Father is concerned. Even though we do fall short sometimes, our total confidence is in Christ's sacrifice, His forgiveness, and His Love for us.

[16] For God so loved the world that he gave his only begotten Son, that whosoever believes in him should not

perish (eternally), but have everlasting life. [17] For God sent not his Son into the world to condemn the world; but that the world through him might be saved. [18] He that believes on him is not condemned: John 3:16-18

All humans were once far from God, and at enmity with Him. Now as a 'pilgrim' on a journey with Him, that is no longer the case. It is imperative that Christians continue to follow His 'Way' with fortitude and diligent work.

[21] You, being in past times alienated and enemies in your mind in your evil deeds, [22] yet now he has reconciled in the body of his flesh through death, to present you holy and without defect and blameless before him (the Father), [23] if it is so that you continue in the faith, grounded and steadfast, and not moved away from the hope of the Good News which you heard, which is being proclaimed in all creation under heaven, of which I, Paul, was made a servant. Colossians 1:21-23

We need not fail, He is always with us.

[20b] Look, I am with you always, even to the end of the age." Amen (so be it) Matthew 28:20b

There is little peace in this present evil world, and Christians have a work to do, to be at peace with themselves and with others, and to be very thankful that we can be at peace with our Father in Heaven.

Now the Lord of peace himself give you peace always by all means. The Lord be with you all. 2 Thessalonians 3:16

The next chapter examines the extent to which we may be entering the beginning of the 'end of the age'.

CHAPTER 10

ARE WE APPROACHING THE 'END OF THE AGE'?

Are we approaching the 'Last Days' of this world as we know it now?

Are we approaching the 'Last Days' of this world as we know it now?

All over the world, in almost every country thousands, if not millions of people, are 'demonstrating' in the streets with varying degrees of aggression because they are unhappy or even angry with the government or the conditions where they live. Discontent is a pandemic malaise, and getting worse.

[1] This know also, that in the last days perilous times shall come. [2] For men shall be lovers of their own selves, covetous, boasters, proud, blasphemers, disobedient to parents, unthankful, unholy, [3] Without natural affection, trucebreakers, false accusers, incontinent, fierce, despisers of those that are good, [4] Traitors, heady, high-minded, lovers of pleasures more than lovers of God; [5] Having a form of godliness, but denying the power thereof: from such turn away. 2 Timothy 3:1-5

[13] But evil men and seducers shall wax worse and worse, deceiving, and being deceived. 2 Timothy 3:13

One way we can know that we are probably approaching the 'time of the end' of the world as we know it now, in 2020 is that all the adjectives in this passage apply so very aptly to the average human being more than at any time in history.

The 'me' generation, 'It's all about me', seriously disobedient kids, some young children are even murderers; a drastic universal lack of natural affection among people, violence and murder are rife. Most people are lovers of worldly pleasures while ignoring God, billions may appear to be 'religious', but by the way they live they actively deny the truths of God's Word, His Power and Sacrifice.

Many educated people in important positions are convinced that unless we make extensive, drastic global changes in the way we treat our planet, total collapse of our entire ecological environment is virtually imminent.

In early 2020 the United Nations and the National Geographical Society, and other eminent scientific bodies estimate that unless world governments take immediate action worldwide on a vast scale, humanity has only about twelve years before the inevitable ecological disaster takes place. If and when this happens, conditions on this earth will become very different, that is if indeed it will be possible for life as we know it to continue.

So, are the far-reaching climate changes immediately beginning to be addressed by governments or industries around the world? No, they are not, and it seems most unlikely that they will be. Most are talking about making some changes to the use of fossil fuels by 2030 or 2050, but currently doing little. The entire world is in the grip of very powerful leaders, self-seeking corrupt politicians, and those who run huge global businesses, virtually all of whom are motivated by lust for power, financial greed, or both.

On the other hand, an increasingly large number of apparently well-educated minds reject the whole notion of ecological collapse, they have pooh-poohed the whole idea of 'Global Warming' for decades. Despite the clear evidence that 'Climate Change' is affecting the world now, most still refuse to believe that it is due to human activities, like the destruction of vast areas of ancient forests which are essential to the maintenance of the balance of gases in our atmosphere.

Nor do scoffers agree that the profligate use of 'fossil' fuels has led to the increase of CO2 and greenhouse gases, or that this is the cause of the significant temperature rise of over 1°C in the oceans over the last few years. This rise means that more water vapour evaporates from the seas, which some meteorologists consider to be the cause of the more dramatically unprecedented extreme weather conditions, like cyclones and tornadoes that are currently occurring, which they think result in unprecedented floods in some places and severe drought in others. The majority just put this down to the natural sequence of the world heating up and cooling down over time. Here are some figures that might make some think again.

World daily oil consumption

There are 10,000 planes carrying 1.25 million people in the air all the time.

There were 1,000,000,000 (a trillion) cars in 2019, plus 250,000,000 more in 2020 but manufacturers are still producing more cars.

What is oil used for? Cars and trucks, heating, aviation fuel, and in the production of plastics, packaging, clothing, furniture, carpets, insulation, kitchen items, and food. 2 billion tons of waste go into landfill worldwide. Plastics are choking the oceans and killing large numbers of whales and other creatures that ingest the rubbish. This has also resulted in the reduction of ocean plankton that produce a large proportion of the Oxygen in the air.

Here are some eye-watering figures of **the amount of oil used on the earth every day, yes every day:**

1.4 trillion, 612 billion, 265 million, 214 thousand, 483 TONS PER DAY... An incomprehensibly large number.

Burning this oil in all its forms would use up the same weight of Oxygen from the air, and produce the same weight of Carbon Dioxide, and experts say that this has not affected the rise in the greenhouse effect of CO2. The increase in CO2 since 1850 almost exactly follows the exponential curve in the chart given earlier, as does the production of oil, gas, coal and other fuels, and in unbelievable millions of tons of waste.

It seems that the majority of the world is unaware of the mathematical certainty of the increasingly destructive nature revealed by the exponential curves we are currently observing in all the above situations which are adversely affecting the earth. If the baseline of that graph represents the last seventy-five years, the rate of the increase of problems is now in an almost vertical straight line. This illustrates that things are actually getting worse a lot faster than most people think.

Here are just a few examples of the damaging impact of the exponential growth over the last 75 years of the use and misuse and abuse of the facilities and the resources of the earth, and how our modern life in 2022 is being affected. In previous times, such changes have taken over hundreds of years to form, not in a few decades like older people have experienced in their lifetimes.

<u>Artificial fertilizers:</u> After the 1939-1945 world war, manufacturers of munitions, bullets, bombs, rockets, etc., had to find new markets for Nitrates and Phosphates used in explosives. So they targeted agriculture. This began the rapid change from organic to inorganic farming. The use of chemicals does make the plants grow faster and produce heavier crops, but that, and the practice of monoculture, depletes organic residues and essential trace minerals in the soil, and produces less healthy food. Pesticides and Herbicides leave poisonous residues in food which are a potential health hazard.

<u>Bread:</u> Wheat is sprayed with chemicals 11 times from planting, during growth and to harvesting. Seed bred for higher yields produce lower quality. Once a staple food,

wheat is now an intestinal irritant that leads to gross overweight and multiple allergies.

Milk from cows fed chemical grass and antibiotics is not natural. Pasteurisation destroys Vitamin C, locks in calcium, makes proteins indigestible, and causes allergies. Children tend to develop allergies and other sensitivities from consuming cow milk instead of being breast fed and weaned onto natural foods.

Herbivore animals were fed meat residues which led to Mad Cow Disease (BSE) and the growth hormones added to feed, made the meat affect people adversely. Chickens are fed their own recycled excrement mixed in their feed to reclaim protein to reduce costs. Terrified animals are slaughtered inhumanely This results in meat that is full of toxic poisons.

Disease is skyrocketing: Are GM and processed foods safe? Or are they and the astronomical exponential rise in Electromagnetic radiation, the cause of the increasing number of people affected by anxiety, autism, heart disease and cancers, diabetes, Parkinson's, Alzheimer's, depression, mental health problems that are all off the chart.

Overuse of pharmaceuticals: Anti-biotics no longer efficiently kill mutant organisms. Huge numbers of children are on Prozac for depression and anxiety, or on Ritalin made from cocaine for ADHD.

Compulsory inoculations

These are actually illegal under International Law which is accepted, but not enforced, by the United Nations, and against the law which forbids discrimination against people for any reason, and forced medical treatment on anyone. Inoculations of 'vaccines' may cause more problems than they solve.

At the end of the Second World War, the Nuremberg Trials held in November 1945 – October 1946, held to account doctors and others who had forced treatments onto the inmates of the Nazi death camps. This led to a new international law being created which states that doctors may not give any treatment to anyone without their consent.

Details of this law are recorded in The British Medical Journal No 7070 Volume 313: Page 1448, 7th December1996, which states:

"Introduction" (To the Nuremberg Law)

"The judgment by the war crimes tribunal at Nuremberg laid down 10 standards to which physicians must conform when carrying out experiments or giving treatments to human subjects in a new code that is now accepted worldwide.

This judgment established a new standard of ethical medical behaviour for the post World War II human rights era. Amongst other requirements, ***this document enunciates the requirement of voluntary informed consent of the human subject. The principle of voluntary informed consent protects the right of the individual to control his or her own body.***

This code also recognizes that the risk must be weighed against the expected benefit, and that unnecessary pain and suffering must be avoided This law is now being flouted by many governments around the world who are coercing those who they control by threats of restricting a number of personal freedoms, including social contact, travel, loss of employment, and financial hardship."

The Media and Covid19 and its 'variants'

For many decades, the public accepted that Influenza, or the 'Flu, was a fact of life. Nobody lived in abject fear of getting the 'flu'. A 'flu' vaccination was available, and some people chose to have it done, and many did not, it was a matter of personal preference. A different vaccination was available each year as the form of the virus changed or had a variant.

For the vast majority, getting the 'Flu' meant a few days in bed, aching with a temperature a few degrees above normal, thoroughly unpleasant, but very rarely life-threatening. A very small percentage of older people, most of whom had pre-existing conditions of one sort or another, died each year, on average about 2% of those who had the 'flu.

The intense media coverage of the Covid19 situation has been on every news bulletin since January/ February 2020 when the outbreak was first broadcast. It was suggested that the 'pandemic' spread of Covid19 originated in the 'wet markets' in Wuhan China where many different types of animal like bats, reptiles, and sea creatures were slaughtered for human consumption. Whether this is true or not is immaterial.

What is of crucial importance is the fact that the media focusses incessantly on the number of new ‘cases’ of the ‘pandemic’ which has grown quickly in many countries. The manner in which the information is presented is that it has spread a wave of deep fear among the population of many countries around the world. This ‘fear’ is very largely unfounded, as the Covid19 and its variants like ‘Delta’ and ‘Omicron’ have actually killed a very small percentage of people, in fact, far less than the ‘flu’ ever did.

They also refer to ‘deaths’ which have been recorded as being due to Covid19 whether they were caused by the virus or not. A careful analysis of the number of ‘cases’ and the ‘number of deaths’ will reveal that less than 1% of Covid19 cases results in death. This is less than the percentage of people who died from the ‘flu’.

The world has been paralysed with fear because of the way the problem of Covid19 has been exaggerated and presented. This ‘fear’ has been capitalised on by governments, who for thousands of years have been proud to be ‘democratic’, which was presented as a being: “Of the people, for the people, and by the people” even when it did not actually operate that way, it did permit a considerable degree of personal freedom.

Governments, almost overnight, have begun to impose ‘draconian’ measures, of laws or their application that are excessively harsh and severe in the restrictions of personal freedoms, in order to reduce the spread of the 'pandemic'. But has it?

One European country has begun to impose a monthly fine on those who refuse the 'jab'. Others are creating inoculation 'Passports'. Anyone who does not have one may not work in certain jobs, or obtain employment without one, be fired without notice, forbidden to enter any shop or business, or travel from one place to another. These are illegal laws.

There is another very sinister threat that is beginning to emerge around the world in 2021.

In 1935, Hitler used his 'Propaganda' minister to publicise that the Jewish people were 'disease .carriers, like rats' and were a health hazard. Within a short time the people of Germany began to persecute the Jewish people verbally, then physically, and ultimately to killing them.

Now in late 2021, previously supposedly 'democratic' governments, and the moguls who control what the media puts into its programs, are beginning to suggest that those who resist, refuse, or demonstrate against vaccination are a danger to the health of others.

This has already begun to spread division between the members of the public, working people, and even in families, where one has been 'fully vaccinated', and the other has exercised their right not to be vaccinated. Demonstrations, resentment, abuse, and even physical violence against the 'anti-vaxers' has begun to rear its ugly head. Where will this end?

Sugar consumption: In 1945 the government allowed ration was 60 gms (2oz) a week, now people eat 1 kilo, or 2.2lbs weekly, or more. The increasing sales of Coca Cola, and other sugary drinks has resulted in more spiralling numbers of diabetics, and contribute to the plague of obesity.

Food Additives: 10-20,000 are “permitted”, long-term effects are ‘not known’.

Huge expansion of ‘Fast food’ chains sell fattening foods that have caused a staggering rise in obesity and heart disease.

ENERGY: Huge increase in the use of electricity. Every current produces an associated magnetic field that affects our aura of bio-energy and causes stress on the body/mind. Rising atomic radiation is potentially damaging and can be lethal. We test nuclear bombs on our own planet!

Microwaves kill all life, render food lifeless, “foodless” food. Computers used to run at 12 MHz, now 1.5 GigaHz++ the higher the frequency the more harmful the radiation. Mobile phones 3G, 4G ARE dangerous, 5G even more so. Look into ‘earthing’ which can reduce the effect of radiation. See below.

Fossil Fuels: Profligate use of fossil fuels causes dangerous air pollution and the reduction of oxygen in the air from 38% to 19% in only 80 years. (!). And the weather changes that are now threatening the destruction of our ecosystem, causing ocean temperature to rise endangering major coastal cities worldwide.

Who is right? The argument between 'experts' is unlikely to be resolved any time soon. Meanwhile there are increasingly alarming scientific reports which insist that the changes in the climate, the temperature of the seas, the melting of the polar ice, and the extinction of species are all accelerating faster than previously thought.

The Flood happened. Christ said so several times

Over four thousand years ago, earth's population was warned of imminent destruction at the time of Noah's flood, but nobody took any notice then, and the governments and people of this present world are ignoring reality and not doing anything significant about the clear and very serious warnings now.

[5] For this they willingly are ignorant of, that by the word of God the heavens were of old, and the earth standing out of the water and in the water: [6] Whereby the world that then was, being overflowed with water, perished: 2 Peter 3:5,6

The world's population, governments, commerce, industry all show by inaction, resistance to change and apathy, that they are willingly ignorant of the increasing adverse consequences of our actions even though they are clearly leading us inexorably towards unprecedented ecological disaster on a global scale.

What can we do personally?

Think about some changes you can make in your life. Because so few will do, it will not make much impact on the global scene, but it will certainly help the individual.

Buy and take 'ACES': Vitamin A, Vitamin C, Antioxidants like Pine Bark, Grapeseed/Pycnogenols, Vitamin E, Chromium, Selenium and Zinc

Take trace minerals that are essential ingredients with which to build amino acids. Iodine helps the body deal with the vast increase in radiation. Use olive oils, not seed oils, they clog arteries. Contrary to popular thinking, saturated fats are good for you.

Reduce daily consumption 'CATS' - Coffee, Alcohol, Tea, and Sugar

Find ways on the Internet to reduce exposure to the invisible electromagnetic radiation from phones, microwave ovens, computers, and electrical devices which cause the production of free radicals that destroy our health slowly but surely. Look into personal 'grounding' or 'earthing', walk barefoot on soil or grass regularly.

Buy and use a water filter, preferably an under-sink variety. Our bodies are 70% water. **Only drink purified water,** not the diluted chlorinated sewage from the tap.

We have twice as much lymph as blood. Lymph feeds tissues and helps excrete toxic waste. Buy a rebounder, exercise gently, and pump your lymph for five minutes a day, or better still, several times a day for a minute or so.

Buy fresh food which will go bad and eat it before it does.

Avoid manufactured foods. If you look at it and you don't know what is in it, don't buy it and eat it!

TAKE BETTER CARE OF YOUR HEALTH WHILE YOU HAVE IT!

A time of trouble is prophesied, worse than anything in history, is coming.

All the above information about the current state of the world in 2022 are strong indications that we are indeed approaching beginning of this time. Worldwide troubles are bad now, but there are worse times ahead.

There are three chapters in Matthew 24, Mark 11, and Luke 21 which include the warnings Christ gives of a time of unprecedented trouble coming on earth shortly before He returns. These warnings specifically directly concerned troubles in the country of Israel, and particularly centred on the area of Jerusalem and the Temple. There is no Temple in Jerusalem now, so Christ's dire prediction concerning the area and the Temple will not happen until one is built sometime in the future.

However Christ's warnings describe many types of problems that also apply to the whole world, and indeed it is easy to observe that there are already global conditions that now threaten life as we know it on earth.

Is this scare-mongering? No, it is not. The following information is not included in this book to frighten or worry people. If someone sees a person about to step into the road in front of a speeding truck, they would want instantly to warn them before they took the fatal step. Those who understand the absolute certainty of prophecy, and know without doubt that they will be fulfilled when it is time, are obliged to warn those who will listen. Forewarned is forearmed. Be comforted that you know that trouble is coming and be prepared for it.

Christ issued these warnings of specific troubles that already apply to us today and will escalate in the next few years. Christ, Yah'Shua the Messiah, was asked by His disciples, what would be the sign of His Second Coming and of the end of the age. The first thing Christ warned about was deception.

[4] And Yah'Shua the Messiah answered and said to them, Take great care that no man deceive you [5] For many shall come in my name, saying, I am Christ; and shall deceive many. Matthew 24:4-5

Christ's first warning is for everyone to be wary of deception in all its forms. We need to be aware that governments, global companies, newscasts, media and television, social media, advertising, religious organisations, and from people in general is pandemic. All this is much more serious than the so-called Covid19 'pandemic', which in fact kills fewer than the 'flu by far, and mostly only the aged who had previous existing conditions died. The real dangers of being deceived by false religions that claim they speak for Him when they do not are all around us. Self-deception is also a problem for many who think they are on the right track with God when they are not. For this reason there are many warnings from the Bible in this book about forms of 'Churchianity' and the religions of this world. Next...

Wars, earthquakes, famines and diseases of increasing ferocity

[6] *And ye shall hear of wars and rumours of wars: see that ye be not troubled: for all these things must come to pass, but the end is not yet.* [7] *For nation shall rise against nation, and kingdom against kingdom: and there shall be famines, and pestilences, and earthquakes, in many different places.* [8] *All these are the beginning of sorrows. Matthew 24:6-8*

Throughout history there have always been wars, famines, disease, pestilence attacking crops and earthquakes, but is it not obvious to everyone that all these things are on the increase? Is it just better reporting as some suggest? No it is not, all these horrendous conditions are definitely on the increase.

World War 1 in which up to 40 million people died was famously said to be "The War to end all wars". It was not. WW1 was followed only twenty years later by WW2 during which 60 million people died. There has been a continuous stream of wars ever since. More people died as a result of war in the 20th century than in all the preceding 19 centuries. Human beings do not learn from history.

What is the 'Great Tribulation'? Unprecedented world problems

[21] *For then shall be great tribulation, such as was not since the beginning of the world to this time, no, nor ever*

shall be. [22] And except those days should be shortened, there should no flesh (human or animal would) be saved (alive): but for the elect's sake those days shall be shortened. Matthew 24:21-22.

When Christ warned of a period some time ahead of us, He made a prophetic prediction which could not have been fulfilled until after 1945. Christ said that things could get so bad that no flesh would survive it. The advent of nuclear weapons signalled the beginning of that possibility.

There are now over 15,000 nuclear bombs stored by several nations, detonation of only a few of which could cause the fulfilment of that prophecy that stated, "Unless those days were foreshortened, no life in the world would survive". It is comforting to know that for the 'elect's sake' those days will be shortened. Who are the 'elect'? They are the 'few there be that find it', that really truly believe in Christ, and live and practice His Way of life in a personal relationship with Him.

All these predictions are not the ramblings of some crackpot. This is Christ, Yah'Shua the Messiah talking, the Word who Created the heavens and the earth, speaking to us today through His Word, and we can be sure His words are true. We had better heed these warnings.

False 'Christs' will appear, the world will think Christ has returned

[23] "Then if any man tells you, 'Behold, here is the Christ!' or, 'There!' don't believe it. [24] For there will arise false

Christs, and false prophets, and they will show great signs and wonders, so as to lead astray, if possible, even the chosen ones. [25] *"Look, I have told you beforehand.* [26] *"If therefore they tell you, 'Behold, he is in the wilderness,' don't go out; or 'Behold, he is in the inner rooms,' don't believe it.* [27] *For as the lightning flashes from the east, and is seen even to the west, so will the coming of the Son of Man be. Matthew 24:23-27*

There may not be many 'false Christs' about, but more than two billion people around the world have been taken in by religions that claim to preach Christ and His way of life called Christianity, but the vast majority of these denominations do not teach or practice Christ's Way of life as has already been covered in this book.

The coming false Christ is the 'man of sin', the 'beast', and false prophet

However, there is coming a time when a man will appear and claim that he is Christ the Messiah. His arrival will be accompanied by dramatic signs and wonders in the heavens and all over the earth. He will sit in the new Temple that will be built in Jerusalem claiming that he is God. Because of the dramatic signs and the miracles that he performs, this man will convince the entire population of the earth that he is actually Christ. He will change times and seasons (the world calendar), he will institute a revival of a version of God's Laws and people will have to observe them under penalty of death.

The world population will be subjugated by the Beast and the False Prophet who will enforce regulations about work and finance, and even about the way people think and express themselves. Freedom of speech, and those who agitate for 'people's rights' will not be tolerated. Nobody will be able to buy and sell without a special 'mark' in the forehead (mind) and in the hand (work).

[16] He causes all, the small and the great, the rich and the poor, and the free and the slave, to be given marks on their right hands, or on their foreheads; [17] and that no one would be able to buy or to sell, unless he has that mark, which is the name of the beast or the number of his name. Revelation 13:16-17

Many have wondered what the 'Mark of the Beast' will be. Strange as it may seem, it will partly be obedience to God's Mosaic Laws, and also possibly an enforced vaccination imprinted with a 'marker' that identifies each person. The false Christ will demand that everyone must obey the Laws of God given to Moses in the Old Testament. So he may enforce the keeping of the Sabbath, Holy days, clean and unclean meats and other Laws of God regarding physical rituals. Those that are obedient will have the 'Mark of the Beast'. Keeping and obeying these Physical Laws will not be a hardship for those that observe them, as part of their religious conduct in obedience to those who rule over us which is commanded of Christians. The 'Mark' may also involve other forms of control over money and health.

Although the neither the 'Beast' nor the 'False Prophet' are on earth yet in 2022. Many are already unable to work or buy or sell due to governments denying personal freedoms, putting people into 'lockdown' and other draconian restrictions. Some think what is happening is like the 'Mark of the Beast, it may look like that, but of course it is not. The issuing of 'passports' to people who are 'fully vaccinated' which enables them to work, enjoy pubs, clubs, and sporting events. Those who resist the Covid19 inoculations cannot do any of these things. They lose their employment, even nurses and others in the health sector, and those in the hospitality industry are put out of work. This is a type of what is to come.

True Christians need have no fear of persecution.

Anyone who chooses to fall in line with the new regime and observe these physical rituals will be safe from persecution. Christians are required to submit to those who have rule over them,

Since Christ's death and resurrection, Christians are no longer required to keep those Mosaic physical laws, but there is nothing wrong with doing so if one is required to keep them in order to have the 'Mark' of approval required to buy and sell.

People who do not obey his dictates, and do not have the 'Mark' will be punished by being unable to buy or sell necessities, and possibly some will even be put to death.

The whole of Revelation is figurative and no doubt some parts also have literal aspects. It is not an easy book to understand, but it is important to be aware of all the predictions is contains.

How will Christians be able to tell that the 'Christ' is false?

We can thank our Friend and Saviour Christ that the elect will not be deceived. From studying God's Word, they know the truth, that when Christ does return, everyone on earth will see Him coming with millions of His angels.

[27] For as the lightning comes out of the east, and shines even unto the west; so shall also the coming of the Son of man be. Matthew 24:27

There is another way the True Christians will realise that the Beast is the False Christ, they will still be in their physical bodies. As when the real Christ, the Messiah arrives, those who are true Christians will experience their physical body rise to meet Him in the air, and will be changed into spirit.

[16] For the Lord himself will descend from heaven with a shout, with the voice of the archangel and with God's trumpet. The dead in Christ will rise first, [17] then we who are alive, who are left, will be caught up together with them in the clouds, to meet the Lord in the air. So we will be with the Lord forever. [18] Therefore comfort one another with these words. 1 Thessalonians 4:16-18

Keep this in mind every day. It is our assurance that true Christians can avoid being deceived by the false 'Christ'

[30] And then shall appear the sign of the Son of man in heaven: and then shall all the tribes of the earth mourn, and they shall see the Son of man coming in the clouds of heaven with power and great glory. [31] And he shall

send his angels with a great sound of a trumpet, and they shall gather together his elect from the four winds, from one end of heaven to the other. Matthew 24:30-31

True Christians will be gathered together from all over the world, and even from outer space, and at the sound of the Trumpet, will rise to meet Christ in the air as He arrives and circles the earth with millions of His angels.

Those who find it hard to live the 'Way of Christ' until all these things come to pass, but keep going diligently on the 'Way' despite all the hardships, will be very well rewarded for their faithfulness and their 'works'. They will spend eternal life with the King, Christ, Yah'Shua the Messiah and God the Father.

[5] *And from Christ YahwehShua the Messiah, who is the faithful witness, and the first begotten of the dead, and the prince of the kings of the earth. Unto him that loved us, and washed us from our sins in his own blood,*
[6] *And has made us kings and priests unto God and his Father; to him be glory and dominion for ever and ever.*
Amen. [7] *Behold, he comes with clouds; and every eye shall see him, and they also which pierced him: and all kindreds of the earth shall wail because of him. Even so, Amen. Revelation 1:5-7*

The next chapter shows why Christianity is truly unique, unlike any other religion, belief system or form of worship of our Creator God.

CHAPTER 11

TRUE CHRISTIANITY IS UNIQUE

ALL THE RELIGIONS IN THE WORLD ARE HUMAN IDEAS ABOUT GOD. CHRISTIANTY IS GOD'S PLAN FOR HUMAN BEINGS BY GOD HIMSELF.

TRUE CHRISTIANITY IS BASED ON BOTH EXTERNAL AND INTERNAL EVIDENCE AND PROOFS THAT PROVE ITS AUTHENTICITY

There are two billion people on our planet who 'believe' and have 'faith' in Christ. However, if most of them were asked for the evidence that proves that God exists, that Christ is His Son, and that the Bible is God's Word, would they be able to offer the questioner those proofs? Unlikely! Very few even read, let alone study the Bible.

This book claims to contain those proofs, and many of them have already been given. Now here from the Bible is more solid evidence that God's Word is 'The Truth'.

[17] Sanctify (set them apart) them through thy truth: thy word is truth. John 17:17

The Bible is chock full of **evidence and testimony** that was inspired by God to be written down by eyewitnesses to Christ's work. All this evidence would be accepted in a court of law as being 'without reasonable doubt', and therefore would provide a sure foundation for any Christian on which to base their true 'Belief' and 'Faith' which are gifts from God.

There are two types of evidence presented in a court of law, direct and indirect.

Direct evidence comes from eyewitnesses and physical evidence, and indirect evidence is that which is given by those who have been told the facts by eyewitnesses or who have seen physical evidence at the scene of the events.

Why do Christians need to establish a case of solid evidence supported by eyewitnesses to undergird their belief? As Christians, it is our responsibility to establish our own 'belief' and 'faith' on the firm foundation of irrefutable evidence in order to give us the confidence to be a light to the world, and to be able to give an answer ***to those who ask*** a reason for the hope that lies within us.

[15] But sanctify (set apart as Holy) the Lord God in your hearts. Always be ready to give an answer to everyone who asks you a reason concerning the hope that is in you, with humility and fear, 1 Peter 3:15

Notice: Give an answer to those who ask. It is not a good idea to offer information to others unless they ask.

Many Biblical passages testify to the evidence of Christ's works

This next passage in the 5th chapter of John, Christ states very clearly that His 'testimony' is not based on His own unsubstantiated words about himself which would be inadmissible or attacked in court, but on the Works He performs for all to observe and witness.

31 "If I testify about myself, my witness is not valid. 32 It is another who testifies about me. I know that the testimony which he testifies about me is true. 33 You have sent (questions) to John, and he has testified to the truth. 34 But the testimony which I receive is not from man. However, I say these things that you may be saved. 35 He (John the Baptist) was the burning and shining lamp, and you were willing to rejoice for a while in his light. 36 But the testimony which I have is greater than that of John, for the works which the Father gave me to accomplish, the very works that I do, testify about me, that the Father has sent me. 37 The Father himself, who sent me, has testified about me. John 5:31-37

So here Christ gives witness testimony, or testifies, to the evidence and proof concerning His actions ten times in a short passage. His declaration of truth is not about Himself, as that would not be valid or acceptable evidence, but that it is His Works, the miracles He performs for all to see that demonstrate the proof of Who He Is and would be proof in any court.

Some of the biggest religions of this world, followed by billions, are based on human beings who claimed they did have 'inspiration' or 'teaching' direct from God

Himself. There is no actual external evidence or reliable proof that those people had that experience, we have only their word for it. This does not stop billions from worshipping those individuals and their teachings.

The vast majority of Christians do not have the confident power of this legal evidence in God's Word living in them either. Their 'belief' and 'faith' is more often based on an emotional feeling, or a set of teachings that they have embraced as a result of listening to fallible human beings of some religious organisation. Here in John 5, Christ further addresses this very problem.

37 The Father himself, who sent me, has testified about me. *You have neither heard his voice at any time, nor seen his form.* 38 *You don't have his word living in you, because you don't believe him whom he sent.* 39 *"You search (superficially) the Scriptures, because you think that in them you have eternal life; and these are they which* testify *about me.* 40 *Yet you will not come to me, that you may have life.* 41 *I don't receive glory from men.*

42 *But I know you that you don't have God's love in yourselves.* 43 *I have come in my Father's name, and you don't receive me. (Yet) If another (person, priest, minister) comes in his own name, you will receive him.*

44 *How can you believe, who receive glory from one another, and you don't seek the glory that comes from the only God? John 5:37-44*

These statements infuriated the Jewish authorities, but they could not refute them.

Christ addresses those who are Christian in name only

Christ speaks vehemently today to 'nominal Christians', which is to those who are Christians in name only, He says in effect, "You do not have God's Word living in you. You may read the Bible, go to church, but you do not have the Love of God in you, how can you believe in Me properly when you get your beliefs from one another (or from ministers of religious organisations) and you don't seek the glory (and the Truth) that comes from the (the Word of the) only God"?

[46] And why do you call me, Lord, Lord, and do not the things which I say? Luke 6:46

The vast majority in 'Churchianity' do not walk the talk. Ministers and evangelists preach to thousands; claim many 'give their heart to the Lord' as a result of their sermons; lay hands on the sick, and claim healing; start missions for lepers; build schools for deprived children in foreign countries; and claim to perform all kinds of charitable acts 'in the name of Jesus', but to how many of them will the following verses apply? Almost all of 'Churchianity' does.

[21] "Not everyone who says to me, 'Lord, Lord,' will enter into the Kingdom of Heaven, but he who does the will of my Father who is in heaven. [22] Many will tell me in that day, 'Lord, Lord, didn't we prophesy in your name, in your name cast out demons, and in your name do many mighty works?' [23] Then I will tell them, "I never knew you. Depart from me, you who work iniquity (evil and sin)." Matthew 7:21-23

Is it time to make a reality check on your life?

If you go to religious services, have you checked the origins of the teachings and practices of the denomination you attend? Have you researched the origins of the special events like Christmas, Easter and Hallowe'en? Or the symbolism of the architecture of the building? Do you think it is important? God most certainly does.

[1] "Now, you priests (originally directed to Levites, but this applies to anyone who claims to represent God), this commandment is for you. [2] If you will not listen, and if you will not take it (my Laws) to heart, to give glory to my name," says Yahweh (God), "then I will send the curse on you, and I will curse your blessings. Indeed, I have cursed them already, because you do not take it to heart. [3] Behold, I will rebuke your offspring, and will spread dung on your faces, even the dung of your feasts; and you will be taken away with it. Malachi 2:1-3

Nobody can choose how they worship God by making up their own 'feast' days or religious events, because God regards pagan and heathen practices as 'dung' which He will figuratively spread on the faces of those who attend them. God cannot make it any plainer about how strongly He feels than that.

God has laid out how to worship Him in His Word the Bible, and those ways are the **only** ways that are acceptable to Him.

'Good works', especially in regard to worship done by our own human power, however sincerely, without obedience to God's Will for us as directed in His Word, may even be seen by God as iniquity, and that is sin.

Christ was a High Priest and taught in the Temple

Remember that Christ was a High Priest who taught in the Temple, so the Jewish authorities more than knew Who they were talking about, they had heard Him preach many times in the Temple beginning when He was twelve years old.

40 And the child grew, and waxed strong in spirit, filled
with wisdom: and the grace of God was upon him. 41 Now
his parents went to Jerusalem every year at the feast
of the passover. 42 And when he was twelve years old,
they went up to Jerusalem after the custom of the feast.
43 And when they had fulfilled the days (of unleavened
bread), as they returned, the child Yah'Shua the Messiah
stayed behind in Jerusalem; and Joseph and his mother
knew not of it. 44 But they, supposing him to have been in
the company, went a day's journey; and they looked for
him among their kinsfolk and acquaintance. 45 And when
they found him not, they turned back again to Jerusalem,
seeking him. 46 And it came to pass, that after three days
they found him in the Temple, sitting in the midst of the
doctors, (Strong's (1320) dida>skalov, — did-as'- kal-
os; from (1321) (dida>skw); an instructor (genitive or
special): doctor [of the Law], master, teacher. At 12 years
old, Christ, Yah'Shua the Messiah was addressing the
very highest Jewish authorities in the land.) both hearing
them, and asking them questions. 47 And all that heard
him were astonished at his understanding and answers.

48 And when they (His parents) saw him, they were amazed: and his mother said unto him, Son, why have you dealt with us like this? behold, your (legal) father and I have looked for you sorrowing. 49 And he said unto them, How is it that you looked for me? did you not know that I must be about my Father's business? 50 And they did not understand the saying which he spoke unto them. Luke 2:40-50

For Christ to even be allowed into the Temple, let alone amaze the top Jewish authorities there, shows they knew His Rank, Status, and witnessed the incredible degree of the maturity of His Knowledge, Understanding and Wisdom that Jesus Yah'Shua had developed, even at such a young age as twelve.

Later in His life, Christ was teaching in the Temple and devout Jews wanted to know if He really was the Messiah, so He explained that His testimony was the evidence that proved His works.

24 The Jews therefore came around him and said to him, "How long will you hold us in suspense? If you are the Christ, tell us plainly." 25 Yah'Shua the Messiah answered them, "I told you, and you don't believe. The works that I do in my Father's name, these ***testify*** *about me. 26 But you don't believe, because you are not of my sheep, as I told you. 27 My sheep hear my voice (as they read My Words in the Bible), and I know them, and they follow me. 37 If I don't do the works of my Father, don't believe me. 38 But if I do them, though you don't believe me, believe the* ***works (the evidence)****, that you may* *know and believe that* ***(they prove that)*** *the Father is in me, and I in the Father." John 10:24-27, 37-38*

Christ's true sheep do not follow human ideas, they follow **His** testimony and the evidence in His Word, and also from inspiration from their direct connection to God through prayer and meditation.

[6] Yah'Shua the Messiah said to him, "I am the way, the truth, and the life. No one comes to the Father, except through me. [7] If you had known me, you would have known my Father also. From now on, you know him, and have seen him." [8] Philip said to him, "Lord, show us the Father, and that will be enough for us." [9] Yah'Shua the Messiah said to him, "Have I been with you such a long time, and do you not know me, Philip? He who has seen me has seen the Father. How do you say, 'Show us the Father?' [10] Don't you believe that I am in the Father, and the Father in me? The words that I tell you, I speak not from myself; but the Father who lives in me does his works. [11] Believe me that I am in the Father, and the Father in me; or else believe me for the very works' sake. John 14:6-11

Christ's disciples and John the Baptist doubted and needed evidence

Philip, one of Christ's own disciples needed more evidence, so once again, Christ points to the evidence of His works that the Father does through Him.

In the book of Acts, evidence of events known to the public abound about Christ's work that prove Who He Was.

1 The first book I wrote, Theophilus, concerned all that Yah'Shua the Messiah began both to do and to teach, 2 until the day in which he was received up, after he had given commandment through the Holy Spirit to the apostles whom he had chosen. 3 To these he also showed himself alive after he suffered, ***by many proofs.*** **(Please read the historic Appendix for more proofs)** *appearing to them over a period of forty days, and speaking about God's Kingdom. Acts 1:1-3*

After His resurrection and ascension to and His acceptance by the Father, and His reinstatement as God the Word, Christ showed many 'proofs'. Forty days is often used in the Bible as a period of emphasis.

2 Now when John (the Baptist) heard in the prison the works of Christ, he sent two of his disciples 3 and said to him, "Are you he who comes, or should we look for another?" Matthew 11:2-3

Even John who had baptised Christ, and heard God say, "This is my Son in whom I am well pleased" Matthew 3:17, was beginning to have doubts. So did Christ say, "Tell John, to pray about it, to have more faith, or just trust God?" No, He did not. Christ says, ***"Go and tell John about My works, they are the evidence that I am He".***

4 Yah'Shua the Messiah answered them (John's two disciples), "Go and tell John the things which you hear and see: 5 the blind receive their sight, the lame walk, the lepers are cleansed, the deaf hear, the dead are raised up, and the poor have good news preached to them. Matthew 11:4-5

Christ here is quoting Isaiah 35:5-6, and 61:1-4 which they would be very familiar with, this **proved** that He was fulfilling prophecy written 400 years previously.

This is confirmed in Luke 7 who gives a second witness account of the event in God's Word.

[21] In that hour he cured many of diseases and plagues and evil spirits; and to many who were blind he gave sight. [22] Yah'Shua the Messiah answered them, "Go and tell John the things which you have seen and heard: that the blind receive their sight, the lame walk, the lepers are cleansed, the deaf hear, the dead are raised up, and the poor have good news preached to them". Luke 7:21-22

Christ said, believe the actual evidence of My miraculous works. Christ goes on to inspire John, the disciple Jesus loved, to write:

*[30] Therefore Yah'Shua the Messiah did many other signs in the presence of his disciples (**for evidence**), which are not written in this book; [31] but these are written, that you may believe (in the evidence) that Christ, Yah'Shua the Messiah, is the Son of God, and that believing (in the evidence) you may have life in his name. John 20:30-31`*

Christ through John is emphasising the need to base their 'belief' on **'evidence'**, not on a fervent religious hope or an emotional feeling.

*[20] Not for these only do I pray, but for those also (Christians now) who will (in the future) believe in me through **(the evidence of)** their word, [21] that they may all be one; even as you, Father, are in me, and I in you, that*

they also may be one in us; that the world may believe ***(the evidence of eyewitnesses)*** *that you sent me. John 17:20-21*

True Christians now who have the Holy Spirit of God, and are 'in Christ' will have the testimony of God's Word, its evidence and proof, flowing in their minds and their hearts.

[26] *"When the Counsellor (the Comforter, the Holy Spirit) has come, whom (that) I will send to you from the Father, the Spirit of truth, who proceeds from the Father, he (it) will* ***testify*** *about me.* [27] *You will also* ***testify,*** *because you have been with me from the beginning. John 15:26-27*

We, in this era, were not there at the beginning with Christ, but we do have the testimony of the many eyewitnesses that were with Him from the beginning to the end of His ministry.

In Acts 3 the Apostle Peter attests to the factual evidence of Christ's death and resurrection.

[14] *But you (Jews) denied the Holy and Righteous One and asked for a murderer to be granted to you,* [15] *and killed the Prince of life, whom God raised from the dead, to which we are (eye)* ***witnesses.*** *Acts 3:14-15*

In Acts 4, Peter and John who were eyewitnesses to His death, resurrection, and His ascension and change into Spirit, gave their evidence to the High Priest and all the Jewish authorities.

[19] But Peter and John answered them, "Whether it is right in the sight of God to listen to you rather than to God, judge for yourselves, [20] for we can't help telling the ***<u>things which we saw and heard.</u>****"... [33] With great power, the apostles gave their* ***<u>testimony</u>*** *(****eyewitness evidence****) of the resurrection of the Lord Yah'Shua the Messiah. Great grace was on them all. Acts 4:19, 23*

Peter gives more evidence in Acts 10:

[39] We (Peter and the other disciples who were there) are **witnesses** *of everything he did both in the country of the Jews, and in Jerusalem; whom they also killed, hanging him on a tree. [40]* ***God raised him up the third day, and gave him to be revealed, [41] not to all the people, but to <u>witnesses</u> who were chosen before by God, to us, who ate and drank with him after he rose from the dead.*** *[42] He commanded us to preach to the people and to testify that this is he who is appointed by God as the Judge of the living and the dead. [43] All the prophets* ***testify*** *about him, that through his name everyone who believes in him will receive remission of sins. Acts 10:39-43*

The **evidence** of the Messiah, Christ's resurrection that is in God's Holy Bible is very clear. In a lifetime of sermons, it is unlikely anyone would have heard anyone mention this subject of 'evidence', as 'Churchianity' does not teach about it.

Christ's resurrection, after the excruciating suffering of His ghastly death, was an event uniquely attested to by secular historians of that time and even more in Acts.

[2] Paul, as was his custom, went in to them, and for three Sabbath days reasoned with them from the Scriptures (the prophecies of the Old Testament), [3] explaining and demonstrating that the Christ had to suffer and rise again from the dead, and saying, "This Yah'Shua the Messiah whom I proclaim to you, is the Christ." Acts 17:2-3

Christ could not have possibly 'managed' in any way His treatment, and the manner of His demise, so as to fulfil all the specific details of His life and death that are foretold in the prophecies we can read in the Old Testament today. All **<u>those prophecies are evidence and proof in themselves as they came to pass exactly as they suggest.</u> In two thousand ears they have <u>never</u> been refuted by any 'scholar' or any sceptic.**

[14] Just as many were astonished at you, his (facial) appearance was (so badly) marred more than any man (that He was unrecognisable), and his form (whole body) more than (any of) the sons of men [15] so he will cleanse (forgive) many nations. Isaiah 52:14-15

In Isaiah 53 there are many more details prophesied about Christ's life which are somewhat difficult fully to understand because of the figurative language, but reveal aspects of His life that are not commonly known. For instance:

Christ was not born, and did not grow up strong and healthy, because He carried the effects of our diseases.

[2] he grew up like a tender plant, a root out of dry ground. He has no good looks or majesty, there is no

beauty that any should desire him. [3] He was despised and rejected by men, a man of suffering and acquainted with sickness and disease. He was despised as one from whom men hide their face; and we didn't respect him. [4] Surely he has borne our sickness and carried our suffering; yet we considered him plagued, struck by God, and afflicted. Isaiah 53:2-4

A study of the entire chapter is shockingly enlightening.

The evidence of many eyewitnesses prove Christ's works

It is also interesting that the books of the Canon of the New Testament were assembled around 98 A.D., under Christ's direct supervision by three Apostles, Peter, James and John who were eyewitnesses to everything Christ did during His ministry and spent time with Him after His resurrection. Their evidence is positive proof.

[24]This is the disciple (John) who ***testifies*** *about these things, and wrote these things. We know that his* ***witness*** *is true. [25] There are also many other things which Yah'Shua the Messiah did, which if they would all be written, I suppose that even the world itself wouldn't have room for the books that would be written. John 21:24-25*

Luke was not an eyewitness, and he makes this clear, however he was a highly respected historian. He states that all he writes, (that Christ wrote through him) is accurately stated by him, **reported from those who were actual eyewitnesses.**

[1] Since many have undertaken to set in order a narrative concerning those matters which have been

fulfilled among us, [2] even as those who from the beginning were **eyewitnesses** *and servants of the word delivered them to us, [3] it seemed good to me also,* ***having traced the course of all things accurately from the first,*** *to write to you in order, most excellent Theophilus; [4] that you might know* ***the certainty*** *concerning the things in which you were instructed. Luke 1:1-4*

Paul became an Apostle because Christ appeared to Him directly, and this was accepted by all the Apostles. Christ inspired him to write fourteen books of the New Testament which Christ led Peter and John to include in the New Testament Canon. In Acts 26, Paul tells the king of his appointed commission from Christ.

[15] "I said, 'Who are you, Lord?' "He said, 'I am Yah'Shua the Messiah whom you are persecuting. [16] But arise, and stand on your feet, for I have appeared to you for this purpose: ***to appoint you a servant and a witness both of the things which you have seen, and of the things which I will reveal to you;*** *[17] delivering you from the people, and from the Gentiles, to whom I send you, [18] to open their eyes, that they may turn from darkness to light and from the power of Satan to God, that they may receive remission of sins and an inheritance among those who are sanctified by faith in me.' Acts 26:15-18*

Paul had the complete and the total authority of Christ who inspired him to write every word of his epistles.

King Agrippa was very impressed at Paul's words, because he knew all about the events that led up to Christ's death, and clearly knew about His resurrection.

[26] "For the king knows of these things, to whom also I speak freely. For I am persuaded that none of these things is hidden from him, for this has not been done in a corner. [27] King Agrippa, do you believe the prophets? I know that you believe." [28] Agrippa said to Paul, "With a little persuasion are you trying to make me a Christian?" Acts 26:26-28

The events of Christ's death, resurrection and ascension were known worldwide at the time to all the eminent people. Even Caesar, who changed the world calendar as a result, made 'Christianity' the official religion of the Roman Empire, but by this time it had become the deadly mixture of truth and error that it has remained to this day.

King Agrippa did not deny that he did indeed know these things. In Corinthians Christ inspires Paul to say of himself:

[3] For I (Paul) delivered to you first of all that which I also received: that Christ died for our sins according to the Scriptures, [4] that he was buried, that he was raised on the third day according to the Scriptures, [5] and that he appeared to Cephas, then to the twelve. [6] Then he appeared to over five hundred brothers at once, most of whom remain until now, but some have also fallen asleep. [7] Then he appeared to James, then to all the apostles, [8] and last of all, as to the child born at the wrong time, he appeared to me also. [9] For I am the least of the apostles, who is not worthy to be called an apostle, because I persecuted the assembly of God. [10] But by the grace of God I am what I am. 1 Corinthians 15:3-10

Paul states that more than five hundred people saw the risen Christ. **They were all eyewitnesses of the evidence of His resurrection**. It is a historical fact that has been attested to by many secular writers of that era. As already stated, the world's Calendar was controlled by the Roman Caesars and changed from B.C. to A.D. Another momentous **evidence** of the impact that Christ's life, death, and resurrection had on the world.

Many of the events recorded in the Old Testament by the Prophets were also prophetic. Prophecies almost always have had more than one fulfilment, and there is no doubt that we are seeing more of them coming to pass in our time now.

There are many other texts written in the second century A.D., that contain truths about Christ's ministry, but they were written by people like Quadratus of Athens in A.D.129, Justin Martyr A.D. 165, Marcus Minucius Felix 197 A.D., and many others who were not eyewitnesses of those events they write about. That is a good reason why these books are not part of the Canon. They may be fine to read about details of historical interest that they write, but they are not inspired.

True Christianity rests on God's evidence, not on human reasoning. The world puts its trust in man's ideas: Philosophy, Science, Religion

[16] For we didn't follow **cunningly devised fables** (which are still an large part of the fabric of beliefs of 'Churchianity') when we made known to you the power and coming of our Lord Christ, Yah'Shua the Messiah, but

we were eye witnesses (on the mount of transfiguration) of his majesty. 2 Peter 1:16

There are two ways of thinking, God's Way, and Satan's way. From the moment that Adam and Eve took the forbidden fruit, they lost sight of God's Way, and their eyes and minds were opened to Satan's way. This way of evil thinking has led to all the problems of humankind ever since. The 'cunningly devised fables' Peter refers to are those concocted by human minds polluted by Satan's thinking and 'wisdom'.

The thinking of the whole world is not based on God's Knowledge, Understanding and Wisdom, but on Satanic reasoning using human ideas of philosophy, science and religion. Satan is the author of confusion, God is the author of peace.

Philosophy, a Greek word meaning love of human knowledge, pursuit of human wisdom;

*[8] Beware lest any man spoil you through **philosophy** (Strong's 5385) and vain deceit, after the tradition of men, after the rudiments of the world, and not after Christ. Colossians 2:8*

(5385) filosofi>a, — fil-os-of-ee'-ah; from **(5386)** (filo>sofov); "philosophy", i.e. (special) Jewish sophistry: philosophy.

The English word 'sophistry' is defined as 'the use of clever but false arguments, especially with the intention of deceiving'. To be 'sophisticated' is thought by many to be something to be attained if possible as being a good thing, but it actually involves false behaviour like the use of makeup in order to 'look better', but is in fact it is to be deceptive to a degree.

The principles of the 'philosophy' of today originated with Socrates, Plato and Aristotle around 400 B.C., by men who were morally perverted and who lived in a society dominated by the worship of Zeus, Apollo, Aphrodite, and many others famous for their version of 'sophos' (love of human 'wisdom') the root of our English words of sophistry, sophistication, etc., **Science,** which is accurately defined in the Bible as being 'falsely so-called'

[20] O Timothy, keep that which is committed to thy trust, avoiding profane and vain babblings, and oppositions of ***science falsely so called****: [21] Which some professing have erred concerning the faith… 1 Timothy 6:20-21*

Science should be the study of everything that exists, which ought to lead to accurate analysis. Instead, much of it progresses by ideas, hunches, notions, vision, and 'intuition'. Most of its changes through time do not record a closer approach to absolute truth. Human science (falsely so called) finds that its previous incorrect opinions and conclusions reported initially as fact, are constantly having to be updated by further investigation which proves them incorrect. True science is a wonderful study of God's Creation which reveals His Glory, but sadly this type of science rarely appears to be the case.

Religion This world is besotted by thousands of religions based on human ideas about a 'God' or 'gods'. The teachings of these religions may approximate to some degree in appearance to being Godly, but all contain human reasoning that is not consistent with God's Word of Truth. The result is worldwide confusion, war instead of peace, pandemic inhumane behaviour, increasing sickness, moral degradation abounds, and now the systematic destruction of the world's delicate ecological balance threatens life on earth. Human reasoning ignores God's Wisdom, and uses these three Satanically inspired human modalities to find answers and solutions to all humanities problems. The result is the confusion and resulting chaos in this world.

[33] For God is not the author of confusion, but of peace, 1 Corinthians 14:33

God speaks in the First Person through His Prophet Isaiah.

[9] Let all the nations be gathered together, and let the peoples be assembled. Who among them can declare this, and show us former things? Let them bring their witnesses, that they may be justified, or let them hear, and say, "That is true." [10] "You are my witnesses," says Yahweh (God the Father and the Word). "With my servant whom I have chosen; that you may know and believe me, and understand that I am he. Before me there was no God formed, neither will there be after me. [11] I myself am Yahweh. Besides me, there is no Saviour. Isaiah 43:9-11

Establish your belief on the sure 'foundation' of the Rock that is Christ the Messiah, the 'I AM' of John 8:58.

These are just some of the **numerous examples of evidence and proofs** that the Bible **attests** to that provides the sure Foundation for a Christian's 'Belief' and

"Faith' that is built, not on the 'cunningly devised fables' of human beings, **but on the solid evidence of the Rock, the Word, which is Christ.**

There is a lot more evidence and proof that could have been mentioned here both in the Old and the New Testament which it is hoped that some will search out for themselves. **The more anyone studies the Word of God, the Holy Bible, the more 'Rock' solid evidence 'appears' that may have previously gone unnoticed.**

This evidence proves that Christianity is unique which can give every earnest Christian great confidence in the integrity of the Bible and of the Knowledge, Understanding and Wisdom they accumulate in their spiritual journey.

The final chapter tells of our Glorious Future as Eternal Beings with God the Father and His Son for Eternity.

CHAPTER 12

ETERNAL LIFE WITH CHRIST AND GOD THE FATHER

The return of Christ to establish His Kingdom

When Christ returns on a white horse together with millions of His angels, sounding a Trumpet, **every eye shall see Him.** The 'dead in Christ', and true Christians who are alive, will rise to meet Him in the air, and be changed into Spirit Beings as full members of God's Family. Here are the words of Christ Himself in Revelation.

[5] ***And from Christ, YahwehShua the Messiah who is the faithful witness,*** *and the first begotten of the dead, and the prince of the kings of the earth. Unto him that loved us, and washed us from our sins in his own blood,* [6] *And has made us kings and priests unto God and his Father; to him be glory and dominion for ever and ever. Amen.* [7] *Behold, he comes with clouds; and* ***every eye shall see him,*** *and they (the Jews) also which pierced him: and all kindreds (inhabitants) of the earth shall wail because of (what they did to) him. Even so, Amen. Revelation 1:5-7*

Christ's angels that come with him will gather the elect from all over the earth, and even from outer space and bring them to Christ in the air.

[31] And he (Christ) shall send his angels with a great sound of a trumpet, and they shall gather together his elect from the four winds, from one end of heaven to the other. Matthew 24:31

Those who are now members of Christ's elect, His 'ekklesia', can give continual thanks to the Word, Christ for their amazing calling and the joy that awaits us.

[24] Now unto him that is able to keep you from falling, and to present you faultless before the presence of his glory with exceeding joy, [25] To the only wise God our Saviour, be glory and majesty, dominion and power, both now and ever. Amen. Jude 1:24-25

Those who are 'dead in Christ' will rise first, and then 'instantaneously', all true Christians that are alive when Christ comes, will rise to meet Him in the air. Here is the promise Christ caused Paul to write:

[15] For this we say unto you by the word of the Lord, that we which are alive and remain unto the coming of the Lord shall not precede them which are asleep. [16] For the Lord himself shall descend from heaven with a shout, with the voice of the archangel, and with the trump of God: ***and the dead in Christ shall rise first: [17] Then we which are alive and remain (Paul thought Christ's return was imminent!) shall be caught up together with them in the clouds, to meet the Lord in the air: and so shall we ever be with the Lord.*** *[18] Wherefore comfort one another with these words. 1 Thessalonians 4:15-18*

Until this day comes, and we do not know when it will be, but come it will as God has promised, **exactly on time.** We can certainly do as Paul suggests and comfort one another with these incredible promises.

[42] So also is the resurrection of the dead. It is (the human body that is) sown in corruption (rots away); it is raised in incorruption: [43] It is sown in dishonour; it is raised in glory: it is sown in weakness; it is raised in power: [44] It is sown a natural body; it is raised a spiritual body… [51] Behold, I shew you a mystery; We shall not all sleep, but we shall all be changed (into Spirit), [52] In a moment, in the twinkling of an eye, at the last trump: for the trumpet shall sound, and the dead shall be raised incorruptible, and we shall be changed. [53] For this corruptible (body of flesh that rots) must put on incorruption, and this mortal must put on immortality. 1 Corinthians 15:42-44: 51-53

[9] But you (true Christians) are a chosen race (type of human, group, ekklesia), a royal priesthood, a holy nation, a special people for God's own possession, that you may proclaim the excellence of him who called you out of darkness into his marvellous light. [10] In the past (before you believed and had faith in Christ), you were not a people, but now are God's people, who (previously) had not obtained mercy, but now have obtained mercy. 1 Peter 2:9-10

True Christians, regardless of their ethnicity are part of the 'Israel of God', those He has chosen to lead the way with Him in His Kingdom.

[9] Christ has made us (true Christians) kings and priests to our God, and we will reign on the earth. Revelation 5:9

Imagine being a King, and ruling with our Elder Brother, Christ. That is more than exciting, it is even an overwhelming thought.

Those who have qualified to be in the Kingdom of God will be blessed with their rewards which Christ will bring with Him. As revealed in the parables of the talents and the pounds, the reward for each person will be a position of responsibility proportionate to the diligence with which they applied themselves to the development of the inherent attributes given to them by God the Father at birth.

[12] And, behold, I come quickly; and my ***reward*** *is with me, to give every man* ***according as his work shall be.*** *Revelation 22:12*

Then follows the Millennial thousand years of them working with Christ to train all those people in His Ways who survived the terrible battles when He arrives.

[4] and they lived and reigned with Christ a thousand years. Revelation 12:4

During that thousand years, the world will be restored and prepared for the coming resurrection at the end of this first Millennium of everyone else who has ever lived.

[5] But the rest of the dead lived not again until the thousand years were finished. This is the first resurrection. 6 Blessed and holy is he that hath part in

the first resurrection: on such the second death hath no power, but they shall be priests of God and of Christ, and shall reign with him a thousand years. Revelation 20:5-6

The fate of the rest of the dead, all who lived since Adam and died over all time without having any personal relationship with God will be referred to later.

As He arrives, Christ will wage war on the world's armies who fight Him.

Just before Christ returns He gives us a situation to watch out for.

[20] *"But when you see Jerusalem surrounded by armies, then know that its desolation is at hand. Luke 21:20*

Then as Christ and His angels are circling the earth in the sky, they will be seen by everyone. The Beast and the False Prophet will have convinced all the nations of the world, that the alien invasion pictured in so many films and television programs is happening, and that they must gather their armies just South of Jerusalem to fight them.

[19] *I saw the beast, and the kings of the earth, and their armies, gathered together to make war against him (Christ) who sat on the horse, and against his army. Revelation 19:19*

Then will follow such devastation from which only Christ could save any life on the planet. The way the armies will die is prophesied in Zechariah written many years before Christ.

[12] And this shall be the plague wherewith the Lord will smite all the people that have fought against Jerusalem; Their flesh will melt away while they stand upon their feet, and their eyes shall disintegrate away in their holes, and their tongue shall shrink away in their mouth. Zechariah 14:12

The 1000 year Millennium – what will it be like?

Those who enter the Kingdom of God will have first to learn what it is like to have God's Powers and Eternal Life. Christ the King will direct His 'Ekklesia' of Spirit Beings to work with the minds of those human beings who survived the holocaust that occurred as He arrived on earth. All the governments of the world will have been eradicated, and replaced by God's Government. So those people who are left on earth will have to learn how to conduct themselves under the Government of God.

Before Christ's Second Advent, the Beast and the False Prophet will have established and enforced a Satanically perverted form of God's Laws on earth. Everyone will now have to be taught God's Way of Truth. Those who are newly arrived in the Kingdom will be their teachers as prophesied by the Word in Isaiah.

[19] For the people will dwell in Zion at Jerusalem. You will weep no more. He will surely be gracious to you at the voice of your cry. When he hears you, he will answer you.
[20] Though the Lord may give you the bread of adversity and the water of affliction, yet your teachers won't be hidden any more, but your eyes will see your teachers; [21]
and when you turn to the right hand, and when you turn

to the left, your ears will hear a voice behind you, saying, "This is the way. Walk in it." Isaiah 30:19-21

This is what the Word inspired Isaiah to write concerning conditions at the beginning of the Millennium:

[1] This is what Isaiah the son of Amoz saw concerning Judah and Jerusalem. [2] It shall happen in the latter days, that the mountain (Government) of Yahweh's (God's) house shall be established on the top (above in power) of the mountains (new human governments), and shall be raised above the hills (local government); and all nations shall flow (be obedient) to it. [3] Many peoples shall go and say, "Come, let's go up to the mountain (Government) of Yahweh, to the house of the God of Jacob; and he will teach us of his ways, and we will walk in his paths. For the law shall go out of Zion, and Yahweh's word from Jerusalem. [4] He will judge between the nations, and will decide (be a judge) concerning many peoples. They shall beat their swords (all weapons) into ploughshares (and other useful implements), and their spears into pruning hooks. Nation shall not lift up sword against nation, neither shall they learn war any more. Isaiah 2:1-4

God will change the nature and diet of the animals, and there will be a complete profound change of God's order on earth.

[17] "For, behold, I create new heavens and a new earth; and the former things will not be remembered, nor come into mind. [18] But be glad and rejoice forever in that which I create; for, behold, I create Jerusalem to be a delight, and her people a joy [19] I will rejoice in Jerusalem, and

delight in my people; and the voice of weeping and the voice of crying will be heard in her no more. [20] "No more will there be an infant who only lives a few days, nor an old man who has not filled his days; for the child will die one hundred years old, and the sinner being one hundred years old will be (thought commonplace). [21] They will build houses and inhabit them. They will plant vineyards and eat their fruit. [22] They will not build and another inhabit. They will not plant and another eat, for the days of my people will be like the days of a tree, and my chosen will long enjoy the work of their hands. [23] They will not labour in vain nor give birth for trouble; for they are the offspring of Yahweh's blessed and their descendants with them. [24] It will happen that before they call, I will answer; and while they are yet speaking, I will hear. [25] The wolf and the lamb will feed together. The lion will eat straw like the ox. Dust will be the serpent's food. They will not hurt nor destroy in all my holy mountain," says Yahweh. Isaiah 65:17-25

[6] The wolf also shall dwell with the lamb, and the leopard shall lie down with the kid; and the calf and the young lion and the fatling together; and a little child shall lead them. [7] And the cow and the bear shall feed; their young ones shall lie down together: and the lion shall eat straw like the ox. Isaiah 11:6-7

The "True" Millennium of Christ will begin with the return of the True Christ to earth, then when after all the battles are over, He sets foot on the Mount of Olives

[2] For I will gather all nations against Jerusalem to battle; and the city shall be taken (by soldiers), and the

houses rifled, and the women ravished; and half of the city shall go forth into captivity, and the residue of the people shall not be cut off from the city. [3] Then shall the Lord go forth, and fight against those nations, as when he fought in the day of battle. [4] And (after the battle) his feet shall stand in that day upon the mount of Olives, which is before Jerusalem on the east, and the mount of Olives shall cleave in the midst thereof toward the east and toward the west, and there shall be a very great valley; and half of the mountain shall remove toward the north, and half of it toward the south… [8] It will happen in that day, that living (fresh) waters will go out from Jerusalem: half of them toward the eastern sea (the Dead Sea), and half of them toward the western sea (the Mediterranean). It will be so in summer and in winter. Zechariah 14:2-4,8

All nations on earth will begin to benefit from Christ's Kingdom's rule of love and service. All those benefits will happen progressively during a period of Christ's judgment on the remaining peoples of the nations of the world, based partly upon their previous treatment of Israel and other people around them.

There will be a period of recovery and rebuilding of all the physical earth back to a condition where it will be able to sustain, and adequately support physical life for the vast number of people who will be raised up in the second resurrection, after the Millennium.

At the end of this 1,000 years Satan will be set free from his chains, again to tempt the nations. He shall succeed. The nations who allow themselves to be influenced by Satan will be judged and punished.

[7] *And* ***when the thousand years are expired, Satan shall be loosed out of his prison.*** [8] *And shall go out to deceive the nations which are in the four quarters of the earth,* **Gog, and Magog,** *to gather them together to battle: the number of whom is as the sand of the sea.* [9] *And they went up on the breadth of the earth, and compassed the camp of the saints about, and the beloved city (Jerusalem): and fire came down from God out of heaven, and devoured them.* [10] *And the devil that deceived them was cast into the (figurative) lake of fire and brimstone, where (they) the beast and the false prophet are, and shall be tormented (not people) day and night for (Hebrew: ahee-ohn' 'an age)'.* [11] *And I saw a great white throne, and him that sat on it, from whose face the earth and the heaven fled away; and there was found no place for them (the Beast and the false Prophet). Revelation 20:7-11*

Another Millennium after Christ's first Millennium

This next period of 1,000 years will inaugurate the 'Great White Throne' judgment. Those not resurrected to spiritual life at Christ's Second Coming will be resurrected to physical life (Revelation 20:5). These individuals resurrected to physical life during this period will live long lives.

The purpose of this period of physical resurrection is to instruct the great mass of humanity about God's plan of salvation for all.

This 1,000 year period of judgment and education will culminate in universal salvation. All intelligent creatures (all children of Adam and all spirit beings) all who had been given the gift of free will and choice, **all will of their own volition** be reconciled to God the Father.

[9] Wherefore God also hath highly exalted him, and given him a name which is above every name: [10] That at the name of YahwehShua the Messiah ***every*** *knee should bow, of things in heaven (Spirit beings), and things in earth (all humans), and things under the earth; [11] And that* ***every*** *tongue should (and ultimately will) confess that Christ YahwehShua the Messiah is Lord, to the glory of God the Father. Philippians 2:9-11*

'Universal Salvation' for all is the Father's Plan

As we know from the word of Yah'Shua, even the hairs on our head are numbered, so interested in every individual is our Father Yahweh. Ultimately, all human beings be saved. Everyone will be recovered from wherever they may have died. Even those who have been lost in space!

If any of thine be driven out unto the outmost parts of heaven, from thence will the Lord thy God gather thee, and from thence will he fetch thee: Deuteronomy 30:4

[9] But if ye turn unto me, and keep my commandments, and do them; though there were of you cast out unto the uttermost part of the heaven, yet will I gather them from thence, and will bring them unto the place that I have chosen to set my name there. Nehemiah 1:9

So at the end of that time, when Christ, YahwehShua the Messiah, having finished His appointed work will give rule over the Kingdom over to the Father. The Kingdom of God will continue without end, but rule and authority that had been delegated to Christ, YahwehShua, will be returned to the Father. God the Father (YHWH) shall then "be all and in all" (1 Corinthians 15:28) and Christ, the Word His Son will as forever has been true will reign under the Father and above all others.

[24] Then the end comes, when he (Christ) will deliver up the Kingdom to God, even (to) the Father, when he will have abolished all rule and all authority and power. [25] For he must reign until he has put all his enemies under his feet. [26] The last enemy that will be abolished is death. [27] For, "He put all things in subjection under his feet. But when he says, "All things are put in subjection", it is evident that he (the Father) is excepted who subjected all things to him. [28] When all things have been subjected to him, then the Son will also himself be subjected to him who subjected all things to him (the Father), that God (the Father) may be all in all. 1 Corinthians 15:24-28

This period of time is known as the Greek "the aeon of the aeons" or "the age of the ages" spoken of in the New Testament (mistakenly translated as "eternity" in several places in various translations).

The two 1,000 year periods of Christ's reign together are called "the aeons [plural] of the aeons" or "the ages of the ages."

[12] And I saw the dead, small and great, stand before God; and the books were opened: and another book was opened, which is the book of life: and the dead were judged out of those things which were written in the

books, according to their works. [13] And the sea gave up the dead which were in it; and death and hell delivered up the dead which were in them: and they were judged every man according to their works.

[14] And death and hell (the 'grave') were cast into the (figurative) lake of fire (to be 'ended for ever'). This is the second death. Revelation 20:12-14

Death and suffering will be no more, only joy for ever and ever, and when and the world is handed back to the Father.

God the Father will reign His entire Kingdom for Eternity.

So Eternity will continue for God's Family with endless "the aeons [plural] of the aeons" or "the ages of the ages", who will enjoy a life of joy and pleasures for evermore.

[11] You wilt shew me the path of life: in Your presence (Father) is fulness of joy; at Your right hand (under Your rule) there are pleasures for evermore. Psalm 16:11

What a glorious future awaits all those who, with God's help, endure to the end.

APPENDIX

The evidence, eyewitness testimony of the books of Luke and Acts

LUKE and ACTS – are trusted books of testimony that prove the validity of the historical evidence of eyewitnesses and other witnesses they contain. Acts uniquely presents the facts of the birth of Christianity in the first century A.D.

The book of Acts is a very special book of history in that it contains an astonishing amount of **irrefutable evidence** of the truths of how Christianity began after the birth, death, resurrection and ascension of Christ Jesus.

Luke the disciple and 'beloved physician', who wrote the book of Luke was a highly educated man and a meticulous historian. In Luke 1:1-4 **he outlines the fact that his gospel was a declaration of all those things recorded by those who were eyewitnesses from the beginning, and who testified to all of Christ's works.** Luke had perfect understanding of all the miraculous events that occurred during Christ's ministry right up until the time when Christ ascended into heaven, and he sets them out **in (scholarly) order** to Theophilus.

The book of Acts begins with the reference to the former 'treatise', that is Luke's gospel, which he had delivered to Theophilus previously. **So Luke undoubtedly wrote the book of Acts between 33**

A.D. and 43 A.D. under the direct inspiration of the ascended Christ Jesus and His Holy Spirit.

Acts begins with repeating that the risen Christ gave commandments to the apostles and appeared to many people showing ***infallible proofs.***

[1] The former treatise have I made, O Theophilus, of all that Jesus began both to do and teach, [2] Until the day in which he was taken up, after that he through the Holy Ghost had given commandments unto the apostles whom he had chosen: [3] To whom also he shewed himself alive after his passion ***by many infallible proofs****, being seen of them forty days, and speaking of the things pertaining to the kingdom of God: Acts 1:1-3*

After Saul's conversion, Luke apparently accompanied Paul on many of his journeys, as is indicated by the use of the personal pronouns 'him' and 'we' in the text from Acts chapter twenty onward.

Acts reveals the facts that Christianity quickly became widely known in Israel and many of the countries ruled by the Roman Empire. The population of the entire known world in 1 A.D. is estimated to be between 100-200 million.

For some time Rome had been expanding its authority in Asia, and in 63 B.C., the Roman triumvirate Pompey the Great captured Jerusalem. Later in the time of Christ, a clash of the occupying Romans with Jewish nationalism was averted for a while by the political skill of a remarkable family whose most illustrious member was Herod the Great.

Many modern lands were once part of the Roman Empire, and were exposed to the events of Christ's life. For example England and Wales (not Scotland), Spain, Portugal, France (Gaul), Italy, Greece, Turkey, Germany, Egypt, the Levant Eastern Mediterranean/Western Asia, Crimea, Switzerland, and the north coast of Africa. All these countries have remnants of the history of paganism and Christianity intertwined in folklore, and in the names of towns, rivers and places.

God's Word, the Bible is the most accurate history ever written

All histories written by human beings are inaccurate to a degree and reflect the opinions and biases of the historian. 'Historians' and other scholars often have contrary opinions about matters in the Bible, and state that they are not supported by the archaeological evidence.

This is the opposite what should be done by honest scholars. Where there appears to be any conflict, the Bible historic account should take precedence and be believed over archaeological ideas, opinions and theories.

The Bible was directly inspired by God, and each word was dictated to His servants by Him, who wrote down exactly what God determined they should. God never lies, and His Word **is** Truth, so the whole Bible both Old and New Testaments (a 'Testament' **is** legal testimony) can be relied upon to be an absolutely accurate historical record.

In a sense, both the Old and New Testaments are ‘bundles’ of testimonial evidence as they would be called in a court today, which all have the hallmark of writings inspired by God Almighty the Father and Christ Jesus His Son.

In courts of law, a ‘bundle’ of evidence is prepared. A trial ‘bundle’ is defined as “all the documents brought together by the claimant for a trial”. Therefore, any document that is likely to be referred to at trial should be placed into a paginated trial bundle for use by the judge, witnesses and other relevant parties.

There are several types of evidence presented in courts of law.

Character evidence: In the case of the Bible, the Book was written by men who were inspired by God who cannot lie, and whose character is totally beyond reproach. The character of all the Old Testament Prophets, Christ’s Apostles and disciples in regard to what is recorded in the Bible is again above reproach.

Eyewitnesses: Many of the events in the Bible were witnessed by the person telling the story of what happened. They recorded those things which they had seen, heard and experienced.

Witness evidence: The entire Bible is full of references to thousands of people who were witnesses of things they saw, heard or experienced, to times, dates, miraculous events and happenings over thousands of years. In the time of Christ, the events recorded were witnessed by a Caesar, Roman officials and ranking officers of the occupying Roman army of Israel at the time, by the top Jewish ruling authorities in the Temple, and by the disciples and followers of Christ Jesus, as well as large numbers of the population.

Physical evidence: All that is physical matter, the universe, our Solar system, all life, the fauna and flora on earth is physical evidence of a Creator that made them. For every effect there has to be a cause. All design had to be designed. All matter had to be made from something by 'Someone'. Logic demands that that cause was an 'Extra Terrestrial Intelligence' outside and separate from the universe we are aware of. The physical evidence of events in the Bible is often mentioned in the record.

Non-physical Evidence: Energy is not physical, and is invisible. It takes many forms like heat, light, atomic, magnetism, electricity, all of which can be converted from one form to another, but cannot be created or destroyed. Without it nothing exists. Energy is the ultimate evidence, and there has to be a Source of all energy. The Source of all energy and power is God.

Testimonial evidence: In the Bible, there are countless testimonials by witnesses to what occurred. This is why both the Old and New testaments are actual legal testimony to everything they contain.

SCOTT'S COMMENTARY ON THE HISTORICAL TRUTH OF ACTS

An extract is given here on the Biblical book of Acts from Scott's Commentary Volume 5 published in 1866 that is in the public domain. It confirms with great authority that the truths of Christianity, its miracles and events were not refuted by any of the writings of Jewish or Israelite authorities, nor by any secular historians like Flavius Josephus, or by kings, Caesars or government officials of that time which supports its historic authenticity.

LUKE, "the beloved Physician," was undoubtedly the writer of this book; and, intending it as an appendix to his gospel, he inscribes it likewise to Theophilus. (Preface to the gospel of St. Luke.) Indeed the whole may be considered as **one publication in two parts:** but the convenience of having the four gospels together, seems to have induced Christians in early times to divide it, by inserting St. John's gospel between these two parts.

As the history in Acts terminates with St. Paul's imprisonment at Rome during two years, which certainly ended before A. D. 65 with his being beheaded; it may fairly be concluded, **that it was written within thirty or thirty-one years,**

after our Lord's crucifixion: for it can hardly be supposed, that the sacred writer would have closed his narrative so abruptly, and not have carried it on something further, had he composed it at a later period.

The early reception also of this book, as authentic and divine, among the primitive Christians, has been sufficiently proved by learned men, from the testimony of ancient writers. But the circumstance which most of all demands our attention, and should raise our expectations respecting it, is this: it records the fulfilment of the ancient prophecies concerning the kingdom of the promised Messiah, and the manner in which it should be established in the world; and also of those predictions, or promises, which our Lord gave to his disciples, " while he was yet with them," concerning the powers with which they should be endued, the success which would attend their labours, and the persecutions which awaited them;

It is a fact, which cannot be doubted, that the religion of Jesus the Nazarene, who expired on a cross at Jerusalem, almost eighteen hundred years ago, was soon very extensively propagated among the nations ; that it obtained a permanent establishment, which it preserves to this day; and that the prophets had foretold that this would be the case, as to the kingdom of the Messiah: but the book before us is the only history, which expressly relates the manner in which this religion was at first promulgated.

Here we are informed, that eleven obscure men, whom Jesus had called to be his attendants and apostles, having continued with him till his crucifixion, saw and conversed with him after his resurrection, and afterwards beheld him ascend from them towards heaven, "till a cloud" received him out of their sight."

In a few days, having appointed one in the room (place) of the twelfth who had betrayed his Lord and destroyed himself, and being accompanied with a small number of disciples, the Holy Spirit, according to the promise of their Lord, descended upon them, in a most extraordinary manner, enabling them to speak divers languages, and work stupendous miracles; and in all respects qualifying them for their arduous undertaking. Accordingly, without further delay, within less than two months from the time when Jesus was crucified ; and at Jerusalem, under the immediate notice of his crucifiers, they began boldly to declare that he was risen from the dead, ascended into heaven, and exalted at the right hand of God; that he was the promised Messiah, the "Prince of Life," the Saviour and Judge of the world, and as such entitled to all confidence, obedience, and adoration; and openly to charge the people, the priests, and the rulers, with murdering "the Lord of glory."

They were themselves unarmed, and unprotected except by a divine power; they possessed neither human learning, eloquence, nor influence: yet they had all the wisdom and the folly, the learning and the ignorance, the religion and the irreligion, with all the obstinate and varied prejudices, and corrupt passions and habits, of the whole world to encounter; as well as the power of rulers and princes to oppose them: notwithstanding which, they became decidedly and permanently triumphant. They employed no weapons, but simple **testimony** to the facts which they had witnessed, cogent arguments, affectionate persuasions, holy beneficent lives, fervent prayers, and patient sufferings even unto death.

With the Jews they reasoned from the scriptures of the Old Testament, and shewed how exactly these had been fulfilled in Jesus of Nazareth; and when they afterwards went among the gentiles, they reasoned with them from such principles as they themselves acknowledged. Proceeding in this manner, and everywhere attended by a divine power, both manifested in undeniable miracles, and by inwardly preparing men's hearts to receive the truth; they had such astonishing success, that many hundreds of thousands, if not millions, not only from among the Jews and proselytes, but also from the grossest and most licentious idolaters, became the avowed disciples of the crucified Jesus, and the devoted worshippers and servants of "the one living and true God."

Thus, in "the Acts of the Apostles," there is given us a history of the manner, in which the most extraordinary revolution that ever took place in the moral and religious state of the world was first begun; the effects of which were afterwards extended far more widely, till Christianity became the religion of powerful and numerous nations, and superseded the idolatries and superstitions, in which they were before enveloped: and if this account be true, the gospel must be divine.

Now one most extraordinary circumstance attends this narrative; namely, if the truth of it be not admitted, there is no other history extant in the world, which can be substituted in its place: and thus an event, productive of far more extensive and important consequences, than any other, which ever yet occurred on earth, took place in a manner, of which no (other) account has been transmitted to posterity!

This book is indeed the report of friends to the cause: but there is no counter report, with which we may compare it. Neither Jewish scribes and priests, nor gentile philosophers, historians, or moralists, ever attempted, that we find, to write a history of the first introduction of Christianity, in order to confront the account given by the Christians.

The things here recorded were not done in "a corner." Jerusalem, Caesarea, Antioch, and Ephesus, all great and celebrated cities, nay, Rome itself, the proud capital of the world, were among the places, in which the miracles are attested to have been wrought, and the success attained, in the full view of vehement and powerful opposers, who never ventured to deny the facts, though they could not account for them, without allowing the truth of the gospel.

Indeed the silence of the scribes and priests, who were loudly called upon to vindicate themselves from the charge of the most atrocious crimes; and even that of the heathen writers, in such a cause, is a plain confession, that they had nothing to say.

Some modern sceptics, however, insinuate in a covert manner, that a very different account might be given of the triumphs of Christianity, than that contained in scripture; but all their observations are grounded in misapprehension or misrepresentation.

The time for giving another history of these events is long since past and there are no materials for composing one. And indeed, to suppose, that such a religion as Christianity, which directly opposes every corrupt passion of the human heart, without making the least allowance, either to persons in the highest stations, or to its most zealous friends, could have prevailed in the world as it has done, by such instruments and means, and in the face of such powerful opposition, without the power of God succeeding it; is to assume, without shadow of proof, a fact immensely more incredible, than any of the miracles recorded in scripture, or all of them combined.

We must not, however, here expect a full and particular history of the labours and successes of the apostles and primitive evangelists: a select specimen alone is given. After the pouring out of the Holy Spirit on the day of Pentecost, and the first successes and sufferings of the apostles, little is recorded in the scripture concerning most of them. Indeed the names of more than half of them are never mentioned after the first chapter: yet it cannot reasonably be doubted, that they laboured, suffered, and prospered, as their brethren did; though most of the ancient records and traditions concerning them are so mingled with fiction, as not to be entitled to implicit or indiscriminate credit.

Some other labourers are likewise brought forward, as Stephen the first martyr, Philip the evangelist, Barnabas, Silas, and others. But the conversion of Saul the persecutor, with his subsequent labours, sufferings, and triumphs, as the apostle of the gentiles, occupies a large proportion of the book; and the mention of the other apostles, in that part of the history, is occasional and brief.

Peter, indeed, the apostle of the circumcision, was chosen to instruct Cornelius and his friends, (the first fruits from among the gentiles,) doubtless to avoid giving needless offence to the Jews; and the martyrdom of James the brother of John is briefly related. Indeed the labours of St. Paul himself are recorded in a very compendious manner. The events of several years are summed up in two or three chapters. And though, after Luke the historian joined the apostle, and became his faithful companion, (which is shewn by his using the first person plural in the narrative,) he is somewhat more circumstantial: yet the epistles of St. Paul prove, that his labours, persecutions, and successes were far greater, and the instructions which he gave his converts, far more particular, than a cursory reading of this history would lead us to suppose.

At the same time, the remarkable coincidence, even in minute particulars, of the history and the epistles, is of such a nature, as could never have taken place, had not both been genuine; which will appear more fully, when the epistles come under our consideration.

But the book, on which we now enter, contains also a specimen of true believers, as illustrating the nature and effects of genuine Christianity: and it should be carefully noted, that in every age, all those multitudes who are called Christians, yet bear no resemblance to this specimen, will be driven away as chaff, at the great decisive day: and that the more we are like these primitive believers, when "great grace was upon them all," the more evident it is, that we shall 'be numbered with them in glory everlasting.'

Some intimations are also given of the manner, in which the primitive church was constituted and governed, its ministers were appointed, and its ordinances administered: yet it can hardly be supposed, but that the eager disputants of all those parties, into which the church is at present unhappily divided, must feel considerably disappointed in this respect; and secretly regret, that more particular and explicit information has not been given on these subjects: but this the Lord for wise reasons has seen good to withhold.

Extract from Volume 5 of Scott's Commentary on Acts

Printed and Published in 1866.

POSTSCRIPT

To the Glory and Praise of God.

13 Keep back your servant also from presumptuous sins.

Let them not have dominion over me. Then I will be upright.

I will be blameless and innocent of great transgression.

14 Let the words of my mouth and the meditation of my

Heart (and writing) be acceptable in your sight, Yahweh, Father; and YahwehShua my rock, and my redeemer.

Psalm 19:13-14

Lightning Source UK Ltd.
Milton Keynes UK
UKHW020028110123
415109UK00007B/585

9 780645 404234